MACROECONOMICS
UNDER DEBATE

MACROECONOMICS UNDER DEBATE

Alan S. Blinder

Ann Arbor
THE UNIVERSITY OF MICHIGAN PRESS

First published in the United States of America in 1989
by The University of Michigan Press

First published in Great Britain in 1989 by
Harvester Wheatsheaf

Printed and bound in Great Britain

1992 1991 1990 1989   4 3 2 1

Library of Congress Cataloging-in-Publication Data

Blinder. Alan S.
  Macroeconomics under debate/Alan S. Blinder.
    p. cm.
  A selection of the author's essays mostly written in the mid and
late 1980s.
  Includes bibliographical references.
  ISBN 0–472–10140–4
  1. Macroeconomics. I. Title.   89–37881
  HB172.5.B59 1989   CIP
  339.5′3–dc20   r89

CONTENTS

INTRODUCTION

Accident rather than design led me into a career as a macroeconomist. In graduate school at MIT, I specialized in what was then called 'advanced theory.' That, in itself, is a measure of how much economics has changed in less than two decades. My PhD dissertation (Blinder (1974)) was on the theory of income distribution. But when Princeton University asked if I could fill their need for someone to teach graduate macro theory, I gave the only answer a job-seeking PhD candidate can give: of course!

Teaching graduate students at Princeton drew me more deeply into macro theory than I had ever been before and kept me on top of current macro issues. Although I have periodically strayed into other fields, the bulk of my research has been in empirical and theoretical macroeconomics. This volume is a nonrandom sample of that work. In selecting items to include, I have not sought to pick out the best papers, but rather to put together a collection with some thematic coherence – and also to include some papers that are relatively inaccessible. (Two are published here for the first time.)

Often I have wondered whether my accidental conversion to macroeconomics was a stroke of good or bad luck. On the one hand, the field has been constantly bubbling with intellectual excitement and draws you naturally into the world of public policy, where I go willingly. Furthermore, macroeconomics is a big and prominent field; so making a splash there earns you notice – or notoriety – on a wide scale. On the other hand, macroeconomic debates during my professional career have been distressingly unrelenting, acrimonious, and even ideological. The constant state of intense disputation takes a personal toll and, more importantly, inhibits scientific progress. Too much of our time, it seems to me, is spent defending obvious positions against preposterous challenges, too little doing what T.S. Kuhn called normal science. Sometimes I wonder if we are doing science at all.

Nothing in my undergraduate or graduate education (1963–71) prepared me for the tumult that was to follow. I was raised on a straight diet of Keynesian economics at Princeton and MIT just before the consensus crumbled. When I left graduate school in 1971, I thought I was joining a cadre of researchers that was pursuing a progressive research agenda that had started in 1936. I knew, of course, all about the Keynesian – monetarist controversy; indeed, two of my earliest papers addressed it (Blinder and

Solow (1973), reprinted here as Chapter 1, and Goldfeld and Blinder (1972)). But this debate seemed to involve a very small number of people, to be greatly overblown, and to be potentially resolvable by empirical evidence. As Milton Friedman (1970) made clear, theoretical divisions among macro-economists back then did not run deep.

The academic world I entered in 1971 was quite different from the one I have inhabited ever since. (The first section of Chapter 7 describes that world briefly.) The monetarist controversy was simmering, but the Keynesian paradigm reigned supreme. None of my teachers had ever assigned a paper by Robert E. Lucas, Jr. Robert Barro was doing fixed-price disequilibrium economics with Herschel Grossman (Barro and Grossman (1971)). MIT professors spoke about money illusion without embarrassment. And the natural rate hypothesis was the new guy on the intellectual block. The wisdom on the natural rate that was received by MIT graduate students back then was simple: the Friedman – Phelps theoretical arguments for a vertical long-run Phillips curve were sound, but the econometric evidence was against it. We believed in econometrics in those days, or at least some of us did; and working on or using large-scale macroeconometric models was a perfectly respectable activity.[1]

When the earliest papers on what is now called new classical economics (Lucas (1973), Sargent and Wallace (1975)) began to appear, I barely looked up from my ongoing research – deciding that new classicism was a passing fancy of limited importance. What foresight! Not only did I fail to jump on the bandwagon, I did not even run alongside. Although many of my subsequent papers have routinely assumed rational expectations, and one or two have even been set in a market clearing context (see, for example, Blinder and Fischer (1981)), my heart was never really in either assumption.

The major influences on my research in the late 1970s and into the 1980s were not the Lucas critique and rational expectations, but rather two real-world events. The first was the realization that the big recession the United States experienced in 1973–75 was, in large measure, an inventory contrac-tion. The second was the apparent collapse of econometric money demand equations in the United States and elsewhere in the 1970s and 1980s.

MONETARY THEORY AND CREDIT

The first six chapters of this collection are contributions to the ongoing debate over the role of money and credit in the economy.

Chapter 1, my 1973 paper with Robert Solow, stands alone from the other five both in publication date and subject matter. I nonetheless welcome the opportunity to reprint it here because the paper continues to be widely cited and the original contained a number of small errors which I here correct. These corrections do not disturb the paper's two main results: first, that the economy is more likely to be stable under money financing of budget deficits than under bond financing; second, that if the economy remains stable under bond financing, the long-run impact of fiscal policy on aggregate demand is greater under bond financing than under money financing. The first of these is obviously relevant to the monetarist debate since monetarist policy amounts to strict bond financing of deficits. Both results have, I think, proven to be extremely robust,[2] and keep reemerging in different contexts.[3]

Chapters 2 through 6 all raise, in one way or another, a possibility not mentioned in Chapter 1: that central bank policy might work through the creation and destruction of *credit* rather than *money*. My interest in this question was piqued by the aforementioned collapse of the empirical demand function for money.

The Keynesian *LM* curve in the United States started showing serious signs of wear and tear in the mid-1970s (Goldfeld (1976)) and pretty much disintegrated in the 1980s. Money demand equations in several other countries suffered similar fates, though not necessarily with the same timing. Yet – and this is what fascinated me – it certainly did not appear that monetary policy lost its bite when economists lost their money demand functions. The Federal Reserve in the United States and the Bank of England in the United Kingdom, to name just two, seemed to have no trouble causing severe recessions with 'tight money' – even if they failed to slow the growth rates of any of the *M*s. By 1982, I had concluded that there must be something seriously wrong with a theory that relies on the Keynesian *LM* curve for its monetary transmission mechanism and started wondering whether 'tight credit' was not a better sobriquet than 'tight money.'

Chapters 2 through 6 display most of my writing on this topic – which is one I am still actively researching. Chapter 2, coauthored with Joseph Stiglitz, is a short 'think piece' originally prepared for the December 1982 meetings of the American Economic Association. In it, we sketch – with no equations! – a transmission mechanism for central bank policy that has nothing to do with either money or interest rates, but is based instead on credit rationing. We mention, with no attempt at formal modeling, the possibility that a credit-rationed firm might be forced to curtail production due to a shortage of working capital. This idea is developed more formally and embedded in several otherwise conventional Keynesian macro models in Chapter 3. It opens the possibility that a restrictive central bank policy might be both contractionary and inflationary at the same time – with potentially destabilizing consequences.

These two papers led directly to Chapter 4, which is published here for the first time. The more I thought about the financial intermediary modeled by Stiglitz and Weiss (1981), the less it looked like a bank. In macroeconomics, as in real life, we think of a bank as an institution that accepts deposits, holds reserves, and makes loans. It is principally through reserves that the central bank exercises control over commercial banks. But the Stiglitz–Weiss bank neither takes deposits nor holds reserves, and hence seems an unsuitable vehicle for examining how central bank policy works. So, while I was writing Chapter 3, I prepared Chapter 4 as the microfoundation of the credit-supply behavior I assumed there. Since there are relatively few models of the banking firm extant, the chapter may also be of some independent interest.[4]

Recently, my work on credit, much of it in collaboration with Ben Bernanke, has proceeded along two lines. One is empirical and is represented by Chapter 5, which is also published here for the first time. When I began to study the empirical dimensions of credit, I quickly learned that there was not much to study – apart from a series of papers by Benjamin Friedman (1983, and others). In particular, almost no one, possibly excluding Friedman, knew what the stylized facts were. Which sorts of credit are most important and most cyclical? Which are most volatile? Questions like these are answered in Chapter 5, as a prelude to more structured research. The chapter also offers a variety of credit aggregates that I have found useful in several contexts.[5]

The other line of research has been on developing macro models in which credit plays an essential role. Bernanke and I have labored over many variants, some based on credit rationing and some not; but most of this work exists only in handwritten notes. Chapter 6 is the one published example to date. It enlarges the *IS/LM* framework to include bank loans and thereby distinguishes theoretically – and to some extent empirically – between 'credit shocks' and 'money shocks.'

THE KEYNESIAN/NEW CLASSICAL DEBATE

For a long time, I worked on issues like inventories, credit, and consumption which were on the periphery of the raging debate between the Keynesians and the new classicals, rather than at its center.[6] But, as many people will testify, I was hardly a shrinking violet in these debates, which often were carried on at conferences and seminars rather than in print.[7]

Then came 1986, the fiftieth anniversary of the publication of Keynes's *General Theory*. The number of symposia, conferences, and other scholarly events marking the occasion must have exceeded the number of professed Keynesians under the age of 50. So those of us who fit the description were besieged with invitations to go here or there to reflect on the rough treatment Lord Keynes's ideas had been receiving of late and/or on where Keynesian economics might be headed. I accepted a few of these invitations, and Chapters 7 and 8 are two of the results.

Chapter 7 originated as an address to the April 1986 meetings of the Eastern Economic Association and is reprinted here along with the lengthy list of references that had to be omitted from the original due to space limitations. The paper includes capsule summaries of the Keynesian consensus *circa* 1972 and the new classical alternative that sought to supplant it, as well as my personal evaluation of the latter's contribution to macroeconomic progress. I think it safe to say that no one would call my account neutral. Nor would anyone apply that adjective to Chapter 8, which was first presented to the meetings of the American Economic Association in December 1986. Knowing that Robert Lucas was my discussant, and reacting in part to his *Models of Business Cycles* (1987), I wrote the paper in the form of eight questions to which Keynesians often give different answers from Lucasians. In each case, I defended the Keynesian position as the more 'scientific.' I still believe they are.

The final three chapters take up three controversial issues that have been associated with the Keynesian/new classical debate but are also of broader interest. Chapter 9 is about the so-called Lucas critique of econometric policy evaluation: the claim that econometric models estimated on historical data may be misleading indicators of the effects of policy interventions. I do not question the validity or value of the critique itself; its logic is impeccable and its insight invaluable. Instead, I raise the possibility that one of the methods most frequently suggested for coping with the critique may lead applied econometricians into grievous errors by imposing a structure on the data that is not there. I illustrate by example how this might happen.

Chapter 10, my Ely Lecture to the American Economic Association in December 1987, is on high unemployment, which no longer plagues the United States but still haunts Europe. It argues that neither policy-makers, macroeconomists, nor microeconomists have coped very well with the phenomenon of persistent, high unemployment and challenges all to do better. It suggests, among other things, that a convincing theoretical model of unemployment may have to come to grips with concerns people have about relative wages and 'fairness.'

Everyone knows that nominal price or wage rigidities are central to Keynesian theory. Indeed, some critics refuse to consider Keynesianism a full-fledged theory because it lacks a theoretical rationale for the nominal rigidities it assumes. However, microeconomic theories of wage or price rigidities virtually always explain *real* rigidities, not *nominal* rigidities. The latter can easily be overcome by indexing. Yet few actual contracts are fully indexed. Why? It is striking how often macroeconomic debates come down to this question. It's a good question, too – one which economists have still not answered satisfactorily. Chapter 11 is my attempt at an answer and a suggestion as to how the difficulty might be overcome by the creation of a new kind of financial intermediary.

A scholar wants little but to have his work read – praised is nice, but read is the essential thing. But I have never been presumptuous enough to suggest to anyone that my papers be collected and reprinted. I am therefore grateful to Harvester Wheatsheaf, and especially to my editor, Peter Johns, for initiating this collection. I hope the reader will find their judgment sound.

NOTES

1. See, for example, Blinder and Goldfeld (1976), which used the MPS model extensively, and without apology.
2. See, for example, Pyle and Turnovsky (1976), Cohen and McMenamin (1978).
3. For example, Sargent and Wallace's (1981) 'unpleasant monetarist arithmetic' is an application of these ideas.
4. The unpublished version of this chapter circulated as 'Notes on the comparative statics of a Stiglitz–Weiss bank,' but I came to realize that this was a bad misnomer. Hence I have changed the title and revised the paper slightly for this volume.
5. See, for example, Blinder (1986), and Chapter 6 in this volume.
6. Some of these papers are collected in *Inventory Theory and Consumer Behavior*, volume 2 of this collection.
7. Two small published examples are in Chapter 5 of Blinder (1979) and in Blinder (1981).

REFERENCES

Barro, R. and Grossman, H. (1971) 'A general disequilibrium model of income and employment,' *American Economic Review*, vol. 61 (March), pp. 82–93.

Blinder, A. S. (1974) *Toward an Economic Theory of Income Distribution*, Cambridge: MIT Press.

Blinder, A. S. (1979) *Economic Policy and the Great Stagflation*, New York: Academic Press.

Blinder, A. S. (1981) 'Supply shock inflation,' in M. J. Flanders and A. Razin (eds), *Development in an Inflationary World*, New York: Academic Press.

Blinder, A. S. (1986) 'Comments on "Debt problems and macroeconomic policies," by L. H. Summers,' in *Debt, Financial Stability, and Public Policy*, Kansas City: Federal Reserve Bank of Kansas City.

Blinder, A. S. and Fischer, S. (1981) 'Inventories, rational expectations, and the business cycle,' *Journal of Monetary Economics* (November), pp. 277–304.

Blinder, A. S. and Goldfeld, S. M. (1976) 'New measures of monetary and fiscal policy, 1958–1973,' *American Economic Review*, vol. 66 (December), pp. 780–96.

Blinder, A. S. and Solow R. M. (1973), 'Does fiscal policy matter?' *Journal of Public Economics*, vol. 2, pp. 319–37, included here as Chapter 1.

Cohen, D. and McMenamin, J. S. (1978) 'The role of fiscal policy in a financially disaggregated macroeconomic model,' *Journal of Money, Credit and Banking*, (August), pp. 322–36.

Friedman, B. (1983) 'The roles of money and credit in macroeconomic analysis,' in J. Tobin (ed.) *Macroeconomics, Prices, and Quantities*, Washington: Brookings.

Friedman, M. (1970) 'A theoretical framework for monetary analysis,' *Journal of Political Economy*, vol. 78, pp. 193–237.

Goldfeld, S. M. (1976) 'The case of the missing money,' *Brookings Papers on Economic Activity*, vol. 3, pp. 683–730.

Goldfeld, S. M. and Blinder, A. S. (1972) 'Some implications of endogenous stabilization policy,' *Brookings Papers on Economic Activity*, vol. 3, pp. 585–640.

Lucas, R. E. Jr (1973) 'Some international evidence on output-inflation tradeoffs,' *American Economic Review*, vol. 63 (June), pp. 326–34.

Lucas, R. E. Jr (1987) *Models of Business Cycles*, Oxford: Basil Blackwell.

Pyle, D. H. and Turnovsky, S. J. (1976) 'The dynamics of government policy in an inflationary economy: an "intermediate-run" analysis,' *Journal of Money, Credit and Banking*, (November), pp. 411–38.

Sargent, T. J. and Wallace, N. (1975) ' "Rational" expectations, the optimal monetary instrument, and the optimal money supply rule,' *Journal of Political Economy*, vol. 83 (April), pp. 241–54.

Sargent, T. J. and Wallace, N. (1981) 'Some unpleasant monetarist arithmetic,' *Federal Reserve Bank of Minneapolis Review*.

Stiglitz, J. E. and Weiss, A. (1981) 'Credit rationing in markets with imperfect information,' *American Economic Review*, vol. 71 (June), pp. 393–410.

1 · DOES FISCAL POLICY MATTER?

Perhaps the most fundamental achievement of the Keynesian revolution was the reorientation of the way economists view the influence of government activity on the private economy. Before Keynes, it was a commonplace that government spending and taxation were powerless to affect the aggregate levels of spending and employment in the economy; they could only redirect resources from the private to the public sector. This, of course, is an immediate corollary of Say's Law. In a full-employment context, each dollar of additional government spending can only 'crowd out' exactly one dollar of private spending; it cannot alter the overall level of aggregate income.

The Keynesian demonstration that with sticky wages unemployment can persist changed all this. Economists began to stress the macroeconomic effects of government spending and taxation. It became a commonplace that not only would a dollar of additional government spending raise national income by the original dollar but that this expenditure would have multiplier effects of perhaps several dollars more. The old view that government spending simply crowded out private spending was banished. At the same time a new question arose: does monetary policy matter, or, at least, does it matter much?

Lately, however, the resurgence of the quantity theory of money – under the new name of 'monetarism' – has brought with it both a renewed belief in the power of monetary policy and a resurgence of interest in the crowding out effect. Both the theoretical and empirical work of the monetarists has called into question the basic Keynesian principle that government spending can alter the aggregate level of employment. The current question appears to be: does fiscal policy matter?[1]

The purpose of this note is to reexamine the underlying basis of the Keynesian multiplier in view of the monetarist critique. We hope to show that there are still good theoretical reasons to believe in the efficacy of fiscal policy in an economy with underemployed resources.

This paper is written with Robert M. Solow and is an outgrowth of work we are doing for The Brookings Institution. Support from Brookings and from the National Science Foundation under Grant GS 32003X is gratefully acknowledged. We are also indebted to A. B. Atkinson for an important suggestion which led to a substantial revision of this paper.

1.1 THE PROBLEM DEFINED

There are several levels at which crowding out has been alleged to occur. The most obvious is the possibility that government will engage in productive activities which would otherwise be provided by the private sector, so that public spending would simply supplant private investment. It can be argued, for example, that total investment in electrical utilities in the Tennessee Valley area would be much the same today had the government never created the Tennessee Valley Authority. However, for the bulk of government expenditure – on national defense, courts, and the like – it is hard to imagine that public-sector outlays are simply replacing potential private outlays on a *dollar-for-dollar basis*. In any case, this is not the sort of crowding out we wish to discuss, and it would occur whether the spending were financed by taxes, bonds or money.

A second level of crowding out is an integral part of the Keynesian tradition and is, in fact, disputed by almost no one. This is the notion that deficit spending *not accompanied by new issues of money* carries with it the need for the government to float debt issues which compete with private debt instruments in financial markets. The resulting upward pressure on interest rates will reduce any private expenditures which are interest-elastic – which may include some spending by state and local governments as well as private spending on consumer durables, business fixed investment and residential construction. This financial side-effect will partially offset the expansionary effect of the original increase in public spending. Thus in a monetary economy the government spending multiplier is certainly lower than the naive Keynesian formula, multiplier = $1/(1 - $ marginal propensity to spend), and is lower for bond-financed spending than it is for money-financed spending.

There is no theoretical controversy over this second level of crowding out. The only contested issues are empirical. How much will interest rates rise in response to the greater demand for money and supply of bonds engendered by the government spending? How much will investment fall in response to the rise in interest rates? It is by now well-known that only a zero interest-elasticity of the demand for money will give rise to a multiplier of zero, that is, make fiscal policy impotent. While this assumption was formerly associated with the new quantity theorists,[2] there is by now an overwhelming accumulation of empirical evidence against it, and the monetarists have more or less disavowed it.[3]

Yet monetarists still cling to the view that fiscal policy is powerless, that is, that the multiplier for bond-financed government spending is approximately zero. How can this be so? A possible answer is that when there are significant wealth effects the simple Keynesian story (as summarized, say, in the *IS–LM* model) closes the books too soon. Any government deficit requires the issuance of some sort of debt instrument – outside money or interest-bearing bonds – and this increase in private wealth will have further reverberations in the economy. It is precisely these wealth effects – which provide the rationale for the third level of crowding out – that we wish to investigate in this paper.

Figures 1.1 and 1.2 illustrate the problem. In Fig. 1.1, IS_0 and LM_0 represent the initial equilibrium of the economy in the ordinary Hicks–Hansen model. Government spending is indicated by an outward shift of the IS curve to IS_1. Income rises by $Y_1 - Y_0$. Income does not rise all the way to Y_2 – which represents the naive multiplier effect – because of the second level of crowding out alluded to above.

This is where the usual textbook story ends, and if there are no significant wealth effects, that is correct. However, when wealth effects exist, Y_1 is not an equilibrium position. Greater wealth will, presumably, mean higher levels of consumption out of any given income flow; thus the IS curve will shift out further to IS_2 in Fig. 1.2. This augments the ordinary multiplier. But the greater wealth will also affect the financial markets. Increased household wealth will presumably mean increased demands for money (and bonds) at any level of income and interest rates, represented by a shift in the LM curve to LM_2 in Fig. 1.2.

The outcome of these last two shifts may be either expansionary or contractionary on balance as Silber (1970) has stressed. Advocates of complete crowding out, of course, believe the results to be contractionary. If they are correct, as long as a budgetary deficit exists there will be increases in private wealth which have deflationary impacts on the level of national income. In the long run, the fiscal policy multiplier is negative.

In response to a recent criticism by Tobin (1972), Friedman has indicated that he now believes that these wealth effects, rather than the oft-cited slope of the LM curve, constitute the main issue separating monetarists from Keynesians. He contrasts the initial impact of fiscal policy in Fig. 1.1 with the wealth-induced shifts in Fig. 1.2 – shifts which continue as long as the budget is unbalanced – and he asks: 'Is there any doubt that this (latter) effect must swamp the once-for-all shift of the IS curve?' (Friedman (1972), p. 916). He summarizes his new view of the monetarist–Keynesian debate as follows (Friedman (1972), p. 922):

> One way to characterize the Keynesian approach is that it gives almost exclusive importance to the first-round effect. This leads it to attach importance primarily to flows of spending rather than to stocks of assets. Similarly, one way to characterize the quantity – theory approach is to say that it gives almost no importance to first-round effects.
>
> The empirical question is how important the first-round effects are compared to the ultimate effects. Theory cannot answer that question.

Friedman believes that the answer for deficit spending financed by printing money is that the subsequent asset effects are: (a) much larger than, and (b) in the same direction as the initial expansionary thrust of government spending. By contrast, if the deficits are financed by floating government bonds, he

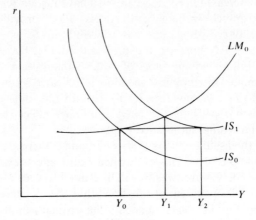

Fig. 1.1 The first-round effects of a rise in government purchases.

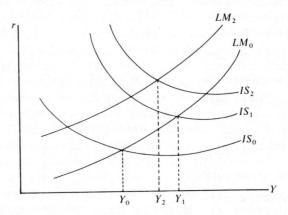

Fig. 1.2 The subsequent wealth effects of a rise in government purchases under bond-financed deficits.

apparently believes that wealth effects are: (a) about equal in magnitude, and (b) opposite in direction to the initial movement of the *IS* curve. On the other hand, it has always been a central tenet of Keynesian macroeconomics that bond-financed government spending has a net expansionary impact on the level of economic activity.[4] After all, if this were not so, symmetry would imply that reducing spending in order to pay off part of the national debt would be expansionary.

But is it only faith that supports this view? In this paper, we hope to show that while Friedman may be correct in describing the issue as an empirical one, certain theoretical arguments can be adduced in support of the conventional view that fiscal policy works. Furthermore, we suggest that it is also an empirical question whether the subsequent wealth effects of bond-financed deficits, while less expansionary than money-financed deficits in the short run (Friedman's 'first round'), are actually more expansionary in the long run.[5]

In the following section we consider the long-run impact of government spending, under the two alternative modes of financing, in an *IS–LM* model with wealth effects. This analysis, however, utilizes a funny concept of the 'long run' since, in conformity with the *IS–LM* rules, the capital stock is held fixed (despite positive net investment) while the stocks of the other two assets (money and bonds) adjust to their final equilibrium. So, in Section 1.3, we rectify this error by considering a true long-run equilibrium where all three asset stocks are free to adjust. We find that, in a sense to be specified later, the case for fiscal policy is somewhat stronger in this more sophisticated model.

1.2 CROWDING OUT IN THE SIMPLE *IS–LM* MODEL

The conventional *IS–LM* model,[6] with wealth effects added, consists of the following ingredients:

(goods–market equilibrium)	$Y \equiv NNP = C + I + G$	(1.1)
(consumption function)	$C = C(Y - T, W)$	(1.2')
(net investment function)	$I = I(r)$	(1.3)
(tax function)	$T = T(Y)$	(1.4')
(demand for real balances)	$M^d/P = L(r, Y, W)$	(1.5)
(exogenous money supply)[7]	$M^s = M$	(1.6)
(money–market equilibrium)	$M^s = M^d$	(1.7)
(definition of wealth)[8]	$W = K + M/P + V(r)/P$	(1.8)

Here $V(r)$ is the nominal market value of the supply of government bonds. The only additions to the classical textbook treatment which we have made are to include wealth as an argument in both the consumption and demand-for-money functions.

To this model, we must append a somewhat different version of what Christ (1967, 1968) has called the 'government budget restraint.' As it usually appears in the work of Christ and others, the restraint is a simple differential (or difference) equation equating the changes in the nominal stocks of bonds and money to the nominal government deficit:

$$P[G - T(Y)] = \dot{B} + \dot{M} \qquad (1.9')$$

where B is the number of bonds (each of face value $1). But (1.9') commits an oversight: it ignores the fact that interest paid on bonds is an expense item in the government's budgetary accounts along with G. If we assume for simplicity that each bond is a perpetuity paying \$1 per year, interest payments will be B and the market value of the stock of bonds will be B/r. The government budget restraint can therefore be written:

$$P[G + B - T] = \dot{B}/r + \dot{M} \tag{1.9}$$

Note that the bond term on the right-hand side is the change in the number of bonds, evaluated at the current market price. This differs from $(\dot{B}/r)$ which is the change in the market value of the stock of bonds, if there are capital gains or losses on pre-existing bonds.

Two other minor alterations in the model are necessary. First, in the definition of wealth we can write B/r for $V(r)$. Second, both consumption and taxes presumably depend upon personal income, which includes the interest paid on the national debt; thus (1.2′) and (1.4′) become:

$$C = C(Y + B - T, W) \qquad \cdot \tag{1.2}$$

$$T = T(Y + B) \tag{1.4}$$

The first model which we shall study consists of equations (1.1)–(1.9). Since we shall treat the price level as fixed throughout, we can set $P = 1$ with no loss of generality and reduce the nine equations to the following three-equation dynamic system:

$$Y = C[Y + B - T(Y + B), M + B/r + K] + I(r) + G \tag{1.10}$$

$$M = L(r, Y, M + B/r + K) \tag{1.11}$$

$$\dot{M} + \dot{B}/r = G + B - T(Y + B) \tag{1.12}$$

Equations (1.10) and (1.11) are the static IS and LM equations which hold at each instant; equation (1.12) drives the model from one instantaneous equilibrium to the next by changing the stocks of money and/or bonds.

The unmodified model which ignores interest payments as a budgetary expense item – equations (1.1), (1.2′), (1.3), (1.4′), (1.5) – (1.8) and (1.9′) – has an implication which has attracted attention in recent years. Suppose that we ignore the dynamics of the model and look only at the long-run steady-state solution. This means that $\dot{M} = \dot{B} = 0$, so that (1.9′) implies: $G = T(Y)$, that is, the government budget must be balanced in long-run equilibrium. But this immediately implies that the steady-state multiplier for government spending not financed by higher tax rates (but ultimately financed by higher tax revenues at unchanged rates) must be, as Christ has pointed out:

$$\frac{dY}{dG} = \frac{1}{T'(Y)}$$

Observe that this long-run multiplier expression holds regardless of how the deficit is financed, and is independent of all functional relations in the model except the tax function. In a word, if the model is stable under each mode of financing (so that it actually approaches its steady state), the long-run multipliers for bond and money-financed deficit spending are identical.

What happens when we add interest to the budget constraint? Setting $\dot{B} = \dot{M} = 0$ in (1.9) gives: $G + B = T(Y + B)$, from which it follows that:

$$\frac{dY}{dG} = \frac{1 + (1 - T')\dfrac{dB}{dG}}{T'}$$

If deficits are financed by money-creation, so that $dB/dG = 0$, we obtain the same long-run multiplier as before. But if bond financing is used, so that $dB/dG > 0$, the long-run multiplier exceeds $1/T'$. In words, contrary to the usual supposition, the long-run multiplier for bond-financed deficit spending exceeds that for money-financed deficit spending.

What is the reason for this paradoxical result? Simply this: starting from any long-run equilibrium income level with a balanced budget, an initial surge in government spending will cause income to rise as in normal IS–LM analysis. It is well-known that, if the LM curve has positive slope, the impact multiplier will be larger if the deficit is financed by creating money. But, this is only Friedman's 'first round.' Since the budget will be in deficit, new assets will have to be created. If financing is by bonds the subsequent deficit financing will have to be larger than in the money case for two reasons. First, income will rise less so the induced increase in tax receipts will be smaller. Second, a larger outstanding debt will require greater interest payments. Provided that the net impact of the wealth effects is expansionary, the 'second round' increase in income will be greater under bond financing than under money financing, and this will continue to be true in subsequent rounds. The basic intuition is that under bond financing any given budgetary gap is harder to close because every increase in the number of bonds outstanding requires more expenditure on debt service. It therefore takes a greater rise in income to induce tax receipts sufficient to close the budgetary gap.

Thus one is tempted to conclude that Friedman's 'empirical question' can be resolved on purely theoretical grounds after all – not only is deficit spending financed by bonds expansionary in the long run, it is even more expansionary than the same spending financed by the creation of new money.[9] However, this would be jumping too hastily to a conclusion which may not be warranted. Steady state equilibria are of interest only if the system under consideration is stable. And it turns out that the stability of the system of equations (1.10)–(1.12) may depend on the way in which deficits are financed. As we shall see, the model is always stable under money finance, but there are three possibilities under bond finance as follows:

1. If the parameters of the system are such that the net wealth effect of a new bond issue is contractionary (as depicted in Fig. 1.2), the mone-

tarists will be vindicated; but the more important consequence is that the system will then be unstable.

2. For some other values of the crucial parameters, bonds will have an expansionary impact on the level of national income (so that the monetarists are wrong), but this impact will not be sufficiently strong to close the budgetary gap. Again the system will be unstable.

3. Finally, if the parameters are such that the system is stable, additional bonds must have a positive net impact on GNP (Y_2 must lie to the right of Y_1 in Fig. 1.2) so that fiscal policy works as expected. Only in this case can we appeal to the steady-state result that bond-financed deficits are more expansionary than money-financed deficits. And it is an empirical question as to which case actually obtains.

To prove these assertions it will be useful to consider the static equilibrium equations (1.10)–(1.11) as defining Y and r as functions of M and B, for given K and G:

$$Y(t) = F(M, B, \bar{K}; G) \tag{1.13}$$
$$r(t) = H(M, B, \bar{K}; G) \tag{1.14}$$

It is a routine exercise in comparative statics to find that the partial derivatives of these functions are:

$$F_M = \mu\alpha \quad H_M = \mu\frac{\lambda}{L_r}(S' - h) \tag{1.I}$$

$$F_B = \mu\left[\frac{\beta}{r} + C_y(1 - T')\right] \quad H_B = -\mu\frac{\lambda}{L_r}\left[\frac{h}{r} + (1 - S')L_y\right]$$

where

$$h \equiv S'L_w + C_wL_y > 0$$

$$0 < S' \equiv 1 - C_y(1 - T') < 1$$

$$\alpha \equiv C_w + (1 - L_w)\sigma > 0 \text{ since } 0 < L_w < 1$$

$$\beta \equiv C_w - L_w\sigma$$

$$0 < \lambda \equiv L_r\left/\left(L_r - \frac{B}{r^2}L_w\right)\right. < 1$$

$$\sigma = \frac{I_r - (B/r^2)C_w}{L_r - (B/r^2)L_w} > 0$$

and μ is the basic multiplier:[10]

$$\mu \equiv 1/(S' + \sigma L_y)$$

So the short-run multiplier for increases in M is $\partial Y/\partial M = \mu\alpha$, which is unambiguously positive; while the corresponding multiplier for bonds is

$\partial Y / \partial B = F_B$ which is ambiguous on a priori grounds. Monetarists, of course, believe $F_B < 0$, but correctly emphasize that the sign of F_B is an empirical question.

We now turn to the issue of stability. Equations (1.13)–(1.14) enable us to reduce the dynamic system (1.10)–(1.12) to a single nonlinear differential equation:

$$\dot{M} = G + \bar{B} - T[F(M, \bar{B}, \bar{K}) + \bar{B}] \tag{1.15a}$$

under money finance, or:

$$\dot{B} = H(\bar{M}, B, \bar{K})\{G + B - T[F(\bar{M}, B, \bar{K}) + B]\} \tag{1.15b}$$

under bond finance.
Under a regime of pure money finance, the stability condition for differential equation (1.15a) is simply:

$$\frac{\partial \dot{M}}{\partial M} = -T' F_M = -T' \mu \alpha < 0 \tag{1.16a}$$

which is obviously satisfied. However, if deficits are financed by floating bonds, the corresponding condition is:

$$\frac{\partial \dot{B}}{\partial B} = r\{1 - T'(F_B + 1)\} + H_B\{G + B - T\} < 0$$

$$= r(1 - T' - T' F_B) \text{ in the neighborhood of equilibrium.}$$

So the necessary and sufficient condition for local stability is:

$$F_B > \frac{1 - T'}{T'} \tag{1.16b}$$

We find that the stability of the *IS–LM* model under bond financing of deficits is indeed an empirical question. However, since $F_B > 0$ is necessary (but not sufficient) for stability, *in a stable system* the discovery of a hitherto unsuspected government bond must lead to a higher level of national income. The three possibilities enumerated above are immediately apparent from condition (1.16b). If $F_B < 0$ as the monetarists claim, fiscal policy does not work, but the system is unstable. The economy does not return to its initial equilibrium before the deficit spending, as monetarist doctrine holds; instead income falls cumulatively and without limit. If $0 < F_B < (1 - T')/T'$, fiscal policy works as Keynesians have always believed, but the increases in GNP are not sufficient to close the budgetary gap. Each new bond leads to a rise in income of $F_B dB$ and a rise in tax revenues of $T' F_B dB$, but costs the government $(1 - T')dB$. Only if $T' F_B$ exceeds $(1 - T')$, i.e. only if (1.16b) is satisfied, will the budget deficit be falling, and thus only in this case will the system approach its new steady state equilibrium.[11]

1.3 CROWDING OUT WHEN THE CAPITAL STOCK MAY VARY

We now wish to make only two small alterations in the *IS–LM* model of equations (1.10)–(1.12). First, we recognize that the change in the capital stock (K) is identical to net investment (I). Second, in line with modern investment theory which envisions an equilibrium demand for capital stock and a disequilibrium demand for investment, we alter the investment function of equation (1.3) to read:

$$I = I(r, K), \quad I_r < 0, \quad I_K < 0 \tag{1.3'}$$

with the property that $I(r^*, K^*) = 0$ if r^* is the long-run equilibrium interest rate corresponding to any long-run equilibrium capital stock, K^*.

With these modifications, our dynamic system becomes:

$$Y = C\left[Y + B - T(Y + B), M + \frac{B}{r} + K\right] + I(r, K) + G \tag{1.17}$$

$$M = L\left(r, Y, M + \frac{B}{r} + K\right) \tag{1.18}$$

$$\dot{M} + \frac{\dot{B}}{r} = G + B - T(Y + B) \tag{1.19}$$

$$\dot{K} = I(r, K) \tag{1.20}$$

Once again, we can treat the static *IS–LM* equations (1.17) and (1.18), as defining Y and r as functions of M, B and K, for a given G:

$$Y = F(M, B, K; G) \tag{1.21}$$

$$r = H(M, B, K; G) \tag{1.22}$$

with the following comparative-static derivatives:

$$F_M = \mu\alpha > 0 \qquad\qquad H_M = \mu \frac{\lambda}{L_r}(S' - h)$$

$$F_B = \mu\left[\frac{\beta}{r} + C_Y(1 - T')\right] \qquad H_B = -\mu \frac{\lambda}{L_r}\left[\frac{h}{r} + (1 - S')L_y\right] > 0$$

$$F_K = \mu(\beta + I_K) < F_B \qquad H_K = -\mu \frac{\lambda}{L_r}(h + I_K L_y) \tag{1.II}$$

Note that the derivatives with respect to M and B are the same as in equation (1.I). In particular, $\partial Y / \partial B = F_B$ remains ambiguous. Substitution of (1.21)–(1.22) into (1.19)–(1.20) reduces our system to two non-linear differential equations:

$$\dot{K} = I[H(M, B, K), K] \tag{1.23}$$

and either:

$$\dot{M} = G + \bar{B} - T[F(M, \bar{B}, K) + \bar{B}] \tag{1.24a}$$

in the case of money financing, or:

$$\dot{B} = H(\bar{M}, B, K)\{G + B - T[F(\bar{M}, B, K) + B]\} \tag{1.24b}$$

in the case of bond financing.

Let us take up the case of monetary finance first. Linearizing the non-linear system (1.23)–(1.24a) about its equilibrium $M^*, \bar{B}, K^*$:

$$T(Y^* + \bar{B}) = G + \bar{B}, \ I(r^*, K^*) = 0$$

gives:

$$\begin{pmatrix} \dot{m} \\ \dot{k} \end{pmatrix} = \begin{pmatrix} -T'F_M & -T'F_K \\ I_r H_M & I_r H_K + I_K \end{pmatrix} \begin{pmatrix} m \\ k \end{pmatrix} \tag{1.25}$$

where $m \equiv M - M^*$ and $k \equiv K - K^*$. Denoting the matrix in (1.25) by D, the stability conditions are:

$$\text{tr}(D) < 0 \tag{1.26a}$$

$$\det(D) > 0 \tag{1.26b}$$

where $\text{tr}(D)$ and $\det(D)$ denote respectively the trace and determinant of D. Substituting from (1.II) into (1.26a) yields:

$$\text{tr}(D) = -T'\mu\alpha - \mu\lambda \frac{I_r}{L_r}(h + I_K L_y) + I_K < 0$$

$$= -T'\mu\alpha - \mu\lambda \frac{I_r}{L_r} h + I_K \left(1 - \mu\lambda \frac{I_r}{L_r} L_y\right) < 0$$

A sufficient condition is therefore:

$$\lambda \frac{I_r}{L_r} L_y < \frac{1}{\mu} = S' + \sigma L_y$$

which is true since $\lambda(I_r/L_r) < \sigma$.

The proof that the determinant is positive is as follows. From equations (1.II):

$$\det(D) = -T'\mu \begin{vmatrix} \alpha & \beta + I_k \\ \mu\lambda \dfrac{I_r}{L_r}(S' - h) & I_K\left(1 - \mu\lambda \dfrac{I_r}{L_r} L_y\right) - \mu\lambda \dfrac{I_r}{L_r} h \end{vmatrix}$$

So we need to prove:

$$\alpha I_K - \lambda \frac{I_r}{L_r} \mu[\alpha I_K L_y + \alpha h + (\beta + I_K)(S' - h)] < 0$$

The term in square brackets can be written:

$$I_K(\alpha L_y - h) + S'(\beta + I_K) + (\alpha - \beta)h$$

$$= I_K(\alpha L_y - h) + S'(\beta + I_K) + \sigma h \quad \text{since } \alpha - \beta = \sigma$$

Expanding this by using the definitions of α, β and h yields:

$$I_K[C_w L_y + (1 - L_w)\sigma L_y - S' L_w - C_w L_y]$$

$$+ S'(C_w - \sigma L_w + I_K) + \sigma(S' L_w + C_w L_y)$$

$$= [I_K(1 - L_w) + C_w](S' + \sigma L_y)$$

$$= \frac{I_K(1 - L_w) + C_w}{\mu}$$

Thus the entire expression simplifies to:

$$\alpha I_K - \lambda \frac{I_r}{L_r}(I_K(1 - L_w) + C_w) < 0$$

$$C_w\left(I_K - \lambda \frac{I_r}{L_r}\right) + (1 - L_w)I_K\left(\sigma - \lambda \frac{I_r}{L_r}\right) < 0$$

which is again true since $\lambda(I_r/L_r) < \sigma$. QED. This establishes (1.26b) and thus the stability of the system (1.25).

Now turn to the system under bond financing of deficits, equations (1.23) and (1.24b). Linearizing around equilibrium as before results in:

$$\begin{bmatrix} \dot{b} \\ \dot{k} \end{bmatrix} = \begin{bmatrix} r(1 - T' - T'F_B) & -T'rF_K \\ I_r H_B & I_r H_K + I_K \end{bmatrix} \begin{bmatrix} b \\ k \end{bmatrix} \tag{1.27}$$

where $\dot{b} = B(t) - B^*$. Defining Δ as the matrix in (1.27), the stability conditions for the system are:

$$\text{tr}(\Delta) < 0 \tag{1.28a}$$

$$\det(\Delta) > 0 \tag{1.28b}$$

It is not possible, in general, to prove that these inequalities must hold. That is, as in the case where the capital stock was fixed, stability under bond finance is an empirical matter. We can, however, derive a set of intuitively plausible sufficient conditions for stability.

Consider first the trace. The upper left term will be negative if and only if condition (1.16b) holds. The lower right term is simply the total effect of an increase in the capital stock on investment, including any indirect effects through changing interest rates. It seems intuitively plausible that this should be negative. If this condition is met, then the model with variable capital stock is 'more stable' than the model with fixed capital stock in the sense that (1.16b) is sufficient but no longer necessary.

Only one other condition is required to insure stability. Let us pose the following question: what would be the effect on aggregate demand of the discovery of an additional dK of capital? First, it would increase consumption through the wealth effect by $C_W dK$. Second, it would decrease investment by $I_K dK$. It seems intuitively plausible that the net effect should be contractionary, that is, $I_K + C_W < 0$. As the reader can verify from (1.II), this assumption suffices to establish that $F_K < 0$, which, in view of the fact that $H_B > 0$ establishes that the determinant is positive.

To recapitulate, two jointly sufficient conditions (neither one necessary) for the stability of the economy under bond finance are:

$$F_B > \frac{1 - T'}{T'} \tag{1.16b}$$

$$I_K + C_w < 0 \tag{1.29}$$

We would argue that both are likely to be satisfied in practice.

The argument for (1.29) has already been given: it asserts that the depressing effect of more capital on investment outweighs the expansionary wealth effect on consumption.[12] In considering (1.16b), the reader is reminded that B is the volume of interest payments on the national debt, so $F_B = dY/dB$ is analogous to an ordinary multiplier for transfer payments. A number between 1.0 and 2.0 seems plausible for F_B, at least for the United States. These limits would imply that T' must exceed some number between 0.33 and 0.50 in order to satisfy (1.16b). The appropriate interpretation of T' is as the *marginal propensity to tax and reduce income-conditioned transfer payments* as GNP rises. According to Modigliani (1971, p. 30), when US GNP rises by $1, the combined increase in federal income taxes, state and local income taxes, social security contributions and corporate income taxes amounts to about 50¢. Since there are also transfer payments which decline automatically with rising incomes – unemployment insurance, welfare payments of various kinds and farm subsidies are just a few examples – it would appear that $T' > 0.50$. And this would imply that any F_B greater than unity would mean that the system is stable.[13]

1.4 SUMMARY AND CONCLUSIONS

The cutting edge of monetarism is the assertion that fiscal policy can not affect aggregate spending; otherwise monetarism is hardly distinguishable from an eclectic Keynesian view. The latest version of the monetarist challenge appears to accept the interest – elasticity of the demand for money and to rest, instead, on the perverse wealth effects associated with bond-financed government spending.

We have analyzed the question in the framework of an *IS–LM* model extended to allow for wealth effects and for the need of the government to finance its budget deficit or surplus. The economy can be at rest only when the budget is balanced, else the stock of financial assets in the hands of the private economy will necessarily be changing, and there will be wealth-effects on private spending. In this context, an analysis of the effectiveness of fiscal and monetary policy has to cover both the comparative-static multiplier for bond-financed or money-financed government spending and the stability of the process touched off by an unbalanced government budget.

As a preparatory exercise, we study a conventional 'short-run' model in which the stock of fixed capital is assumed to be constant, although net investment may be going on for as long as it takes the economy to reach a new equilibrium. Our conclusion is that if such an economy is stable at all under bond finance, fiscal policy is normally effective. If the monetarists are right, the system must be unstable. And then fiscal policy is worse than impotent: bond-financed spending drives income down without limit. Both the stability of the economy and the effectiveness of fiscal policy are in principle empirical matters. But equation (1.16b) provides an empirically plausible condition that guarantees both. The case of monetarist instability – deficit spending contracts the economy, thus enlarging the deficit and contracting the economy still more, thus . . . – hardly sounds plausible.

Allowing the capital stock to vary complicates the story, but changes the result only slightly. It remains true that both the stability of the economy and the positivity of the multiplier for bond-financed deficit spending are empirical matters. But (1.16b) and (1.29) are a pair of plausible restrictions on the behavior functions that suffice to insure both. In this extended model, $dY/dB > 0$ is no longer a necessary condition for convergence, so that it is logically possible for the economy to be stable and fiscal policy ineffective. However, we regard this as a curiosum rather than as a vindication of monetarism. For the empirical values characteristic of the United States, at least, the evidence seems to require a comfortable 'yes' in answer to the question posed in the title of this paper.

1.5 NOTES

1. See, for example, L. C. Andersen and J. L. Jordan (1968); R. W. Spencer and W. A. Yohe (1970); and many of the writings of Milton Friedman.
2. See Friedman (1956, 1959).
3. Friedman (1966, 1972), Fand (1970).
4. There is no controversy over government spending financed by printing money. Both sides agree that it will be expansionary; but one group likes to call it fiscal policy, while the other prefers to call it monetary policy. Nothing much hinges on

this distinction. In terms of Fig. 1.2, the *LM* curve would shift outward instead of inward if financing were by money instead of by bonds.

5. So far as we know, this conclusion was first suggested in a paper by Sean Murray (1972).

6. The *IS–LM* model usually treats the price level as exogenously fixed, and we shall adhere to this convention. However, it should be noted that we do this strictly for simplicity. There are no real difficulties in adding a production function and a labor market and allowing the price level to be endogenously determined. The result would be that expansionary fiscal policy causes some inflation of the price level which reduces the value of the multiplier for (at least) three reasons:

   1. With prices higher, the real value of the money stock is lower, which shifts the *LM* curve inward.
   2. Higher prices reduce the real wealth of the private sector, which has a negative 'Pigou effect' on consumption, shifting the *IS* curve inward.
   3. If taxes are progressive in terms of money income, inflation will increase the real yield of the tax system at each level of real income, again lowering the *IS* curve.

   While each of these serves to reduce the absolute value of the fiscal multiplier, none of them has any bearing on its sign, which is what is at issue here.

7. This is again a simplification, made solely for the purpose of notational convenience. We here ignore the banking system, and thus the distinction between inside and outside money, and we treat the money stock as exogenous. These complications could all be brought in, and would in no way affect the central conclusions.

8. This includes government bonds as a net asset to the public. We are well aware of, but not persuaded by, the arguments which hold that such bonds are not seen as net worth by individuals because of the implied future tax liability. If that view were correct, the wealth effects of new bonds, illustrated in Fig. 1.2, would simply not occur.

9. An interesting corollary of this is that an open-market purchase, i.e. a swap of *B* for *M* by the government with *G* unchanged, will be contractionary! This is because, with less debt service, the existing levels of *G* and *Y* will imply a budgetary surplus which, in turn, must lead to a reduction in the supplies of money and/or bonds.

10. Note that if, as is typically done in *IS–LM* analysis, we ignored the capital gains on bonds when interest rates change, σ would simplify to I_r/L_r so that μ would be the more familiar $1/(S' + I_r L_y/L_r)$.

11. In a model where interest payments are omitted from the budget restraint, the stability condition turns out to be simply $F_B < 0$, so that there is a direct correspondence between whether fiscal policy works as expected and whether the system is stable.

12. Note that this is not *necessary* for stability since more capital also has a contractionary impact through the *LM* curve.

13. In the oversimplified model which omits interest payments from the budget restraint, stability under bond finance can be established on purely theoretical grounds in the case where the capital stock varies. The proof is given in the original working draft upon which the present paper is based: 'Does Fiscal Policy Matter?' Econometric Research Program Memorandum no. 144, Princeton, New Jersey, August 1972.

1.6 REFERENCES

Andersen, L. C. and Jordan, J. L. (1968) 'Monetary and fiscal actions: a test of their relative importance in economic stabilization,' *Federal Reserve Bank of St. Louis Review*, vol. 51 (November), pp. 11–24.

Christ, C. F. (1967) 'A short-run aggregate – demand model of the interdependence of monetary and fiscal policies with Keynesian and classical interest elasticities,' *American Economic Review*, vol. 57 (May), pp. 434–43.

Christ, C. F. (1968) 'A simple macroeconomic model with a government budget restraint,' *Journal of Political Economy*, vol. 76, pp. 53–67.

Fand, D. I. (1970) 'A monetarist model of the monetary process,' *Journal of Finance*, vol. 25, pp. 275–89.

Friedman, M. (1956) 'The quantity theory of money – a restatement,' in M. Friedman (ed.) *Studies in the Quantity Theory of Money*, Chicago: University of Chicago Press, pp. 3–21.

Friedman, M. (1959) 'The demand for money: some theoretical and empirical results,' *Journal of Political Economy*, vol. 67, pp. 327–51.

Friedman, M. (1966) 'Interest rates and the demand for money,' *Journal of Law and Economics*, vol. 9, pp. 71–85.

Friedman, M. (1972) 'Comments on the critics,' *Journal of Political Economy*, vol. 80, pp. 906–50.

Modigliani, F. (1971) 'Monetary policy and consumption,' in Federal Reserve Bank of Boston, *Consumer Spending and Monetary Policy: The Linkages*, Conference series no. 5 (Boston), pp. 9–84.

Murray, S. (1972) 'Financing the government budget deficit', unpublished paper, University of Essex.

Silber, W. L. (1970) 'Fiscal policy in *IS–LM* analysis: a correction', *Journal of Money, Credit and Banking*, vol. 2, pp. 461–72.

Spencer, R. W. and W. P. Yohe (1970) 'The "crowding out" of private expenditures by fiscal policy actions,' *Federal Reserve Bank of St. Louis Review* (October), vol. 52, pp. 12–24.

Tobin, J. (1972) 'Friedman's theoretical framework', *Journal of Political Economy*, vol. 80, pp. 852–63.

2 · MONEY, CREDIT CONSTRAINTS, AND ECONOMIC ACTIVITY

When government expenditures exceed current tax revenues, the resulting deficit must be financed either by issuing bonds, which imply obligations to levy future taxes, or by creating high-powered money. The choice between money and bonds is often thought to be of great moment for both real and nominal variables; that is, monetary policy matters.

There is by now a wide empirical consensus that monetary policy has effects on real variables like output and employment, but there is far less agreement about why this is so. The purpose of this paper is to take issue with some currently fashionable views of why money has real effects, and to suggest a new theory, or rather resurrect an old one – the loanable funds theory – and give it new, improved micro foundations.

2.1 SOME NEW IRRELEVANCE THEOREMS

In classical monetary theory, prices are fully flexible and the future tax liabilities implied by government bonds are fully discounted. In such a world, government spending has identical effects whether it is financed by bonds (thus creating a 'deficit') or by current taxation, and an open-market purchase of bonds is equivalent to a money rain. Consequently, a swap of future for current taxes has neither real nor nominal effects, and a swap of money for bonds affects only the price level.

But these irrelevance theorems rest on micro foundations that are not well specified. For example, classical monetary theory presumably applies to a frictionless world of certainty and lump sum taxes, and mostly ignores the dynamic effects on real rates of return that arise when monetary policy changes the expected path of the price level.

If an explicitly dynamic, general equilibrium model in which people form (rational) expectations about the uncertain future is constructed, a number

Written with Joseph E. Stiglitz, Princeton University. We gratefully acknowledge financial support from the National Science Foundation and helpful discussions with Benjamin Friedman, Bruce Greenwald, Laurence Kotlikoff, and Andrew Weiss. A longer version of this chapter appears as an NBER working paper.

of irrelevance theorems about government financial policy can be established, provided that financial changes do not redistribute the tax burden (see Stiglitz (1981)). For example, let the government reduce current taxes, issue bonds, and sometime later raise taxes to retire the bonds. Not only will such a policy leave real consumption and investment by all individuals in all states of nature unchanged, but neither will it change any prices. The reason is Say's Law of Government Deficits: the increase in the supply of government debt gives rise to an identical increase in the demand.

Other irrelevance propositions can be established. For example, if the government changes the maturity structure of its debt, or exchanges indexed for nonindexed bonds, such changes will be irrelevant because of exactly offsetting changes in the demands for different government securities. Similarly, a change in the rate of inflation that is matched by a change in the nominal interest paid on government debt does not disturb equilibrium in any market.

Some of these irrelevance results are familiar. Others contrast sharply with the implications of traditional portfolio theory. For example, a standard argument holds that a change in the maturity structure of the government debt will require a change in the term structure of interest rates to equilibrate the demands and supplies of different types of bonds. But this argument ignores the tacit, and exactly offsetting, changes in liabilities implied by the structure of taxes across time and states of nature. Perhaps individuals also ignore the implied tax changes. But to use this as a major theoretical underpinning of the effectiveness of monetary policy is to ground the theory in irrationality, an anathema to economists of the modern school.

2.2 THE IRRELEVANCE OF IRRELEVANCE THEOREMS

If these irrelevance theorems are correct, then neither swaps between current and future taxes (nonmonetized budget deficits) nor open-market operations (creation of high-powered money) should matter.

To put these notions to a crude test, standard 'causality' tests were run by regressing three critical US time-series on their own lagged values, lagged values of changes in bank reserves, and lagged values of changes in government debt. Specifically, the regressions took the form:

$$\Delta X/X = a(L)(\Delta X/X) + b(L)(\Delta R/R) + c(L)(\Delta D/D) + e$$

where Δ is the first-difference operator; $a(L)$, $b(L)$, and $c(L)$ are polynomials in the lag operator; R is bank reserves; D is the government debt; and X is alternatively nominal GNP (Y), real GNP (y), or the GNP deflator (P).[1] Regressions were run with the maximum lag set alternatively at two or three years.

If open-market operations were irrelevant, then changes in reserves should not 'cause' any of the left-hand variables, once we control for changes in debt; that is, all the bs should be zero. In the case of nominal GNP, this hypothesis is easily rejected with F values of 6.9 and 9.2 (See Table 2.1). But for real GNP and prices, the evidence is mixed. In each case, one regression rejects the irrelevance proposition while the other does not.

If pure swaps between current and future taxes were irrelevant, then changes in debt should not 'cause' any of the left-hand variables, once we control for changes in reserves, that is, all the cs should be zero. The regressions for nominal GNP overwhelmingly reject this hypothesis (with F values of 10.5 and 14.6). And the regressions for inflation also reject it, though less decisively. However, we cannot reject the hypothesis that non-monetized deficits are irrelevant for real GNP growth.

On balance, the evidence calls the strong forms of the irrelevance theorems into question and suggests a need to examine the assumptions that underlie them. Full rationality has already been mentioned. Equally obvious is the assumption that all taxes are lump sum; no one ever claimed that swaps among distorting taxes would be neutral.

The theorems also assume that taxes are distributionally neutral. It is well known that changes in the distribution of income and wealth across individuals can have real effects. Analogously, redistributing the tax burden across generations can have real effects if individuals have no heirs or fail to incorporate fully their heirs' welfare into their own utility functions. While these effects are probably present, one wonders about their empirical importance. Is redistribution across generations really the driving force behind monetary policy?

The irrelevance theorems also ignore the difference between interest-bearing government debt and non-interest-bearing money, which is held for transactions purposes. Traditional monetary theory has focused on this difference. Surely paper money and checking balances have advantages in transactions over other potential media of exchange. But are these advantages sufficiently large to explain the effectiveness of monetary policy by arguing, for example, that a contrived scarcity of the medium of exchange will constrain economic activity? In Italy, when there was a shortage of small change, candy became a medium of exchange. And now, with computerized banking, it should be relatively easy for velocity to change quickly to compensate for any shortage of money. Recent innovations like CMAs suggest that the transactions costs of providing a medium of exchange paying a market rate of interest cannot be very large. We believe that only regulation and lack of full rationality prevented checking accounts from paying slightly less than market interest rates for so long.

Another assumption pertains to the informational content of monetary or debt policy: the irrelevance theorems assume that policy actions do not

Table 2.1 F tests of irrelevance propositions[a]

	Equation explaining:		
	Nominal GNP growth	Inflation rate	Real GNP growth
Hypothesis: All $b_i = 0$	$6.9^b/9.2^b$	$3.5^c/2.8$	$2.6/4.0^c$
Hypothesis: All $c_i = 0$	$10.5^b/14.6^b$	$3.5^c/4.2^c$	$2.6/2.4$

Notes:
[a] Results from regressions with 3 lags are reported before the slash; results from regressions with 2 lags are reported after the slash.
[b] Denotes significant at 1 percent level.
[c] Denotes significant at 5 percent level.

change people's beliefs about the different states of nature. But if the government has superior information (which it does not make public), and uses this information in formulating policy, then policy might have real effects because of the information it conveys to the private sector. In addition, if monetary policy has a random element, individuals will have trouble distinguishing between price movements that are the consequence of real shocks and those that are the consequence of monetary shocks. This, too, can give money the power to influence real variables.

But can these informational issues be empirically important? We are skeptical. In addition to the weekly money supply number, a firm can look at its inventories, sales data, the national unemployment rate, and many other facts and figures that help it distinguish between real and nominal shocks. Besides, at low and moderate rates of inflation, people always know the current price level within a very small margin of error, and therefore can easily convert any absolute price into a relative one with great accuracy. It therefore seems implausible that the issues emphasized by the new classical macroeconomics can rationalize sizable effects of monetary policy on output.

A final, and very critical, assumption that underlies the irrelevance theorems is that capital markets are perfect. But people cannot borrow freely at the government's interest rate and for a very good reason: they might default. The probability of default, and the informational imperfections that it implies, lie at the heart of our alternative theory of how monetary policy works.

2.3 IMPERFECT INFORMATION AND CREDIT RATIONING

Imperfect information about the probability of default has several fundamental implications for the nature of capital markets. First, it gives rise to institutions – like banks – that specialize in acquiring information about default risk. Such information is valuable. A lender with superior information can more easily distinguish between good and bad risks, thereby raising his own net (of default losses) rate of return. But such information is very specific (knowing that Company A is a good risk may tell us little about Company B) and, for a variety of reasons, is also difficult to sell.

Second, banks will devise nonprice mechanisms for screening out untrustworthy borrowers. As Stiglitz and Weiss (1981) have argued, reacting to excess demand for loans by raising the rate of interest may lower the bank's expected return because of adverse effects on the mix of applicants, and by inducing borrowers to undertake riskier projects. Thus credit rationing arises as an equilibrium phenomenon, an observation that plays a crucial role in the theory we develop here.

Third, banks will try to devise contracts that provide strong incentives not to default. This may lead to contingency contracts in which both the rate charged and the availability of credit at a later date depend on the borrower's previous performance. In conjunction with the specialized knowledge mentioned above, this type of contract ties particular borrowers to particular lenders, that is, creates a 'customer market' of the sort described by Okun (1981). Thus, although the credit market is 'competitive' in the usual sense (free entry, many buyers and sellers), lenders will view different borrowers as highly imperfect substitutes, and borrowers will have the same attitudes about different lenders – at least in the short run. There may, in particular, be classes of borrowers (like small businesses) for whom denial of credit by 'their' bank has the effect of making credit inaccessible.

2.4 THE EFFECTIVENESS OF MONETARY POLICY

We are now prepared to see how monetary policy affects real activity in this model. Consider what happens if the central bank sells bonds in the open market, causing a drain of reserves from the banking system.

If banks were essentially 'loaned up' before, they will have to contract their loan supply. Some borrowers will not have their loans renewed. As we have just argued, many of these borrowers will be unable to secure credit from other banks. Investment activities will be curtailed and, if the loans were providing working capital, even current operations may have to be reduced. Thus tight money can depress real economic activity. Note also that, because of credit rationing, all this may happen with little increase in interest rates. So the effectiveness of monetary policy in this model does not rely on large interest elasticities, which often cannot be found empirically.

Two important questions remain. First, what stops prices from falling so fast that neither the real supply of credit nor real output has to decline, thereby robbing monetary policy of its real effects? Second, why do borrowers that are denied credit by the banks not turn elsewhere, for example, to the auction market?

The first question is as old as monetary theory itself, and bedevils any attempt to provide a deep explanation of the real effects of monetary policy. Part of the answer is simple and quite general: expected price changes affect the expected returns on holding financial assets (such as money), and therefore have real effects.[2] But we have just expressed doubts about the empirical importance of interest elasticities of this sort.

The rest of the answer has to do with the fact – the unexplained fact – that many long-term contracts without complete indexation exist. We do not have a good explanation for this phenomenon. Neither does anyone else.[3] But that does not imply that the consequences of nominal rigidities should be ignored. This paper seeks to explain how monetary policy works in the presence of such rigidities.

The second question is more specific to our approach. Recall that we rejected the transactions mechanism as an explanation for the real effects of money on the grounds that there were too many close substitutes. Analogously, our theory would not hold up if close substitutes for bank credit were readily available. Are there close substitutes?

If information were perfect (or cheaply acquired), then a reduction in bank credit would be offset by an increase in nonbank credit. Central bank policy would change the locus of borrowing, but would change neither the total volume of credit nor who gets it. However, we have argued that costly and specialized information is the essence of the credit market, so that good substitutes for bank credit do not exist, at least in the short run.

What about the market for commercial paper, for example? For some large firms (like General Motors) this is a real option, and they use it. For these firms, curtailments of bank credit may be offset by expansions of open market credit. But the fact of the matter is that for many firms, including all the small ones, commercial paper is simply not an option; if the banks are forced to contract, they end up credit constrained. Thus, like Stiglitz and Weiss (1981), we view the credit market as divided into clienteles. Very low-risk borrowers can use the open market, and are rationed only by price. Very high-risk borrowers cannot get credit at any price. Those in between may encounter quantity constraints, and this rationing becomes more severe when the central bank drains reserves from the banking system.

Notice that the segmentation of credit markets should become particularly severe during recessions, when even large, well-known firms face the possibility of default. Since investors assume that banks have superior knowledge about their customers, a firm that comes to the open market because it was rationed by its bank will be viewed as a bad risk, and therefore either charged a higher interest rate or denied access to the market.

Not much has been said so far about money; the emphasis has been on credit. To relate the two, consider a typical bank which has liabilities (deposits, D, and net worth) equal to assets (reserves, R, loans, L, and government bonds, B). Under a system of fraction reserve banking in which lending institutions also provide the medium of exchange (deposits), L and D will be closely related. Take our previous example in which the central bank makes an open market sale of government bonds: B rises and R falls by an equal amount. Banks then find themselves short on reserves and, as mentioned above, must contract L. But if R and D are held in fixed proportion, then the decline in deposits – and therefore in the money supply – must match the decline in loans.

Thus, while we have two competing theories – one based on credit, the other on money – that are conceptually distinct, the data will have difficulty distinguishing between them because credit and money normally are highly collinear. Given an institutional structure in which the same institutions supply loans and the medium of exchange, devising tests to distinguish between the 'credit' theory and the 'money' theory is no easy matter. And we do not pretend to have done this. However, we can make some suggestive remarks.

First, Benjamin Friedman (1981) has documented the facts that (1) a broad measure of credit (far broader than bank credit) does just as well as money in forecasting future movements in nominal GNP, and (2) credit is just about as closely related to the Federal's Reserve instruments as is any of the monetary aggregates.

Second, Bernanke's (1983) study of detailed data from the Great Depression suggests that the decline in money was too small to account for the sharp drop in output, but that a proxy for credit stringency does rather well.

Third, the particular factors that have led to the breakdown of the demand function for money in recent years – deregulation and financial innovation – ought not to have destroyed the demand function for credit, according to the arguments presented here. In a period of rapid financial innovation, the ability of the central bank to curtail economic activity by causing a scarcity of the medium of exchange should be severely limited. Yet the Federal Reserve seems to have caused a severe disruption of economic activity, and has even done so without reducing the growth rate of money very much. We suggest that restrictions on the availability of credit, via the mechanisms discussed here, may provide a better explanation of how the Federal Reserve killed the economy.[4]

Finally, we should observe that, just as financial innovation has impaired the link between money and economic activity, further innovation might impair the link between bank credit and the economy. According to our arguments, it is the unique position of banks in the credit system that gives the central bank such strong leverage over the real economy. But if banks prove to be an unreliable source of funds, alternative institutions may arise that serve the same functions as banks. If such institutions do develop, the effectiveness of monetary policy might be seriously reduced.

2.5 NOTES

1. Time was measured in fiscal years, and the sample period covered 1952–81. The term R is adjusted bank reserves, as calculated by the Federal Reserve Bank of St Louis, and ΔD is the increase in government indebtedness to the public during the fiscal year. For more detailed results, see Blinder (1982).
2. Real effects can be avoided only by an exactly offsetting change in the nominal interest rate on financial assets. Naturally, this cannot occur in the case of currency.
3. The analogy between the short-run rigidities imposed by multiperiod nominal wage contracts and those imposed by multiperiod nominal loan contracts should be apparent. For one attempt to explain why wages and interest rates may not be fully indexed, see Blinder (1977), reprinted here as Chapter 11.
4. During the four years from 1978 through 1981, the December-to-December growth rate of what we currently call M1 fell gradually from 8.3 to 6.4 percent, which hardly suggests a savage monetary squeeze. However, the growth rate of commercial bank loans fell from 18.1 to 6.4 percent.

2.6 REFERENCES

Bernanke, B. (1983) 'Nonmonetary effects of the financial collapse in the propagation of the Great Depression,' *American Economic Review* (June), vol. 73.

Blinder, A. S. (1982) 'On the monetization of deficits,' Working paper No. 1052, National Bureau of Economic Research (December).

Blinder, A. S. (1977) 'Indexing the economy through financial intermediation,' in K. Brunner and A. H. Meltzer (eds) *Stabilization of The Domestic and International Economy*, vol. 5, Carnegie-Rochester Conferences on Public Policy, *Journal of Monetary Economics*, Suppl.

Friedman, B. M. (1981) 'The roles of money and credit in macroeconomics analysis,' Working Paper No. 831, National Bureau of Economic Research (December).

Okun, A. M. (1981) *Prices and Quantities: A Macroeconomic Analysis*, Washington: Brookings.

Stiglitz, J. E. (1981) 'On the relevance or irrelevance of public financial policy: indexation, price rigidities and optimal monetary policy,' paper presented to a conference at Rio de Janeiro (December).

Stiglitz, J. E. and Weiss, A. (1981) 'Credit rationing in markets with imperfect information,' *American Economic Review* (June) vol. 71, pp. 393–410.

3 · CREDIT RATIONING AND EFFECTIVE SUPPLY FAILURES

The topic of this paper is among the oldest and most fundamental in monetary theory: how and why does monetary policy affect real economic activity? Traditional answers hold that the central bank can manipulate aggregate demand by engineering expansions or contractions of the medium of exchange.

In its monetarist variant, this story posits a direct link between something called M and aggregate spending. In its Keynesian variant, the story holds that adjustments in asset prices brought about by a change in M lead to more spending, especially on capital goods. In either case, short-run stickiness of prices is needed to translate some of the changes in demand into movements of real output.

In recent years, these conventional stories have become increasingly implausible, as Stiglitz and I (Blinder and Stiglitz (1983)) have argued elsewhere. With 'money' becoming more and more difficult to define, it is becoming increasingly difficult to believe that the central bank can cause a recession by contriving a shortage of an arbitrary subset of assets called M. Put differently, the point seems both simple and compelling: if there are ready substitutes for money, control of money will not give the authorities much leverage over the real economy.

Hence this paper develops an explanation for how central bank policy affects real economic activity that has nothing to do with money. Instead, credit rationing is the operative mechanism. In order to make the credit-rationing mechanism stand out in bold relief, most other channels of monetary policy (such as interest elasticities and expectational errors) are banished from the model. The reader should understand that this is merely an

The research reported here has been supported by the National Science Foundation. Parts of the work were done while I was a visiting fellow at the Institute for International Economic Studies in Stockholm and at the Brookings Institution. I am grateful for comments received at seminar presentations at the Institute, Princeton, Harvard, Columbia, Brown, the Center of Planning and Research in Athens, and the National Bureau of Economic Research; and for comments and suggestions from Costas Azariadis, Willem Buiter, Rudiger Dornbusch, Stanley Fischer, Benjamin Friedman, Michael Horgan, Leonard Nakamura, Elias Salama, John Seater, Dennis Snower, Robert Solow, Joseph Stiglitz, Lawrence Summers, and several referees. Finally, it was a remark made at a seminar some years ago by Robert Mundell which first got me scratching my head about the concept of 'effective supply.'

expositional device. I do not wish to deny, for example, that investment depends on interest rates. But interest-rate channels have been well understood for decades, and the spirit of this paper is that interest elasticities do not seem large enough to explain the deep recessions that are apparently caused by central bank policy. There must be something else.

The idea that credit availability impinges on economic activity is, of course, hardly new. But it does seem to have gone out of style in recent years under the pressure of the classical revival. Blinder and Stiglitz (1983) suggested that this fashion change may have been a mistake; and this paper is an attempt to give analytical substance to the ideas sketched there.

The basic idea is simple enough to be stated at once. Firms may have a desired or 'notional' supply based on relative prices, expectations, and other variables. But they may need credit to produce the goods. If the required credit is unavailable, there may be a 'failure of effective supply' in which firms fail to produce as much as they can sell. The idea of a supply failure contains a hint of what is to come: if recessions are initiated by declines in supply, rather than by declines in demand, then prices may rise, not fall, as economic activity contracts.

Where, then, does money enter the story? The banking system both connects credit to money and creates a kind of 'credit multiplier.' Suppose demand rises. Firms, seeing higher expected marginal value products, borrow more and expand production. As economic activity expands, higher transaction balances are required; so bank deposits rise. As funds flow into the banking system, the supply of bank credit expands further. This credit expansions fuels both the increase in demand and the increase in supply by easing credit constraints, and so the expansion is amplified. This credit multiplier – whereby more credit leads to more hiring of factors, more production, more bank deposits, and then to more credit – operates alongside the standard Keynesian income – expenditure multiplier. The interaction of the Keynesian and credit multipliers is at the heart of this paper.[1]

The paper is organised as follows. Section 3.1 outlines the essential elements of the model, including microfoundations for some of the assumptions. Section 3.2 sketches a rough version of the model, comments on the empirical relevance of the approach and relates the paper to an important strand of literature on credit rationing in less developed countries. The next two sections present and analyse two formal models in which credit rationing impinges on the behavior of firms. In the first (Section 3.3), credit rationing restricts the use of working capital and thus reduces aggregate supply. While this mechanism is the focus of the paper, credit rationing in the real world also has important effects on aggregate *demand*. Therefore, in the second model (Section 3.4), credit rationing restricts investment spending, which naturally cuts into both aggregate demand and aggregate supply. In both models, I show that credit rationing enhances the power of monetary policy but reduces the power of fiscal policy. Section 3.5 is a brief summary.

3.1 ELEMENTS OF THE MODELS

While the models considered in this paper differ in some important ways, they share the following eight common elements:

1. *Firms need credit for working capital* (and for other purposes). They must pay their factors of production *before* they receive revenues from sales, and must borrow in order to do so. To eliminate the possibility of equity finance on the margin, all profits are assumed to be paid out to shareholders. These assumptions – which are, of course, overly strong – make credit an essential ingredient in the production process. Firms that cannot get credit must cut back their hiring, which is what I mean by an *effective supply failure*. Naturally, there are other ways to introduce demand for credit, such as for financing inventories (which will appear in Section 3.3) or for fixed investment (which will appear in Section 3.4).

2. *There is no auction market for credit*, that is, no commercial paper market. So, firms wishing to borrow must borrow from banks. This assumption, of course, gives banks primacy in the credit market in a very stark way. It perhaps needs some motivation.

    The modern literature on credit rationing stresses the moral hazard and adverse selection problems that arise when information is imperfect and default is possible.[2] In response to these problems, specialized institutions develop to acquire information about default risk. Such information is valuable because it enables a lender to distinguish more easily between good and bad risks. But it is very specific (knowing that Company A is a good risk may tell us little about Company B) and, for a variety of reasons, is also difficult to sell. Hence, the institution that gathers the information tends also to make the loans. We call these institutions banks.[3]

    To reduce the incentive to default, banks will try to devise contingency contracts that, for example, make the future cost and availability of credit depend on the borrower's previous performance. In conjunction with the specialised knowledge mentioned above, this type of contract ties particular borrowers to particular lenders, creating a 'customer market' of the sort described by Okun (1981). Thus, although the credit market is 'competitive' in the usual sense (free entry, many buyers and sellers), lenders will view different borrowers as highly imperfect substitutes, and borrowers will have the same attitudes about different lenders – at least in the short run. There may, in particular, be classes of borrowers (like small businesses) for whom denial of credit by 'their' bank has the effect of making credit inaccessible.

    For simplicity, this paper assumes that all firms are in this situation, so there is no substitute for bank loans. That is certainly not a realistic assumption for large firms. A better model would recognise the existence of two kinds of firms: large firms that can borrow either at the bank or in the auction market, and small firms that can borrow only at the bank. In such a world, when bank credit is restricted, small firms may borrow in the form of trade credit from large firms who can, in turn, go to the open market and are rationed only by price.[4] The best way to think of this paper is as a stepping-stone that includes only the small firms.[5]

3. *Banks normally ration credit.* As Stiglitz and Weiss (1981) argued, it may be unprofitable for a bank to raise its lending rate to clear the market; if so, credit rationing arises as an equilibrium phenomenon. Whether or not banks will ration credit depends on the nature of the rate-of-return function and on the availability of funds to the bank. In a system of fractional reserve banking (see just below), the central bank has considerable leverage over the latter.

4. *Credit expands as economic activity expands.* This is the idea behind the 'credit multiplier' sketched above and is justified as follows. Assume that banks, in addition to making customer loans, hold auction-market securities as a buffer stock, as suggested by Tobin (1982). Since deposit flows are stochastic, banks might hold liquid assets either because customer loans are fixed commitments and they face a penalty cost for borrowing from the central bank (King, (1986)) or because they are loath to renege on tacit loan commitments to their regular customers (Blinder, (1984)).

Regardless of the motive for holding securities, the flow of deposits (net of required or desired reserves) determines how many assets any single bank can acquire in both the customer and auction markets. For the banking system as a whole, however, the supply of deposits is generated endogenously from the available reserves and required reserve ratio. Thus, for the system as a whole, reserves, not deposits, are the binding constraint.

Consider the behavior of a single bank in a fractional reserve system. When it receives the deposit inflows, it sets aside reserves, invests some of the proceeds in government bonds, and lends the rest to customers, perhaps without changing the interest rate it charges – for reasons sketched by Stiglitz and Weiss (1981). As the economy expands, the probability of default declines and business loans become less risky.[6] So banks hold smaller excess reserves (thereby raising the deposit multiplier) and also shift their optimal portfolio proportions away from riskless government bonds toward risky (but higher yielding) business loans.[7]

Specifically, suppose that banks hold real excess reserves, E/P, that are a decreasing function of real national income:

$$E_t = \beta_1(\bar{y} - y_t) P_t \tag{3.1a}$$

where $\beta_1 > 0$ and $\bar{y}$ are constants. If M is bank deposits, the reserve identity is:

$$R_t = rM_t + E_t \qquad (3.1b)$$

where R_t is bank reserves and r is the required reserve ratio. The banks' balance sheet identity (ignoring net worth) is:

$$R_t + C_t + B_t = M_t \qquad (3.1c)$$

where B is the banks' holdings of government bonds and C is customer loans. The assumption that desired portfolios shift away from bonds toward loans as economic activity expands is:

$$C_t = h(1-r)M_t + \beta_2(y_t - \bar{y})P_t \quad (\beta_2 > 0)$$
$$\hat{B}_t = (1-h)(1-r)M_t - (\beta_2 - \beta_1)(y_t - \bar{y})P_t \qquad (3.1d)$$

where $\hat{B}_t$ is the banks' *notional* demand for government bonds.[8] Substituting from (3.1a) and (3.1b) into (3.1d) yields:

$$C_t = \frac{h(1-r)}{r}R_t + \left[\beta_2 + \frac{\beta_1 h(1-r)}{r} \right](y_t - \bar{y})P_t$$

which can be written compactly as:

$$\frac{C_t}{P_t} = \frac{L_t}{P_t} + \alpha y_t \qquad (3.1)$$

where L_t/P_t is a linear function of real bank reserves, R_t/P_t. For convenience, I hereafter treat L, not R, as the central bank's policy instrument. It is L that controls the availability of customer-market credit. Note the important assumption that there is no substitute for bank reserves.

5. As mentioned already, *all interest elasticities are banned from the model*, as are other responses to relative prices such as input substitutions among labor, materials and capital in response to changes in relative factor prices.[9]

6. *A simple Keynesian income – expenditure multiplier* augmented by a real balance effect comprises the entire demand side of the model. There are no explicit investment goods in the models of Sections 3.2 and 3.3. Investment appears in Section 3.4, but does not depend on interest rates. These assumptions are strictly expositional – to close off the standard Keynesian channel for monetary policy. The real balance effect on consumption is included only as a way to make the price level determinate when there is no credit rationing; in several places I assume that it is 'small.'

7. *Money plays no essential role in the models.* Firms hold money to

facilitate production. But money adjusts passively to income, as in King and Plosser (1984), and not the other way around.[10] However, high-powered money, that is, bank reserves, is central to the model.

8. In those places in which expectations enter the models, I assume *perfect foresight*. So expectational errors also play no role in the analysis.

3.2 CREDIT RATIONING AND SUPPLY: THE BASIC IDEAS

3.2.1 A preliminary model

I begin with a preliminary 'finger exercise' model that embeds in an otherwise conventional macro structure the idea that credit rationing might create a shortage of working capital, and thereby force firms to cut back on production. While seriously deficient in many respects, the model has the virtue of making the links from credit rationing to working capital to output completely transparent. There will be time for subtlety later.

Firms hire factors of production at constant relative prices that are normalized to unity. Thus, the quantity of factors hired and real factor payments are represented by the same symbol, F_t, which should be thought of as an amalgam of labor, materials and capital. Since relative prices do not change, neither should factor proportions. It is important to note that, unlike many other models of monetary policy, the expansions and contractions of real output in this model do not stem from any policy-induced change in the real wage.

Factors hired at time t are paid immediately and go to work. One period later, they produce output. Assuming constant returns to scale and fixed factor proportions, the production function is:

$$y_t = vF_{t-1} \tag{3.2}$$

where v is a measure of productivity $(v > 1)$

Aggregate demand comes from a simple linear consumption function with a real balance effect:

$$x_t = a + by_t + s(L_t/P_t) \quad (0 < b < 1, s > 0) \tag{3.3}$$

where x_t is real final sales. Here, a is Keynesian 'autonomous expenditure,' b is the marginal propensity to consume, and s indicates the wealth effect of outside money. I presume s to be small.

Credit rationing is the critical element of the model. Under the assumption that firms expectations are correct, firms today expect to sell x_{t+1} next period. To produce this much output, they must hire x_{t+1}/v factors today. Hence, if unconstrained, their hiring today would be x_{t+1}/v, which constitutes the *notional* demand for credit:

$$\frac{C_t^d}{P_t} = \frac{x_{t+1}}{v} \tag{3.4a}$$

where P_t is the price level and C_t is nominal credit.[11, 12] However, as noted above, banks may ration credit to a maximum volume C_t. Hence actual credit is:

$$C_t^a = \min(C_t^d, C_t) \tag{3.4b}$$

Since factor hiring and borrowing are taken to be equal (recall: there is no substitute for bank credit), we have, in real terms:

$$F_t = \min\left(\frac{x_{t+1}}{v}, \frac{C_t}{P_t}\right) \tag{3.4}$$

Finally, the price level adjusts according to the 'law of supply and demand':

$$P_{t+1} - P_t = \lambda(x_t - y_t), \quad (\lambda > 0) \tag{3.5}$$

Consider the credit-rationed regime. If the credit constraint is binding, then (3.1), (3.2) and (3.4) imply the following difference equation for factor payments:

$$F_t = (L/P)_t + uF_{t-1} \tag{3.6}$$

where $u = \alpha v$. Subtracting F_{t-1} from both sides gives a dynamic equation for real factor payments:

$$F_t - F_{t-1} = \frac{L_t}{P_t} - (1-u)F_{t-1} \tag{3.7}$$

Substituting (3.2) and (3.3) into (3.5) gives the other dynamic equation, for the price level:

$$P_{t+1} - P_t = \lambda\left[a + s\frac{L_t}{P_t} - v(1-b)F_{t-1}\right] \tag{3.8}$$

By setting both equations equal to zero, we obtain the stationaries $\Delta P = 0$ and $\Delta K = 0$ in Fig. 3.1. (It is convenient to put L/P rather than P on the vertical axis.) The $\Delta P = 0$ locus is steeper so long as:

$$v(1-b) > s(1-u) \tag{3.9}$$

which is assumed.[13]

As can be seen by inspection, the credit-rationed equilibrium, point R, is a saddle point. If L/P starts at just the right level (given F_{t-1}), the system will converge to point R along the stable arm indicated in the diagram. Otherwise, the system will explode.[14] In sharp contrast to many modern models with rational expectations, however, there is no optimising agent that sets L/P at just the right level to put the economy on the convergent path. The price level is a state variable, inherited from the past. While the central bank could, in principle, manipulate L to keep the economy on the saddle path, I find this a bizarre way to characterize actual monetary policy. Hence I view the convergent path as a knife-edge solution, obtained only by coincidence. Instability is the more likely, and therefore the more interesting, outcome.

There are two possibilities. Explosion in the north-easterly direction means that output is rising while the price level is falling (L/P is rising) – a deflationary boom! With the supply of real credit rising, you might expect that the credit constraint would soon cease to be binding. When the model is fleshed out, this will be shown to be the case.

Explosion in the south-westerly direction is stagflationary: output falls as prices rise (L/P falls). The dynamic mechanism in this case is interesting and important enough to merit attention. Why is the model unstable?

Ignore the financial parameters s and u for the moment (that is, set $s = u = 0$), and suppose that, starting from equilibrium, credit is reduced by one unit. Demand *next period* will fall by bv, but *supply* next period will fall by v, which is bigger. Hence the credit restriction causes *excess demand* as long as $b < 1$.[15]

Excess demand drives prices higher, according to (3.5). But with L fixed *in nominal terms*, rising prices lead to further reductions in real credit, and the whole cycle repeats: less credit leads to excess demand which leads to higher prices which leads to less credit... This chain of events, which may lead to dynamic instability under credit rationing, is the basic message of this paper.

Is this mechanism realistic? I think so. Credit restrictions do reduce effective supply in the real world (e.g. through investment). And if these effects are bigger than the effects of tight credit on demand, inflationary pressures will result. Section 3.4 will consider a model in which credit rationing impinges on fixed investment. Section 3.3 will elaborate the 'finger exercise' model based on working capital. This elaboration is necessary because Fig. 3.1 raises more questions than it answers. What happens in the case of upward explosion into the 'unrationed' region? What factors determine whether credit is rationed or not? Is the model still unstable under alternative price-adjustment mechanisms?

We can answer the last question right away. Suppose we replace the law of supply and demand by a Phillips-curve equation with a natural rate at F^*, namely:

$$P_{t+1} - P_t = \gamma(F_t - F^*) \tag{3.10}$$

Using (3.6), it can be seen that the $\Delta P = 0$ locus is now:

$$\frac{L_t}{P_t} + uF_{t-1} = F^*$$

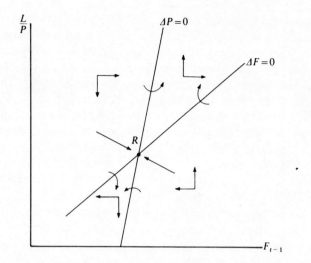

Fig 3.1 Saddle-point equilibrium in the preliminary model.

which is the downward-sloping line shown in Fig. 3.2. Evidently, the credit rationed equilibrium is now stable. What has changed? Notice that the demand parameters b and s from (3.3) are now irrelevant because demand no longer enters the picture. If inflation is determined by (3.10), a reduction in credit reduces factor-hiring, which is deflationary. (By contrast, under (3.5) a reduction in supply is inflationary.) The price level falls, thereby raising the real supply of credit back toward its original level. The equilibrium is stable. (See Fig. 3.2.)

In Section 3.3, when we elaborate and complicate the model, the relative importance of price adjustment according to (3.5) versus (3.10) will turn out to be critical to the nature of the credit-rationed equilibrium (if one exists). Figures 3.1 and 3.2 show, in the simplest possible terms, why this is so.

3.2.2 Empirical relevance

Economics is not an art form, so a theoretical model needs to be justified. Precisely where is this kind of analysis applicable? Is it an important factor in macroeconomic fluctuations? There are several possible answers.

In the contemporary US and UK economies, there seems to be a strong *a priori* case that quantity rationing is important in the housing sector – where builders are mostly small, undercapitalised firms that rely on banks for working capital. Also, if we think of households as producing services from durable goods (which they buy on credit), a similar story would apply to consumer durables. In addition, the story of firms curtailing their activities for lack of credit rings true for the small business sector (but not for

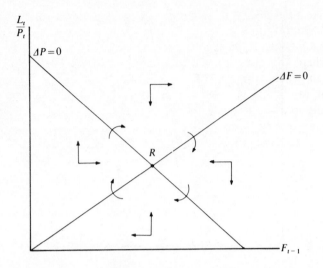

Fig. 3.2 Stable equilibrium with an alternative price equation.

giant corporations). The importance of housing and durable goods industries in business fluctuations is too well known to require recitation.

It is also worth remembering that the complex, fluid financial markets that exist in the United States and the United Kingdom are not typical of other industrial countries, where securities markets may be rudimentary and much investment is financed by banks. Indeed, the US economy in the 1980s is quite different in this regard from the US economy in earlier decades. In other times and places, close substitutes for bank loans were not readily available and credit rationing may have played a dominant role in business cycles.[16]

Finally, it is not only in the industrial countries that business fluctuations are apparently linked to central bank policy. There is a growing literature in development economics that argues – on both institutional and econometric grounds – that credit restrictions, which reduce the supply of credit for either working capital or investment, are a major channel through which financial policies have real effects. This line of research derives from the seminal insights of McKinnon (1973), who suggested that financial repression may lead both to credit rationing and to inadequate savings in LDCs.

Notice that the rationing discussed by McKinnon and others is a disequilibrium phenomenon caused by legal ceilings on interest rates; and empirical work in this spirit has stressed the high interest rates that consequently arise in the 'curb market.'[17] By contrast, the models developed in this paper are based on the modern theory of imperfect information. They envisage credit rationing as an equilibrium phenomenon and do not rely on the 'cost-push' effects of interest rates on aggregate supply. Nor can the supply-reducing effects of equilibrium credit rationing be eliminated by financial liberalization. In all these ways, the approach of this paper differs from the LDC literature. But the two are clearly related. This is a place, I think, where the disconnected literatures on LDCs and macroeconomic theory can benefit from cross-fertilisation.

In sum, I think the approach sketched above at least potentially applies to several important sectors of the US economy today, to most of the economies of many other countries today, and to almost all economies in earlier times. That strikes me as sufficient justification to proceed to more formal analysis.

3.3 CREDIT RATIONING AND WORKING CAPITAL

In the finger-exercise model of Section 3.2, demand (sales) and supply (production) can differ. If they do, then inventories must be changing. In order to add inventories to the model while keeping the dynamics to second-order (so as to permit graphical analysis), I switch to continuous time, thereby eliminating the lags present in the preliminary model.[18] Hence, equations (3.1)–(3.4) become:

$$\frac{C_t}{P_t} = \frac{L_t}{P_t} + uF_t \tag{3.11}$$

$$y_t = vF_t \tag{3.12}$$

$$x_t = a + by_t + s\left(\frac{L}{P}\right)_t \tag{3.13}$$

$$F_t = \min\left[\frac{x_t + \theta(\bar{H} - H_t)}{v}, \frac{C_t}{P_t} - (H_t - \bar{H})\right] \tag{3.14}$$

where H is the stock of inventories and $\bar{H}$ is the (constant) desired stock.

Compared to equations (3.1) and (3.2), equations (3.11) and (3.12) eliminate the lag of production behind factor payments, effectively removing the previous short-period dynamics of F_t. The dynamics now come exclusively from inventory change and gradual price adjustment. Owing to the elimination of the one-period production lag, the need for working capital now becomes entirely allegorical. Those obsessed with a need for precision should think of factor payments as being paid 'just before' output is produced, so that credit is only for a fleeting instant. Those not so obsessed should think of the one-period lag as still present in spirit, but suppressed to allow a convenient graphical exposition of the ideas.

Equation (3.14) requires explanation. As before, x_t is assumed equal to expected sales. Now, however, a firm whose initial inventories (H_t) differ from its desired inventory stock ($\bar{H}$) will not wish to produce what it expects to sell. Instead, as indicated in Blinder and Fischer (1981) and in Blinder (1982), it will produce expected sales plus some fraction, θ, of its inventory shortfall. This explains the first-term in (3.14), which applies when credit is not rationed.

The second-term recognises that financing inventories is a second use of credit, in addition to providing working capital. The assumption is that the firm's equity is sufficient to finance its steady-state inventory stock, $\bar{H}$, but that bank credit is used to finance any deviation of inventories from this norm. The available credit is still C_t/P_t, but now $(C_t/P_t)-(H_t-\bar{H})$ is available to finance working capital and hence is the second term of (3.14).

Two further amendments to the model are needed. First, we need the identity that inventory change is the difference between production and sales:

$$\dot{H}=y-x \qquad (3.15)$$

The price adjustment specification combines the 'law of supply and demand' (3.5) and the 'Phillips curve' (3.10):

$$\dot{P} = \lambda(x-y)+\gamma(y-y^*) \qquad (3.16)$$

where y^* is the (exogenous) natural rate of output. Obviously, the special cases $\lambda=0$ and $\gamma=0$ merit special attention, for the preliminary model suggests that they could lead to quite different dynamics under credit rationing.[19]

I proceed by analysing the model separately in the two regimes defined by (3.14) and then putting the two regimes together.

3.3.1 The Keynesian regime

I call the regime in which the credit constraint is not binding 'Keynesian' because it yields a familiar Keynesian solution. From (3.15) and (3.16), it is clear that steady-state equilibrium requires that $x=y=y^*$. By (3.14) and (3.12), then, $H=\bar{H}$. Hence, the Keynesian equilibrium is defined by the pair of equalities:

$$y = \frac{a+s(L/P)}{1-b} = y^* \qquad (3.17)$$

The first equality is the simple Keynesian multiplier formula. The second pins down the price level. (As mentioned earlier, this is the only role of the real balance effect.) Obviously, one requirement for a Keynesian equilibrium to exist is that:

$$y^* > a/(1-b) \qquad (3.18)$$

I assume hereafter that this condition holds; but it will be false if a is large enough relative to y^*.

Away from the steady state, output is given by:

$$y = \frac{a + s(L/P) - \theta(H - \bar{H})}{1 - b} \tag{3.19}$$

which follows from (3.13) and (3.14). Output is higher the higher autonomous expenditure is, the higher real bank reserves are and the lower inventories are. Since, by (3.13) and (3.19), the difference $x - y$ is $\theta(H - \bar{H})$, it follows from (3.15) that the $\dot{H} = 0$ locus is the vertical line at $\bar{H}$ in Fig. 3.3. Similarly, Appendix 3.1 shows that the $\dot{P} = 0$ locus is a straight line which crosses $H = \bar{H}$ at a positive value of L/P so long as a Keynesian equilibrium exists (i.e. if (3.18) holds) and whose slope has the sign of :

$$\rho \equiv \gamma - \lambda(1 - b) \tag{3.20}$$

(See the two panels of Fig. 3.3.)

The sign of ρ depends on the relative sizes of λ and γ. If $\gamma = 0$ (pure law of supply and demand), ρ is negative; if $\lambda = 0$ (pure Phillips curve), ρ is positive. The parameter ρ has the following meaning. If higher inventories reduce prices, then ρ is positive; if higher inventories raise prices, then ρ is negative. In what follows, I will assume that $\rho > 0$ is the normal case, but will allow for the possibility that $\rho < 0$ as well. Figure 3.3 shows that the Keynesian equilibrium is stable regardless of the sign of ρ.

3.3.2 The credit-rationed regime

Under credit rationing, (3.11), (3.12), and (3.14) imply that output is given by:

$$y = \frac{v}{1 - u}\left[\frac{L}{P} - (H - \bar{H})\right] \tag{3.21}$$

Notice the differences between (3.21) and the Keynesian multiplier formula (3.19). When credit is rationed, autonomous expenditure has no effect on output, but bank reserves have a larger effect (assuming that (3.9) holds). In terms of the issues that motivated this paper, we see that monetary policy is more powerful, and fiscal policy (a rise in 'a' might represent a balanced-budget rise in government purchases) is less powerful in the credit-rationed regime than in the Keynesian regime. In fact, if the real balance effect is absent ($s = 0$), monetary policy has no real effects in the Keynesian regime while fiscal policy has no real effects in the credit-rationed regime![20]

Equations (3.15) and (3.16) continue to require that $x = y = y^*$ in steady-state equilibrium, but H need not be equal to $\bar{H}$ when credit is rationed. Specifically, some algebraic effort (displayed in Appendix 3.1) shows that an equilibrium with credit rationing exists only when $H < \bar{H}$ and:

$$y^* < \frac{a}{1 - b - (s/v)(1 - u)}$$

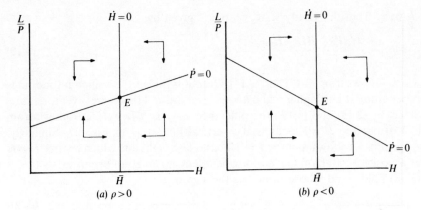

Fig. 3.3 Stable equilibrium in the Keynesian regime.

Since (3.18) continues to be the requirement for a finite price level, there can be an equilibrium with credit rationing only if:

$$\frac{a}{1-b} < y^* < \frac{a}{1-b-(s/v)(1-u)} \tag{3.22}$$

Appendix 3.1 shows that the $\dot{H}=0$ locus in the credit-rationed regime has a positive slope that exceeds unity (see Fig. 3.4), while the $\dot{P}=0$ locus is a straight line with slope:

$$\frac{\rho v}{\rho v + \lambda s(1-u)} = v\left[\frac{\gamma - \lambda(1-b)}{\gamma v - \lambda q}\right] \tag{3.23}$$

where:

$$q \equiv v(1-b) - s(1-u) > 0 \tag{3.24}$$

This is clearly positive if either $\lambda = 0$ (pure Phillips curve) or $\gamma = 0$ (pure law of supply and demand). To avoid a taxonomic treatment, I will hereafter assume that (3.23) is positive regardless of the sign of ρ.

The two alternative phase diagrams for the credit-rationed regime are shown in Fig. 3.4. They are as follows:

1. *Panel (a)*. If ρ is positive, which must be so if $\lambda = 0$, Appendix 3.1 shows that the slope of the $\dot{H}=0$ locus must exceed that of the $\dot{P}=0$ locus. The credit-rationed equilibrium (if one exists) is stable.

2. *Panel (b)*. If both ρ and $\rho v + \lambda s(1-u)$ are negative (which must occur if $\gamma = 0$), Appendix 3.1 shows that the slope of the $\dot{P}=0$ locus is positive and larger than that of the $\dot{H}=0$ locus, In this case, the credit-rationed equilibrium may be stable or unstable, depending on initial conditions

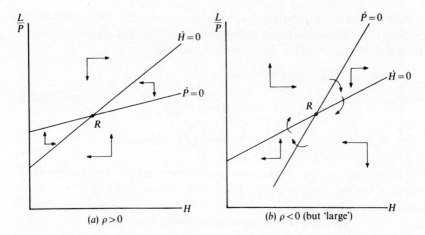

Fig. 3.4 Two possible equilibria in the credit-rationed regime.

and parameter values. The unstable case here is the analog, in this more complicated model, of Fig. 3.1 above.

3.3.3 The borderline between the regimes

To complete the phase diagram, it only remains to locate the border between the Keynesian and credit-rationed regions. This is easily done. The demand for credit in the Keynesian regime is:

$$\frac{a + s(L/P) - \theta(H - \bar{H})}{v(1-b)}$$

The supply of credit in the rationed regime is:

$$\frac{(L/P) - (H - \bar{H})}{1 - u}$$

Setting them equal defines the border. The appendix shows that the border and the $\dot{H} = 0$ locus of the credit-rationed region intersect at $H = \bar{H}$, with the former having the smaller slope. Since the slope of the border can be either positive or negative, and is immaterial to the analysis anyway, I will simply draw the border as horizontal for convenience.

Given the equation for the border, it is straightforward to show (see Appendix 3.1) that the Keynesian equilibrium (point E in Fig. 3.3) occurs above the border if:

$$y^* > \frac{a}{1 - b - (s/v)(1 - u)} \tag{3.25}$$

Similarly, some truly horrendous algebra shows that the credit-rationed equilibrium (point R in Fig. 3.4) lies below the border if and only if (3.25) is reversed. Hence, we have the following possibilities:

1. $y^* < a/(1-b) \rightarrow$ no equilibrium

2. $a/(1-b) < y^* < \dfrac{a}{(1-b)-(s/v)(1-u)} \rightarrow$ a credit-rationed equilibrium

3. $y^* > \dfrac{a}{1-b-(s/v)(1-u)} \rightarrow$ a Keynesian equilibrium

Notice that if s, the real balance effect, is very small, there is little 'room' between the two bounds in (2). This makes the existence of an equilibrium with credit rationing unlikely. So, the likely case is that a Keynesian equilibrium, but no credit-rationed equilibrium, exists.

3.3.4 Dynamics when $\rho > 0$

I now put the two regions together and analyze the dynamics of the complete system. Consider first the case $\rho > 0$ which, as already mentioned, seems the more likely case. (It is the only possibility if $\lambda = 0$.)

Combining Figs. 3.3(a) and 3.4(a) gives the phase diagram shown in Fig. 3.5, which shows a Keynesian equilibrium but no equilibrium with credit rationing. Should a decline in L lead to a period of credit rationing (see point B), a process of deflation would begin, thereby raising L/P. This deflation would continue until the price level fell by enough to restore L/P to its original value (see point E). Hence, the model is globally stable and credit rationing is a self-curing malady.[21]

Let us consider the effects of central bank policy, starting from equilibrium at point E. If L rises, real output will rise (according to (3.19)), putting the economy in a position like D, where the price level is below equilibrium. A period of inflation will ensue, and will continue until L/P is restored to its equilibrium level. During the inflationary adjustment, y will be falling because L/P is falling.[22] But all of this 'action' induced by a contraction of bank reserves is presumably minor because the impact multiplier for monetary policy is:

$$\frac{dY}{d(L/P)} = \frac{s}{1-b}$$

and s is assumed to be small.

The effects of a decline in L are symmetric *unless* the decline is large enough to push the economy into the credit-rationed region. In the rationed region, the impact multiplier for monetary policy is much larger, according

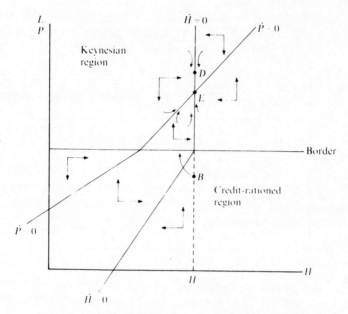

Fig. 3.5 The full model with $\rho > 0$: Keynesian equilibrium.

to (3.21). Specifically, it is:

$$\frac{dY}{d(L/P)} = \frac{v}{1-u}$$

If L is reduced starting from a point like B, prices and output start to fall. Since output declines by more than sales, inventories start to fall. Falling inventory stocks tend to push output back up toward equilibrium. Eventually, inventories reach a minimum and begin to be replenished. But deflation continues until L/P is restored to its original level.

So we conclude that the effects of monetary policy, while qualitatively similar in the two regimes, may be rather weak in the Keynesian regime and rather strong in the credit-rationed regime. Translated into real-world terms, a tightening of monetary policy may have strong effects on the real sector when money is already tight, but weak effects when credit is initially plentiful.

What happens if autonomous expenditure, a, rises? The multiplier formula shows that y rises strongly if the economy is in the Keynesian regime. Inspection of the equations that underlie Fig. 3.5 shows that (see Fig. 3.6):

1. The $\dot{P}=0$ locus shifts to the right in both regions, so the equilibrium point, E, shifts down vertically (to a higher equilibrium price level).
2. The border shifts up.

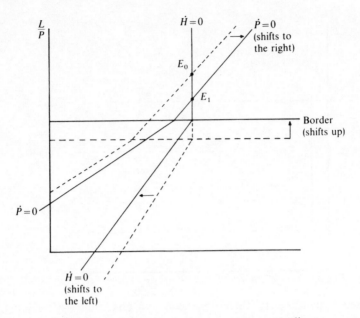

Fig. 3.6 The effects of a rise in autonomous spending.

3. The $\dot{H}=0$ locus shifts to the left in the credit-rationed region, but does not move in the Keynesian region. These shifts are depicted in Fig. 3.6, in which the 'old' lines are drawn broken and the 'new' lines are drawn solid. We see that a rise in 'a' leaves the economy at a point qualitatively similar to point D in Fig. 3.5. The adjustment process from D to E – which entails rising P and falling y – has already been described.

Now consider the possibility that autonomous spending grows so large that the Keynesian equilibrium depicted in Fig. 3.5 ceases to exist, but that s is large enough so that an equilibrium with credit rationing arises. This is shown in Fig. 3.7.

If that happens, the economy initially finds itself at a disequilibrium point like C or, if the border shifts up strongly enough, like B in Fig. 3.7. A substantial inflation ensues – enough to drive L/P down to the new equilibrium level indicated by point R. As the economy moves from point C down to point D, y is falling (slightly). Once the border is crossed, it is no longer clear whether y is rising or falling because the contractionary effects of declining L/P are counteracted by the expansionary effects of falling H.

3.3.5 Dynamics when $\rho < 0$

Now assume that γ is so small that $\rho < 0$ and the $\dot{P}=0$ locus in the credit-rationed region is positively sloped. Since it must be steeper than the $\dot{H}=0$

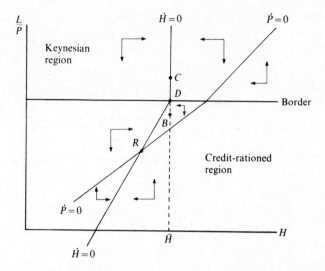

Fig. 3.7 The full model with $\rho > 0$: credit-rationed equilibrium.

locus (see Appendix 3.1), there are again two possibilities, depending on whether the equilibrium is Keynesian or credit rationed. The case of a Keynesian equilibrium, which combines Fig. 3.3b and 4.4b, is qualitatively similar to Fig. 3.5 and need not be analyzed further; the economy can be credit rationed for a period, but it always returns to the Keynesian equilibrium.

Figure 3.8 depicts the more interesting possibility. The economy's only equilibrium here is credit-rationed; but it might not be stable. Following a perturbation, the economy exhibits a cyclical adjustment period which might alternate between periods of rationed and unrationed credit. The adjustment process could be stable (spiralling in to point R) or unstable (spiralling away). The unstable case tells a story that is similar to that told by our preliminary model in Section 3.2.

3.4 CREDIT RATIONING AND FIXED CAPITAL

One valid objection to the model of Section 3.3 is that credit rationing there affects only aggregate supply, whereas in reality it is commonly believed that rationing has important effects on aggregate demand (such as for housing and consumer durables). To meet this objection, this section develops a model in which credit rationing impinges on capital formation, and therefore affects both aggregate demand (in the short run) and aggregate supply (in the long run). Since the capital stock adds an additional dynamic variable, and since I want to keep the dynamics to second order, I eliminate inventory changes by assuming that firms always produce to meet demand ($y = x$).

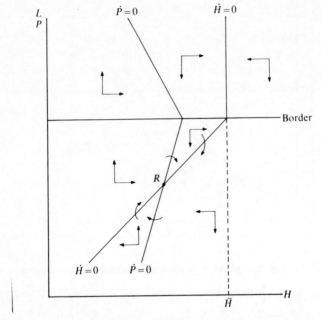

Fig. 3.8 The full model with $\rho < 0$: credit-rationed equilibrium.

To allow for capital accumulation, it is, of course, necessary to distinguish between fixed capital, K, and other factors of production—which I call 'labor', N. Hence, the simple production technology of Sections 3.2 and 3.3 will no longer do. The supply side of the investment model is best understood by referring to Fig. 3.9, which is a standard isoquant diagram. Ray OE shows the expansion path of a firm with constant returns to scale under the given wage-rental ratio. Since the wage-rental ratio is assumed constant throughout the analysis, the cost-minimizing input combinations all lie along OE.

Suppose the firm wants to produce y_0, because that is the amount demanded. The optimal capital stock for this level of output is ϕy_0 (point A). Suppose the firm's actual capital stock is only K_0. Its short-run strategy, I assume, is to produce y_0 by using K_0 units of capital and N_0 units of labor (point B), where N_0 is obtained from the production function. This is a disequilibrium situation in two respects. First, output is above normal 'capacity'—which is most naturally defined as K_0/ϕ. The firm is not producing y_0 at minimum cost, and so will want to acquire more capital. Second, while I assume that workers supply as much (or as little) labor as is demanded in the short run, the level of employment, N_0, may not match the notional supply of labor. If it does not, there will be either upward or downward pressure on wages and prices. (The real wage is constant.)

The long-run equilibrium is determined by the notional supply of labor, N^* in the diagram. To employ the labor force fully, output must be y^* (point

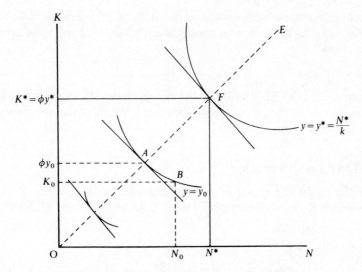

Fig. 3.9 Isoquants for the investment model.

F); and the capital stock must be $K^* = \phi y^*$. Hence, while output is demand-determined in the short run, it is supply-determined in the long run.

A set of equations that captures these ideas is:

$$\bar{y} = K/\phi \qquad \text{(capacity)} \qquad (3.26)$$

$$N = N(y, K) \qquad \text{(employment)} \qquad (3.27)$$

$$\dot{K} = I = \beta(\phi\ y - K) \qquad \text{(investment)} \qquad (3.28)$$

where output is determined by (3.13), augmented by the addition of investment:

$$y = a + by + s(L/P) + I \qquad (3.29)$$

and the function $N(.)$ in (3.27) is obtained by inverting the production function.

Two factors influence prices (and wages): the pressure of output (y) on normal capacity ($\bar{y}$) and the pressure of employment (N) on the available supply of labor (N^*). Hence, the price equation is:

$$\dot{P} = \lambda(y - \bar{y}) + \gamma\ (N - N^*) \qquad (3.30)$$

where N^* is the (exogenous) natural level of employment and $\bar{y}$ is the (endogenous) capacity level.

The model is completed by specifying the credit market. The credit constraint now says that the volume of working capital, N, and end-of-period fixed capital ($K + I$) cannot exceed the real supply of credit.[23]

$$C/P \geqslant N + K + I \qquad (3.31)$$

(Here the real wage is normalized to unity and the price of a capital good is assumed equal to the price of a consumption good.) The supply of credit is still given by:

$$C/P = L/P + \alpha y \tag{3.32}$$

Equations (3.26)–(3.32) constitute the entire model. If (3.31) holds as an equality, we are in the credit-rationed regime; if it holds as an inequality, we are in the Keynesian regime.

3.4.1 The Keynesian regime

When the credit constraint is not binding, output is determined by the conventional Keynesian multiplier formula. From (3.28) and (3.29)

$$y = \frac{a + s(L/P) - \beta K}{1 - b - \beta\phi} \tag{3.33}$$

In the steady-state, of course, y will be equal to the natural rate, y^*, which is defined implicitly by $N^* = N(y^*, \phi y^*)$. Similarly, K will be equal to $K^* = \phi y^*$; so (3.33) becomes:

$$y^* = \frac{a + s(L/P)}{1 - b} \tag{3.34}$$

which determines the price level so long as the existence condition (3.18) holds.

Using (3.28) and (3.33), investment in the model will be:

$$\dot{K} = I = \beta(1 - b - \beta\phi)^{-1} [\phi[a + s(L/P)] - (1 - b)K] \tag{3.35}$$

so that each dollar of autonomous expenditure 'crowds in':

$$\frac{\partial I}{\partial a} = \frac{\beta\phi}{1 - b - \beta\phi} > 0$$

dollars of investment. Equation (3.35), of course, defines the $\dot{K} = 0$ locus which appears in Fig. 3.10.

The rest of the dynamics of the model follow by substituting (3.33) into (3.30) to get a nonlinear equation for $\dot{P}$. Appendix 3.2 shows that the $\dot{P} = 0$ locus can be linearized around equilibrium to get a line whose slope is less than the slope of the $\dot{K} = 0$ locus. Hence the phase diagram for the Keynesian region looks like Fig. 3.10. The Keynesian equilibrium at E is stable (if it exists).

3.4.2 The credit-rationed regime

Two possible variants of credit rationing can be accommodated within the structure of this model, depending on whether it is fixed or working capital

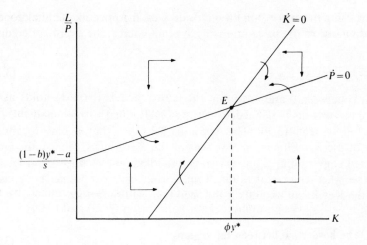

Fig. 3.10 Stable equilibrium in the Keynesian regime: investment model.

that is rationed. Since rationing of working capital was studied in Section 3.3, I assume here that it is investment that gets rationed when the credit constraint is binding. Hence, when (3.31) holds as an equality, we have:

$$C/P = N(y, K) + K + I$$

which, using (3.32), means that investment is rationed to:

$$I = (L/P) + \alpha y - N(y, K) - K$$

Of course, a reduction of I will make y fall as well, as is standard in Keynesian analysis. Substituting for I into (3.29) gives an equation for the level of output under credit rationing:

$$y = a + by + s(L/P) + L/P + \alpha y - N(y, K) - K$$

which implicitly defines:

$$y = Y(\underset{+}{a}, \underset{+}{L/P}, \underset{-}{K}) \tag{3.36}$$

with the signs of the partial derivatives as indicated.

Appendix 3.2 shows that $\partial Y/\partial a$ is smaller than the corresponding multiplier in the Keynesian case (see equation (3.33)), and that $\partial Y/\partial(L/P)$ is larger. These comparisons echo those of Section 3.3, though the multiplier for autonomous expenditure is no longer zero when credit is rationed.

Using (3.36), the constrained rate of investment is found to be:

$$\dot{K} = I + L/P - K + \alpha Y(a, L/P, K) - N[Y(a, L/P, K), K] \tag{3.37}$$

Hence, using the expression for $\partial Y/\partial a$ derived in Appendix 3.2, the degree of crowding out is:

$$\frac{\partial I}{\partial a} = \frac{N_y - \alpha}{1 - b + N_y - \alpha}$$

which is between 0 and -1.

The $\dot{K} = 0$ locus is defined by setting (3.37) equal to zero, and the $\dot{P} = 0$ locus follows from (3.30). The Appendix 3.2 shows that, at least locally, the slope of the $\dot{P} = 0$ locus exceeds that of the $\dot{K} = 0$ locus. Hence, the credit-rationed equilibrium, if one exists, is a saddle point such as R in Fig. 3.11.

To see whether a credit-rationed equilibrium can exist, we need to consider how the Keynesian and credit-rationed regions fit together.

3.4.3 The borderline between the regions

The borderline is determined as before, by equating the real demand for credit in the Keynesian regime:

$$N(y, K) + K + \beta(\phi y - K)$$

to the real supply of credit:

$$L/P + \alpha y$$

where in both cases y is given by (3.33). Even after linearization, the slope of the border could have either sign; in the graphs to follow, I draw it as horizontal.

3.4.4 Dynamic analysis

Combining Figs. 3.10 and 3.11 leaves two main possibilities, depending on whether or not a credit-rationed equilibrium exists. (I assume that a Keynesian equilibrium does exist.)

If the two stationaries intersect outside the positive quadrant, there will be a stable Keynesian equilibrium, but no credit-rationed equilibrium. In this case, if shocks propel the economy into the credit-rationed region, deflation eventually forces L/P up until credit is no longer rationed. The comparative dynamics are essentially identical to Fig. 3.5 for the working capital model, so I will not bother to repeat the analysis.

Figure 3.12 shows the other possibility. Here, the economy has two equilibria: a Keynesian equilibrium at E which is locally stable, and a credit-rationed equilibrium at R which is (locally) a saddle point. Depending on the initial value of L/P, the model can converge to the Keynesian equilibrium, converge to the credit-rationed equilibrium (a knife-edge possibility), or explode in the south-westerly direction with prices rising and capacity falling.

Some properties of the credit-rationed equilibrium are worth mentioning. Since investment is rationed, and is zero in equilibrium, K is naturally below

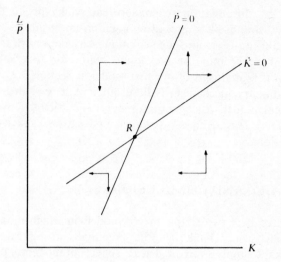

Fig. 3.11 Saddle-point equilibrium in the credit-rationed regime: investment model.

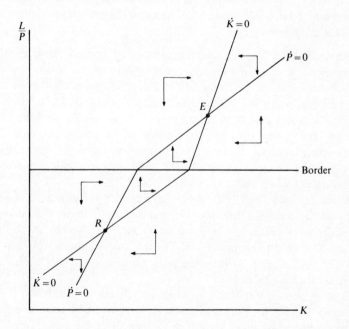

Fig. 3.12 Investment model with both Keynesian and credit-rationed equilibria.

K^*. K is also below ϕy ('desired capital'), but investment is inhibited by rationing. Thus, output is above capacity, even though it is below the natural rate: $\bar{y} < y < y^*$.

The latter inequality means that there is unemployment in equilibrium. This unemployment puts downward pressure on the price level, but that is exactly offset by the inflationary pressure caused by production beyond capacity. If that sounds like a precarious equilibrium, it should – because the rationed equilibrium is a knife-edge solution. Any departure from equilibrium will lead either into the Keynesian region or to a stagflationary explosion that is reminiscent of our first model in Section 3.2.

The stagflationary mechanism is little different here than it was in the working capital model. Rising prices reduce L/P, thereby making credit rationing tighter. This reduces investment and causes capacity to shrink, which is inflationary.

3.5 SUMMARY AND CONCLUSIONS

I have presented here two simple macro models in which money plays no role, but in which central bank policy has potentially strong real effects via its influence over the supply of credit. The real effects of monetary policy do not derive from interest elasticities or from expectational errors, but from credit rationing. And it is not hard (for me, at least) to imagine that this channel of influence might be quite powerful. The central conclusions from the two models are as follows:

1. Depending on the relative magnitudes of central bank credit and aggregate demand, the economy may or may not be credit constrained. Its behavior is qualitatively different depending on whether or not the credit constraint is binding. For example, when credit is rationed the effect of autonomous spending on output is smaller, and the effect of monetary policy is larger than when credit is not rationed. In the investment model, autonomous expenditure crowds out investment only when credit is rationed (and then only partially); it crowds in investment when credit is not rationed.
2. When the economy is credit-constrained, it is subject to a kind of instability owing to inflation. If it reduces supply more than demand, a reduction in credit can be inflationary and can thereby make the real supply of credit shrink further. The inflationary impact of tight credit found here is different from the more familiar cost-push mechanism of higher interest rates.[24]
3. Despite this destabilizing mechanism, dynamic instability is by no means inevitable. Potential instability from credit rationing may be overwhelmed by other stabilizing influences in the model (represented here by the real balance effect and the Phillips curve). If so, credit rationing is a self-correcting malady.

I believe these conclusions are quite robust, and hence are more interesting than the particular models used to derive them. The paper is, nonetheless, only a fragment of a more complete model. Its most important contribution,

I hope, is to start down the road toward a theory of effective supply, based on credit rationing (and perhaps on other phenomena as well). When more fully developed, the principle of effective supply may take its place alongside the Keynesian principle of effective demand as the twin pillars of nonclassical macroeconomics.

3.6 NOTES

1. Bernanke (1981) sketches a similar scenario.
2. See Stiglitz and Weiss (1981), who in turn built on the work of Jaffee and Russell (1976).
3. Nakamura (1984) argues that there is an important economy of scope in banking: banks get information from managing a firm's deposit account that is unavailable to others and that enables banks to reduce the riskiness of their loans.
4. Empirically, however, we do not observe a negative correlation between (detrended) bank loans on the one hand and either (detrended) trade credit or (detrended) commercial paper on the other. So this 'escape hatch' may not be as important as many economists have supposed.
5. Or as a model of an economy without a developed capital market. In fact, after circulating a first draft of this paper, I learned about several papers in development economics that are based on the use of bank credit to finance working capital. More on this below.
6. Bernanke and Gertler (1989) derive this idea from cyclical fluctuations in the soundness of collateral.
7. Banks sell the bonds to households, who pay with money. (Households do not care how much money they hold.) Presumably, interest rates would have to rise to clear the bond market. But interest rates play no role in the model, so this is ignored.
8. If the rationing is effective, then $\hat{B}_t = B_t$. If firms do not take up all the available credit, then B_t is found residually from (3.1c).
9. Of course, it is always possible to associate a shadow price – in this case, a shadow interest rate – with any quantity rationed equilibrium and thereby translate the quantity story into a price story. In general, I think allowing interest rate channels would mainly reinforce the phenomena discussed in this paper.
10. If firms enlarge their holdings of money as output expands, they must sell some other asset. Implicitly, this 'other asset' (whose market is suppressed by Walras's Law) is government bonds. Banks may buy some of these bonds, but there are two conflicting effects: inflows of deposits lead banks to expand their holdings of all assets (including government bonds), but decreases in riskiness lead to portfolio shifts away from bonds. The remainder of the bonds are presumed to be bought by households, whose money holdings are purely passive. See note 7 to this chapter.
11. Notice that 'credit velocity,' which I take to be constant, is normalized to unity.
12. Equation (3.4a) oversimplifies a more complex (and messier!) reality. At time t, the firm realizes $p_t x_t$ from sales and pays back last period's loan in the amount $(1 + i_{t-1}) p_{t-1} x_t / v$, where i is the nominal interest rate. So its actual need for credit is the sum of (3.4a) plus: $[p_{t-1} (1 + i_{t-1})/v - p_t] x_t$. This additional term, which differs from zero to the extent that the real interest rate differs from $v - 1$, would create quite horrendous dynamics, and hence is ignored in the interests of

tractability. However, since $v-1$ ought to approximate the real rate of interest, this simplification should not introduce much error.

13. Recall: the real balance effect is assumed to be 'small.' This is one specific definition of 'small.'

14. Mathematically, these statements are not quite correct. Since the system is discrete rather than continuous, finite jumps from period to period are possible. In the formal modeling, I switch to continuous time to avoid the mathematical complexities inherent in discrete analysis.

15. When s and u are not zero, excess demand eventually arises as long as condition (3.9) holds.

16. For example, Bernanke's (1983) analysis of the Great Depression in the US is based on this idea.

17. See, for example, the interesting work on Korea by van Wijnbergen (1983), who attributes the idea to Cavallo (1977). Other relevant references are Kapur (1976), Taylor (1981) and Leff and Sato (1982).

18. Continuous time also reduces the mathematical complexities alluded to in note 14 to this chapter and those caused by regime switching. See below, especially note 21 to this chapter.

19. Actually, γ cannot be zero, for then the model becomes degenerate because $x=y$ defines both stationaries (see equations (3.15) and (3.16)). Hence, when I speak of $\gamma=0$, I really mean a very small value of γ.

20. The latter would not be true if banks' assessment of risk were more forward-looking than assumed in equations (3.1) (in which only today's output matters).

21. The regime change creates problems in analyzing the dynamics. However, Honkapohja and Ito (1983) point out that, if the directions of motion are the same on both sides of the border (as is true here), the trajectory will pass through the border. Under certain other conditions, the 'patched' system will be stable if the component systems are. See Honkapohja and Ito (1983).

22. In this model, there is perfect foresight and no lags. As a result, inventories do not change during the adjustment period. If production lagged, then the surge in demand would lower inventories, creating an initial point somewhat to the left of D and kicking off an inventory cycle.

23. This constraint is not quite right because it ignores the firm's equity. Since equity is assumed fixed throughout the analysis, it would just add a negative constant to the right-hand side of (3.31). To simplify the notation, this constant is suppressed. In principle, however, it is present.

24. But see note 9 to this chapter.

3.7 REFERENCES

Bernanke, B. S. (1981) 'Bankruptcy, liquidity and recession,' *American Economic Review*, vol. 71 (May), pp. 155–9.

Bernanke, B. S. (1983) 'Non-monetary effects of the financial crisis in the propagation of the Great Depression.' *American Economic Review*, vol. 73 (June), pp. 257–76.

Bernanke, B. S. and Gertler, M. (1989) 'Agency costs, net worth and business fluctuations,' *American Economic Review*, vol. 76, no. 1, pp. 14–31.

Blinder, A. S. (1982) 'Inventories and sticky prices: more on the microfoundations of macroeconomics.' *American Economic Review*, vol. 72 (June), pp. 334–48.

Blinder, A. S. (1984) 'Notes on the comparative statics of a Stiglitz–Weiss bank.' Mimeo, Princeton University, (December).

Blinder, A. S. and Fischer, S. (1981) 'Inventories, rational expectations, and the business cycle.' *Journal of Monetary Economics*, vol. 73 (November), pp. 277–304.
Blinder, A. S. and Stiglitz, J. E. (1983) 'Money, credit constraints, and economic activity,' *American Economic Review* vol. 73 (May), pp. 297–302.
Cavallo, D. F. (1977) 'Stagflationary effects of monetarist stabilization policies.' Unpublished PhD dissertation, Harvard University.
Honkapohja, S. and Ito, T. (1983) 'Stability with regime switching,' *Journal of Economic Theory*, vol. 29, pp. 22–48.
Jaffee, D. M. and Russell, T. (1976) 'Imperfect information and credit rationing,' *Quarterly Journal of Economics*, (November), pp. 651–66.
Kapur, B. K. (1976) 'Alternative stabilization policies for less-developed countries,' *Journal of Political Economy*, vol. 84, (August), pp. 777–95.
King, R. G. and Plosser, C. I. (1984) 'Money, credit, and prices in a real business cycle.' *American Economic Review*, vol. 74 (June), pp. 363–80.
King, S. R. (1986) 'Monetary transmission: through bank loans, or bank liabilities?' *Journal of Money, Credit and Banking*, (August), pp. 230–303.
Leff, N. and Sato, K. (1982) ' Macroeconomic disequilibrium and short-run economic growth in developing countries,' in M. Syrgiun (ed.) *Trade, Stability, Technology, and Equity in Latin America*, New York: Academic Press, pp. 290–303.
McKinnon, R. I. (1973) *Money and Capital in Economic Development*. Washington: Brookings.
Nakamura, L. (1984) 'Bankruptcy and the informational problems of commercial bank lending.' Mimeo, Princeton, September.
Okun, A. M. (1981) *Prices and Quantities.* Washington: Brookings.
Stiglitz, J. E. and Weiss, A. (1981) 'Credit rationing in markets with imperfect information.' *American Economic Review*, vol. 71 (June), pp. 393–410.
Taylor, L. (1981) '*IS/LM* in the tropics: diagrammatics of the new structuralist macro critique,' in *Economic Stabilization in Developing Countries*. Washington: W. Cline and S. Weintraub (eds), Brookings, pp. 465–506.
Tobin, J. (1982) 'The commercial banking firm: a simple model.' *Scandinavian Journal of Economics*, vol. 84, pp. 495–530.
Van Wijnbergen, S. (1983) 'Credit policy, inflation and growth in a financially repressed economy,' *Journal of Development Economics*, vol. 13, pp. 45–65.

APPENDIX 3.1 · THE WORKING CAPITAL MODEL

THE $\dot{P}=0$ LOCUS IN THE KEYNESIAN REGION

By (3.16) and (3.19):

$$\dot{P} = \lambda\theta(H-\bar{H}) + \frac{\gamma}{1-b}\left[a+s\frac{L}{P}-\theta(H-\bar{H})\right] - \gamma y^* \tag{A3.1.1}$$

Setting $\dot{P}=0$ yields:

$$s\frac{L}{P} = y^*(1-b) - a + \theta\left(1-\frac{\lambda}{\gamma}(1-b)\right)(H-\bar{H}) \tag{A3.1.2}$$

This is a straight line with slope $(\theta/s\gamma)(\gamma-\lambda(1-b))$, and with $H=\bar{H}$ 'intercept' $y^*(1-b)-a$, which is >0 if (3.18) holds.

THE $\dot{P}=0$ AND $\dot{H}=0$ LOCI IN THE CREDIT-RATIONED REGION

To find the $\dot{H}=0$ locus, substitute (3.13) into (3.15) to get:

$$\dot{H} = y - x = (1-b)y - \left(a+s\frac{L}{P}\right) = 0$$

$$0 = \frac{v(1-b)}{1-u}\left[\frac{L}{P}-(H-\bar{H})\right] - \left(a+s\frac{L}{P}\right)$$

or:

$$\frac{L}{P} = \frac{1}{q}[a(1-u)+v(1-b)(H-\bar{H})] \tag{A3.1.3}$$

where:

$$q \equiv v(1-b) - s(1-u) > 0 \tag{3.24}$$

To find the $\dot{P}=0$ locus, substitute (3.13) and (3.21) into (3.16) to get:

$$\dot{P} = \lambda\left[a - \frac{q}{1-u}\frac{L}{P} + \frac{v(1-b)}{1-u}(H-\bar{H})\right] + \gamma\left[\frac{v}{1-u}\left(\frac{L}{P}-(H-\bar{H})\right) - y^*\right]$$

Setting $\dot{P}=0$ yields:

$$\frac{L}{P} = [\rho v + \lambda s(1-u)]^{-1} \{(1-u)\gamma y^* - \lambda(1-u)a + \rho v(H-\bar{H})\} \tag{A3.1.4}$$

which has the slope given in the text as (3.23).

The $\dot{H}=0$ locus is steeper than the $\dot{P}=0$ locus if:

$$\frac{v(1-b)}{q} > \frac{\rho v}{\gamma v - \lambda q} \tag{A3.1.5}$$

Suppose $\rho > 0$, then (A3.1.5) is equivalent to:

$$\gamma v(1-b) > \gamma[v(1-b) - s(1-u)]$$

which is obviously true. This is Fig. 3.4a. If, on the other hand, $\rho < 0$ and $\gamma v - \lambda q < 0$, (A3.1.5) becomes:

$$\gamma v(1-b) < \gamma[v(1-b) - s(1-u)]$$

which is false. This is Fig. 3.4b.

THE BORDERLINE

The borderline is given in the text as:

$$\frac{L}{P} = \frac{a(1-u) + [v(1-b) - \theta(1-u)](H-\bar{H})}{q} \tag{3.25}$$

so its value at $H = \bar{H}$ is the same as that of the $\dot{H}=0$ locus for the credit rationed regime (equation (A3.1.3)). That its slope is larger follows by inspection of the two equations.

THE KEYNESIAN AND CREDIT-RATIONED EQUILIBRIA

Keynesian equilibrium

Look at Fig. 3.5. Point E is above the border if the value of (A3.1.2) when $H = \bar{H}$, which is:

$$\frac{y^*(1-b) - a}{s}$$

exceeds the value of (3.25) when $H = \bar{H}$, which is:

$$\frac{a(1-u)}{q}$$

This is true if:

$$\frac{q(1-b)}{s} y^* > \frac{v}{s}(1-b)a$$

or:

$$y^* > \frac{a}{1-b-(s/v)(1-u)}$$

which is condition (3.26) in the text.

Credit-rationed equilibrium

Solve simultaneously the $\dot{H}=0$ and $\dot{P}=0$ conditions, equations (A3.1.3) and (A3.1.4), to get:

$$s\frac{L}{P} = y^*(1-b)-a \qquad\qquad\qquad (A3.1.6)$$

$$s(H-\bar{H}) = \frac{q}{v}y^* - a \qquad\qquad\qquad (A3.1.7)$$

Thus a credit-rationed equilibrium can exist only if $y^* > a/1-b$, which is the same as condition (3.18) for the Keynesian region. Notice that $H < \bar{H}$ if:

$$y^* < \frac{a}{1-b(s/v)(1-u)} \qquad\qquad\qquad (A3.1.8)$$

which is the second inequality in (3.22).

For this to be a legitimate equilibrium, it must lie *below* the border (equation (3.25)). Substituting (A3.1.6) and (A3.1.7) shows (after some algebra) that the inequality goes the right way if (A3.1.8) holds. Hence a credit-rationed equilibrium exists only if (A3.1.8) holds, and H must be below $\bar{H}$ at such an equilibrium (see Fig. 3.7).

APPENDIX 3.2. · THE FIXED CAPITAL MODEL

DERIVATION OF THE $\dot{P}=0$ LOCUS IN THE KEYNESIAN REGION

The $\dot{P}=0$ locus defined by (3.31) and (3.34) is:

$$\dot{P} = \lambda \left[\frac{a + s(L/P) - \beta K}{1 - b - \beta\phi} - \frac{K}{\phi} \right] + \gamma \left[N\left(\frac{a + s(L/P) - \beta K}{1 - b - \beta\phi}, K \right) - N^* \right] \equiv 0$$

(A3.2.1)

Linearize the $N(y, K)$ function around (y^*, K^*) to get:

$$N(y, K) \doteq N^* + N_y(y^*, K^*)(y - y^*) + N_K(y^*, K^*)(K - K^*)$$

Now, since $N(y, K)$ comes from inverting the production function:

$$N_y = \frac{1}{F_N}, \; N_K = -\frac{F_K}{F_N}$$

We have normalized the real wage to be unity. Hence, around equilibrium $F_N = 1$. Letting $r \equiv F_K$, we have:

$$N(y, K) - N^* \doteq y - y^* - r(K - K^*)$$

(A3.2.2)

Since $1/\phi$ is the *average* product of capital, it must exceed $F_K = r$, which is the *marginal* product. Hence $\phi r < 1$.

Using the linear approximation (A3.2.2), (A3.2.1) becomes:

$$0 = \left[\frac{a + s(L/P) - (1 - b)(K/\phi)}{1 - b - \beta\phi} \right] + \gamma \left[\frac{a + s(L/P) - \beta K}{1 - b - \beta\phi} - y^* - r(K - \phi y^*) \right]$$

Multiplying through by $1 - b - \beta\phi$ and simplifying leads to:

$$(\lambda + \gamma) s \frac{L}{P} = -(\lambda + \gamma)a + \gamma(1 - r\phi)(1 - b - \beta\phi)y^*$$

$$+ \left[\frac{\lambda(1 - b)}{\phi} + \gamma\beta + \gamma r(1 - b - \beta\phi) \right] K$$

(A3.2.3)

SLOPE OF THE $\dot{P}=0$ LOCUS IN THE KEYNESIAN REGION

By (A3.3.3), the slope of the $\dot{P}=0$ locus is:

$$\frac{\dfrac{\lambda(1-b)}{\phi}+\gamma[(1-b)r+\beta(1-\phi r)]}{s(\lambda+\gamma)}$$

We need to show that this is less than

$$\frac{1-b}{s\phi}$$

which is the slope of the $\dot{K}=0$ locus (see equation (3.36)). This is easily done. Multiplying both expressions by s makes the condition:

$$\frac{\lambda(1-b)+\gamma[\phi r(1-b)+\beta\phi(1-\phi r)]}{\lambda+\gamma}<1-b$$

Now multiply through by $\lambda+\gamma$ and regroup terms to get:

$$(1-\phi r)\gamma(1-b)>(1-\phi r)\gamma\beta\phi$$

Since $1-\phi r>0$, this is equivalent to:

$$1-b-\beta\phi>0$$

which has been assumed true.

THE FUNCTION $Y\left(a,\dfrac{L}{P},K\right)$ (EQUATION 3.37)

Equation (3.37) is defined by:

$$(1-b-\alpha)y=a+(1+s)\frac{L}{P}-N(y,K)-K$$

Take the total differential to get:

$$(1-b-\alpha)dy=da+(1+s)d\left(\frac{L}{P}\right)-N_y dy-(1+N_K)dK$$

It follows that:

1. $\dfrac{\partial y}{\partial a}=\dfrac{1}{1-b+N_y-\alpha}$

2. $\dfrac{\partial y}{\partial(L/P)}=(1+s)\dfrac{\partial y}{\partial a}$

in the credit-rationed regime. By contrast, in the Keynesian regime (3.34) holds so:

3. $\dfrac{\partial y}{\partial a} = \dfrac{1}{1 - b - \beta\phi}$

4. $\dfrac{\partial y}{\partial (L/P)} = \dfrac{s}{1 - b - \beta\phi}$

Thus (3) exceeds (1) so long as $N_y - \alpha > -\beta\phi$, which must be true since $N_y \approx 1$ and $\alpha < 1$. And (2) exceeds (4) so long as:

$$1 - b - \beta\phi > s(N_y - \alpha + \beta\phi)$$

which will be true for small enough s.

SLOPES OF THE $\dot{P} = 0$ AND $\dot{K} = 0$ LOCI IN THE CREDIT-RATIONED REGION

The $\dot{K} = 0$ locus follows from (3.38):

$$\frac{L}{P} + \alpha Y\left(a, \frac{L}{P}, K\right) = K + N\left(Y\left(a, \frac{L}{P}, K\right), K\right)$$

Linearized around equilibrium, the locus is:

$$\left[1 + \alpha\left(\frac{1+s}{1 - b + N_y - \alpha}\right)\right] d\left(\frac{L}{P}\right) - \frac{(1-r)(1-b)}{1 - b + N_y - \alpha} dK = 0$$

Hence the slope is:

5. $\dfrac{(1-r)(1-b)}{1 - b + N_y + \alpha s}$

The equation of the $\dot{P} = 0$ locus is given in the text. Since:

$$\frac{\partial \dot{P}}{\partial (L/P)} = \lambda Y_{L/P} + \gamma N_y Y_{L/P} \quad \text{and}$$

$$\frac{\partial \dot{P}}{\partial K} = \lambda Y_K + \gamma N_K + \gamma N_y Y_K - \frac{\lambda}{\phi}$$

the slope of the linearized locus is:

$$\frac{\lambda/\phi + ((\lambda + \gamma N_y)(1-r))/(1 - b + N_y - \alpha) + \gamma r}{((\lambda + \gamma N_y)(1+s))/(1 - b + N_y - \alpha)}$$

$$= \frac{\lambda/\phi + \gamma r(1 - b + N_y - \alpha) + (1-r)(\lambda + \gamma N_y)}{(1+s)(\lambda + \gamma N_y)}$$

To show that the $\dot{P}=0$ is steeper (locally), we must establish that (6) exceeds (5). Take the case $s=0$. Then (6) becomes:

6. $$\frac{((\lambda/\phi)+\gamma r)(1-b+N_y-\alpha)}{\lambda+\gamma N_y}+(1-r)$$

The first term is positive. The second term is bigger than (5). Hence (6) must exceed (5) for $s=0$ and, by continuity, for small enough s.

4 · THE COMPARATIVE STATICS OF A CREDIT-RATIONING BANK

4.1 MOTIVATION

Recent empirical and theoretical developments have rekindled the interest of macroeconomists in credit, as opposed to money. On the empirical front, the standard demand function for money apparently has collapsed more than once in the past decade (see Goldfeld (1976) and Judd and Scadding (1982)), while a series of papers by B. Friedman (1982,1983) has demonstrated a strong statistical association (defined in a variety of ways) between credit and GNP – at least as strong as that between money and GNP.

On the theoretical front, Stiglitz and Weiss (1981), picking up a line of thought originated by Jaffee and Russell (1976), showed that (non-price) rationing of credit might be a profit-maximizing strategy for an imperfectly-informed bank – even in equilibrium. Both Bernanke (1983) and Blinder and Stiglitz (1983) appealed to this (or a similar) model of bank behavior as an ingredient in constructing a verbal model of the macroeconomy in which financial intermediation and credit rationing credit play important roles. Although neither presented a formal macro model, Bernanke did provide empirical evidence for the Great Depression. In Blinder (1987) (Chapter 3 in this volume), I formalized some of the ideas expressed verbally in Blinder and Stiglitz, and developed a macro model in which credit rationing is the main channel for monetary policy.

If the Stiglitz–Weiss theory of banking is to be used as a microfoundation for a macroeconomic model with credit rationing, it is imperative that the comparative statics of such a bank be worked out. Similarly, if the theory is to be subjected to empirical testing, its testable implications must first be drawn out. These are the purposes of this short paper.

4.2 A MODEL OF A FINANCE COMPANY

In thinking about this problem, one of the first things one notices about a Stiglitz–Weiss (henceforth, SW) bank is that it is not a bank at all. The SW

Written in December 1984, and revised in June 1988. Helpful conversations with Joseph Stiglitz and financial support from the NSF are gratefully acknowledged.

bank does not take deposits nor make portfolio choices between customer loans and securities. Instead, it borrows money in the open market at a given rate and makes loans to customers (at a rate it sets). The SW bank seems closest in character to a finance company.

So I start this paper with a simple model of a finance company which performs one of the principal functions of a bank (making loans), but not the other (taking deposits. This model, which is close in spirit though not in details to Stiglitz and Weiss (1981), serves as a building block toward the construction of a model of a financial institution that looks more like a bank.

Suppose a finance company can borrow as much money as it wishes on the open market at interest factor I (that is, I is one plus the interest rate). It posts a lending factor R (R is one plus the loan rate), which attracts a pool of applicants wishing to borrow $Q(R)$, where $Q(.)$ is a downward sloping demand curve for loans. But, because of adverse selection problems, the quality of the loan pool depends negatively on the posted loan rate. Specifically, the average probability of repayment, q, is assumed to be a decreasing function of R:

$$q = q(R) \qquad 0 < q < 1, \quad q'(R) \leqslant 0$$

As a consequence, the SW bank does not lend to all who wish to borrow at the posted rate. Instead, it lends out only:

$$L = zQ(R) \tag{4.1}$$

where $0 < z < 1$ indicates the degree of *rationing*.

All this is familiar. The main difference between this model and that of Stiglitz and Weiss (1981) is that I assume that the bank has some limited ability to judge credit-worthiness. Hence, its screening process is not random, but actually makes the quality of the loans granted *better* than the quality of the loan pool. The actual fraction repaid is therefore $s(z)q(R) > q(R)$, where $s(.)$ indicates the gains from screening and has the properties:

$s(1) = 1$ (the no-rationing case)

$s'(z) < 0$ (rationing improves the quality of the pool)

$$\lim_{z \to 0} s(z)q(R) < 1$$

The slope of $s(z)$ indicates the effectiveness of the firm's screening process; $s'(z) = 0$ is the special case dealt with by Stiglitz and Weiss (1981). Presumably, a bank could improve its $s(z)$ function by investing more resources in screening. But I do not pursue this thought further and simply take $s(z)$ as given.

With this notation, one plus the expected rate of return to the bank is:

$$p = s(z)q(R)R \tag{4.2}$$

so expected profits are:

$$P = (p - I)L = (s(z)q(R)R - I)zQ(R)$$

The first-order conditions for optimal z and R are (second-order conditions are assumed to be satisfied):

$$dp/dz = Q(R)[(s(z)q(R)R - I) + zs'(z)Rq(R)] = 0 \qquad (4.3)$$

$$dp/dR = z[Q'(R)(s(z)q(R)R - I) + s(z)Q(R)(q + Rq'(R))] = 0 \qquad (4.4)$$

These first-order conditions do not necessarily imply that a higher value of I (the cost of funds to the 'bank') will induce the bank to raise its R (its posted loan rate) – which is perhaps the central point of Stiglitz–Weiss. To see this, consider a special case in which the demand curve $Q(R)$ and the screening function $s(z)$ are (locally) constant elasticity functions, with elasticities $-\varepsilon$ and $-\eta$ respectively (so both ε and η are positive numbers). Then, a little manipulation of (4.3) and (4.4) leads to:

$$1 + Rq'(R)/q(R) = \varepsilon\eta \qquad (4.5)$$

which establishes that the optimal choice of R is independent of I in this case. While the constant-elasticity case is of limited interest in itself, it shows clearly that by making the elasticities vary in the right way we can construct examples in which R either rises or falls when I rises.

There is one other preliminary result that is useful to derive here. Consider the artificial problem of maximizing the expected rate of return for any given volume of loans; that is:

$$\max \, p = s(z)q(R)R \quad \text{subject to} \quad zQ(R) = \bar{L} \qquad (4.6)$$

With a little algebraic effort, it can be shown that the first-order conditions for (4.6) imply:

$$1 + Rq'(R)/q(R) = \varepsilon(R)\eta(z) \qquad (4.7)$$

where $\varepsilon(R)$ and $\eta(z)$ are the (nonconstant) elasticities of the functions $Q(R)$ and $s(z)$ respectively. This is obviously the generalization of (4.5), and will prove useful in the next section.

4.3 A MODEL OF A BANK WITH STOCHASTIC DEPOSITS

I now consider the loan decision of a bank which takes deposits, D, on which it pays interest factor C, and holds riskless bonds in its portfolio, on which it earns the market interest factor I. While it is a price-*maker* in the loan market, it is a price-*taker* in both the markets for deposits and bonds.

A preliminary question must be addressed. Presumably the expected return on customer loans exceeds the return on riskless bonds. Why, then, would a bank ever invest in bonds? One possible explanation is risk aversion. This no doubt explains why individuals hold risk-free assets in their portfolios despite low yields. But a large bank with thousands of small loans should be virtually self-insured; so only extreme risk aversion could justify any sizable deviation from the portfolio that maximizes expected profits.

A better explanation may be a 'buffer stock' motive for holding bonds. Deposits are of short (often zero) maturity and fluctuate from period to period. Loans must be made for a longer duration and cannot easily be called in – at least not without losing the 'customer relations' with borrowers that the bank prizes. To protect itself against a sudden outflow of deposits, a bank may find it optimal to keep a fraction of its assets in highly liquid form, even though the most liquid assets pay a relatively low return.

To incorporate this idea literally, the model would have to be dynamic and stochastic. I adopt a short-cut procedure here that seems to capture the basic idea while sticking to the one-period static framework. Assume that bank loan decisions are made in two stages. Before deposits are known, tentative loan *commitments* are made. Then deposits (which are random) are observed. If deposits are large enough, the bank honors all of its commitments – selling bonds, if necessary, to do so. Transactions costs in selling securities are taken to be negligible. But, if deposits are too small, it sells all its bonds and then cancels some of its loan commitments. Loan cancellations, however, involve penalty costs (specified precisely below). It is to avoid such penalty costs that the bank holds securities as a buffer.

4.3.1 The objective function

I am now ready to write down the objective function for a bank whose balance sheet is as follows:

Assets	Liabilities
Reserves $= mD$	Deposits $= D$
Bonds $= B$	Capital $= O$
Loans $= L$	

For simplicity I assume that the bank begins with no capital (capital would just add an inessential constant to the analysis), and that it holds exactly the required amount of reserves; m is the required reserve ratio. Hence the balance sheet identity is:

$$B + L = (1 - m)D \tag{4.8}$$

This must hold both *ex ante* (in expected values) and *ex post* (in actual values), despite the randomness of D. If π is the inflation rate, the real net worth of the bank after one period is:

$$(1 - \pi)mD + (I - \pi)B + (p - \pi)L - (C - \pi)D - g(L^* - L) \tag{4.9}$$

The first three terms are, respectively, the real returns on reserves, bonds, and (actual) loans. The fourth term deducts the costs of deposits. And the last term deducts the penalty costs (if any) which are a convex function of the difference between loan commitments, L^*, and actual loans, L, if $L^* - L$ is positive. To keep the solution simple, I assume that $g(.)$ is quadratic, *viz.*:

$$g(L^* - L) = (a/2)(L^* - L)^2 \qquad \text{if} \quad L^* > L$$

$$= 0 \qquad\qquad\qquad \text{if} \quad L^* = L \tag{4.10}$$

The bank's two-stage decision problem works as follows. Before D is known, it makes loan commitments L^*. Then D is realized. If $(1-m)D > L^*$, it meets all its loan commitments and puts the remaining funds into bonds. If $(1-m)D < L^*$, it cancels enough commitments so that it lends only $L = (1-m)D$, holds no bonds, and pays the penalty cost in (4.10). Thus:

$$L = L^* \qquad\qquad \text{if } D > L^*/(1-m) \tag{4.11}$$

$$= (1-m)D \qquad \text{if } D < L^*/(1-m)$$

Actually, the bank's decision variables are its posted loan rate, R, and its degree of rationing, z, as in Section 4.2. But it is more convenient here to re-parameterize the problem by taking loan commitments, L^*, and the rate of return on loans, p, as the decision variables. Remember, however, that p cannot be chosen in an unconstrained manner; L^* and p are related to R and z by (4.1) and (4.2).

The expected value of net worth comes in two pieces. Suppose first that D exceeds $L^*/(1-m)$. Then $L = L^*$ and there is no penalty cost, so (4.9) becomes:

$$(1-\pi)mD + (I-\pi)((1-m)D - L^*) + (p-\pi)L^* - (C-\pi)D$$

$$= (p-I)L^* + [I - C - m(I-1)]D$$

On the other hand, if D falls short of $L^*/(1-m)$, then $B=0$, $L=(1-m)D$, and there is a penalty given by (4.11). Hence (4.9) becomes:

$$(1-\pi)mD + (p-\pi)(1-m)D - (C-\pi)D - (a/2)[L^* - (1-m)D]^2$$

$$= [p - C - m(p-1)]D - (a/2)[L^* - (1-m)D]^2$$

Putting these two pieces together, the objective function of the bank is seen to be:

$$J = \int_{\frac{L^*}{1-m}}^{D_2} \left\{ (p-I)L^* - \mu(I)D \right\} f(D)dD$$

$$+ \int_{D_1}^{\frac{L^*}{1-m}} \left\{ \mu(p)D - \frac{a}{2}[L^* - (1-m)D]^2 \right\} f(D)dD$$

where D is distributed on (D_1, D_2) according to density $f(D)$, and where $\mu(X) \equiv X - C - m(X - 1)$.

4.3.2 The optimal solution

The first-order condition for optimal L^* is:

$$\frac{\partial J}{\partial L^*} = \int_{\frac{L^*}{1-m}}^{D_2} (p - I) \, f(D) dD - \frac{1}{1-m} \left[(p - I)L^* + \mu(I)\frac{L^*}{1-m} \right] f\left(\frac{L^*}{1-m} \right)$$

$$+ \frac{1}{1-m} \left[\mu(p)\frac{L^*}{1-m} \right] f\left(\frac{L^*}{1-m} \right) - \int_{D_1}^{\frac{L^*}{1-m}} a[L^* - (1-m)D] \, f(D) dD = 0$$

which, after some manipulation, can be written:

$$p - I = F\left(\frac{L^*}{1-m} \right) (p - I + aL^*) - a(1 - m) \int_{D_1}^{\frac{L^*}{1-m}} D f(D) dD \tag{4.12}$$

where $F(.)$ is the cumulative distribution function corresponding to density $f(.)$.

The derivative with respect to p need not be written down explicitly, because the objective function is obviously always increasing in p. Economically, given any choice of L, it is always optimal to maximize p. Thus the second condition for expected profit maximization is that the firm solve the artificial problem (4.6) above. Hence we know from Section 4.2 that (4.7) must hold, which means that the optimal posted loan rate is not affected by the parameters of the model in the constant-elasticity case.

It is obvious from equations (4.1) and (4.2), and from the structure of the problem, that the maximal p is a decreasing function of L^*, viz:

$$p = H(L^*) \quad H'(L^*) < 0 \tag{4.13}$$

This graphs as a decreasing function in (p, L) space. See Fig. 4.1. I will complete the (qualitative) solution by showing that (4.12) graphs as an upward-sloping function in this space.

Proof
Integrate (4.12) by parts and simplify to get:

$$(p - I)\left[1 - F\left(\frac{L^*}{1-m} \right) \right] = a(1 - m) \int_{D_1}^{\frac{L^*}{1-m}} F(D) dD \tag{4.14}$$

Since $F(D)$ is a distribution function, the left-hand side of (4.14) is a decreasing function like that in Fig. 4.2a. It is shifted vertically upward (downward) by a rise in $p(I)$ and is shifted rightward by a rightward shift in the density function $f(D)$, i.e., by 'an increase in expected deposits.' The right-hand side of (4.14) is an increasing function like Fig. 4.2b. It is

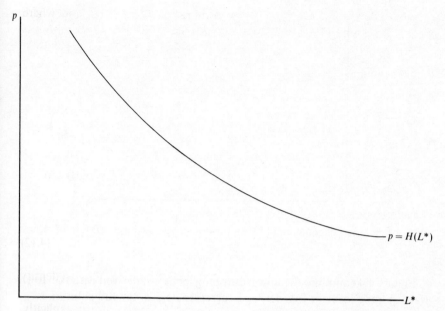

Fig. 4.1 The return on loans (p) as a function of the volume of loans (L).

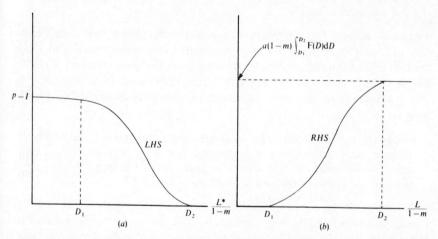

Fig. 4.2(a) Graph of the left-hand side of equation (4.14), **(b)** Graph of the right-hand side of equation (4.14).

unaffected by changes in p or I; but it also shifts rightward if f(D) shifts rightward.

Figures 4.2a and 4.2b are put together in Fig. 4.3, which shows the determination of the optimal L^* for any given p. (Remember, Fig. 4.1 shows the optimal p for any given L^*.) It is easy to see that L^* must be an increasing function of p, which was to be shown. QED.

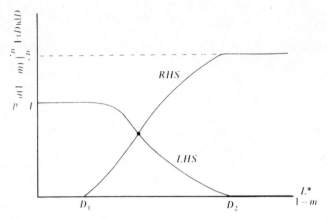

Fig. 4.3 Solution of equation (4.14): optimal loan volume for given rate of return.

Figure 4.4 combines the upward-sloping locus just derived with the downward-sloping locus in Fig. 4.1, and therefore depicts the full solution.

4.3.3 Comparative statics

I can now address the concerns that motivated this paper: how does a bank like this react to changes in its environment? First, consider a rise in I, the market rate of interest on bonds. As just noted, the curve marked 'LHS' in Fig. 4.3 shifts *down*, so the optimal L^* corresponding to any p falls. In Fig. 4.4, this means that the upward-sloping line shifts inward. The conclusion is:

> **Proposition 1:** If the interest rate on bonds rises, a bank plans to make fewer customer loans and to earn a higher average rate of return on them. It is not clear, however, whether it will raise or lower its posted loan rate. (In the constant-elasticity case, the loan rate will not change.)

Next consider an increase in bank deposits, that is, a rightward shift of the density function $f(D)$. As noted before, both of the curves in Fig. 4.3 shift to the right. So the optimal L^* corresponding to any particular p certainly rises. Translated to Fig. 4.4, this means that the upward-sloping locus shifts outward. Hence I conclude:

> **Proposition 2:** If there is an increase in expected deposits, banks plan to make more customer loans and to earn a lower average return on them. Again, the movement of the posted loan rate is not clear (and is zero in the constant elasticity case).

Finally, consider the effect of actual realized deposits on actual loans, once L^* is selected by the bank. We know that L is independent of D if D exceeds

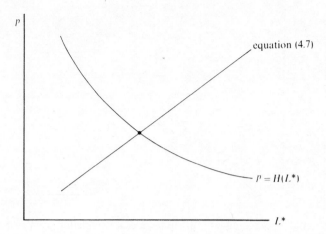

Fig. 4.4 Full solution: optimal loan volume and optimal rate of return.

$L^*/(1-m)$ and that $dL/dD = 1-m$ if D is less than this amount. Thus the dependence of loans on deposits *ex post* looks like Fig. 4.5. At the macro level, when deposits fluctuate, some banks will raise their loans (those on the upward-sloping portion of Fig. 4.5) while others will not (those on the horizontal portion). I therefore conclude that:

Proposition 3: If there is an unanticipated increase in deposits, bank loans rise, but not by as much as they would have risen in response to an anticipated increase in deposits.

4.4 THE INFLUENCE OF AGGREGATE ECONOMIC ACTIVITY

The notion that a deterioration in macroeconomic activity raises the perceived riskiness of customer loans, and thereby reduces loan volume, is prominent in the verbal models of Bernanke (1983) and Blinder and Stiglitz (1983). This section seeks to formalize that idea. To do so, I return to the simpler model of a finance company (Section 4.2) and restrict myself to the constant-elasticity case (in which the posted lending rate does not change when market interest rates change).

I parameterize loan 'safety' by adding a shift parameter, y (think of it as GNP), to the adverse selection function:

$$q = q(\underset{-}{R}, \underset{+}{y})$$

A rise in y raises the probability that loans will be paid back. Let us ask, then, how a rise in y affects the bank's decision variables: R, z, and L.

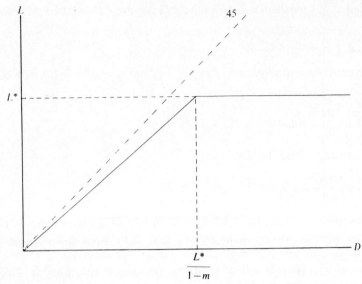

Fig. 4.5 Bank loans as a function of bank deposits.

In the constant-elasticity case, the first-order conditions imply (4.5), which now reads:

$$1 + (R/q)q_R(R, y) = \varepsilon\eta \qquad (4.15)$$

This defines R as an implicit function of y with derivative:

$$\frac{dR}{dy} = \frac{(1-\varepsilon\eta)q_y + Rq_{Ry}}{-(2-\varepsilon\eta)q_R - Rq_{RR}} \qquad (4.16)$$

Consider first the special case in which the $q(.)$ function is linear in R ($q_{RR} = 0$) and a change in y shifts it in a parallel manner ($q_{Ry} = 0$). Then (4.16) specializes to:

$$\frac{dR}{dy} = \frac{(1-\varepsilon\eta)q_y(R, y)}{-(2-\varepsilon\eta)q_R(R, y)} \qquad (4.17)$$

Since $\varepsilon\eta < 1$ (see (4.15)), this expression is positive, meaning that banks actually raise the loan rate in booms. This may seem paradoxical. (It did to me!) The explanation is that the fear of adverse selection, which is what inhibits banks from raising R, is less important in a boom than in a slump.

In more general cases, (4.16) cannot be signed unequivocally, but a positive sign seems more likely. $q_{Ry} > 0$ means that a rise in GNP reduces (in absolute value) the slope q_R of the adverse selection function. This seems plausible. $q_{RR} < 0$ if q is a concave function of R – which also seems plausible (It means that adverse selection is worse, at the margin, when R is high than when R is low.) If $q_{Ry} > 0$ and $q_{RR} < 0$, then (4.16) is surely positive.

What about the degree of rationing, z? Equation (4.3) can be manipulated into:

$$Rq(R, y)s(z) = I/(1-\eta) \qquad (4.18)$$

in the constant-elasticity case. Taking the total derivative with respect to y gives:

$$Rqs'(z)\frac{dz}{dy} + Rq_y s(z) + s(z)[q + Rq_R]\frac{dR}{dy} = 0$$

Now substitute from (4.7) to obtain:

$$Rqs'(z)\frac{dz}{dy} + Rq_y s(z) + s(z)q\,\varepsilon\eta\,\frac{dR}{dy} = 0$$

On the left-hand side, the last two terms are positive. Hence the first term must be negative, which implies that $dz/dy > 0$. In words, banks become less selective and do less rationing when the economy improves.

The volume of loans follows from our previous results, since $L = zQ(R)$. After some algebra, we find:

$$\frac{dL}{dy} = \frac{\eta L}{q}\,q_y(R, y) > 0$$

So loan volume rises when the economic outlook brightens.

In sum, at least in the special case considered here, a reduction in economy-wide risk reduces rationing, raises loan volume, and actually raises the posted loan rate.

4.5 EMPIRICAL IMPLICATIONS

The preceding theoretical model of bank lending decisions suggests an empirical lending function for a single bank of the form:

$$L_t = L(\underset{-}{I}_t, \underset{+}{y}_t, E_{t-1}(\underset{+}{D}_t), D_t - \underset{+}{E}_{t-1}(D_t)) \qquad (4.19)$$

where E_{t-1} is the expectation's operator conditional on information available at time $t-1$ and the signs of derivatives are indicated below each argument. It also suggests (see Section 4.3) that anticipated deposits should have a stronger effect on loans than do unanticipated deposits. Notice that the rate of interest paid on deposits does not enter, owing to the assumption that D is exogenous to the bank.

The corresponding equation for the posted lending rate says that R is an increasing function of y, but carries no particular implications about the signs of any other derivatives.

In principle, when combined with an auxiliary model of expectation formation, equation (4.19) could be estimated on time series data.

4.6 REFERENCES

Bernanke, B. (1983) 'Non-monetary effects of the financial collapse in the propagation of the Great Depression,' *American Economic Review*, vol. 73 (June).

Blinder, A. S. (1987) 'Credit rationing and effective supply failures,' *Economic Journal*; Chapter 3 in this volume.

Blinder, A. S. and Stiglitz, J.(1983) 'Money, credit constraints, and economic activity,' *American Economic Review* (May); Chapter 2 in this volume.

Friedman, B. (1982) 'Debt and economic activity in the United States,' in B. Friedman (ed.), *The Changing Roles of Debt and Equity in Financing US Capital Formation*, Chicago: University of Chicago Press.

Friedman, B. (1983) ' The roles of money and credit in macroeconomic analysis,' in J. Tobin (ed.), *Macroeconomics, Prices and Quantities*, Washington: Brookings, 1983.

Goldfeld, S. (1976) 'The case of the missing money,' *Brookings Papers on Economic Activity*, vol.3.

Jaffee, D. and Russell, T. (1976) 'Imperfect information, uncertainty, and credit rationing,' *Quarterly Journal of Economics* (November).

Judd, J. and Scadding, J. (1982) 'The search for a stable money demand function,' *Journal of Economic Literature* (September).

Stiglitz, J. and Weiss, A. (1981) 'Credit rationing in markets with imperfect information,' *American Economic Review* (June), vol. 71, pp. 393–410.

5 · THE STYLIZED FACTS ABOUT CREDIT AGGREGATES

5.1 INTRODUCTION

Recent years have witnessed a resurgence of interest in credit, both in microeconomic and macroeconomic contexts. As often happens in economic research, theorizing has raced well ahead of empirical evidence.[1] The purpose of this short paper is to help remedy this imbalance by sorting out the relevant facts about credit aggregates and subaggregates as a logical prelude to further theorizing. The outcome of the paper is a list of stylized facts about credit in the United States, some of which are well known, others of which are not.

The data investigated here are seasonally adjusted end-of-quarter stocks from the Federal Reserve's flow of funds accounts, and cover the 1952–83 period. The flow of funds cover a great many lending and borrowing activities. I decided to work with a very broad definition of 'credit' that includes all debt obligations that bear interest, are dischargeable at par (which eliminates equities), and do not serve as a medium of exchange (which eliminates items included in M1 or M2).

The main definitional decisions, therefore, revolved around how much netting out to do. For example, if a finance company floats commercial paper in order to make consumer loans, should the finance company's debt count as part of total borrowing or not? Initially, there was no netting out so that, for example, both the lending and borrowing of the finance company were included.[2] Each item of credit, so defined, was classified into one of eight types of security (or bookkeeping entry), one of six types of borrower, and one of six types of lender listed in Table 5.1. Table 5.1 also shows the sample mean shares in total borrowing or lending of each – to give an idea of the size of each market. While most of the entries in the table are self-explanatory, a few merit comment.

First, while borrowing (a liability) and lending (an asset) are normally equal, there is one important exception. In the trade credit market, the

I am indebted to Leonard Nakamura for research assistance and discussions, to the National Science Foundation for financial support, to Stephen Taylor for help in deciphering the flow of funds data, and to Peter Hartley, Carl Walsh, and Kenneth West for useful suggestions. This paper was written in June 1985.

Table 5.1 Types of credit by market, borrower and lender

By market		By borrower		By lender	
Bonds	(0.398)	Nonfinancial business	(0.321)	Financial institutions	(0.576)
excluding government	(0.107)	Households	(0.272)	Households	(0.162)
Mortgages	(0.256)	Federal government	(0.225)	Nonfinancial business	(0.126)
Loans	(0.132)	Financial institutions	(0.073)	Federal government	(0.060)
Trade credit borrowing	(0.076)	State/local government	(0.075)	State/local government	(0.050)
Trade credit lending	(0.098)	Foreigners	(0.033)	Foreigners	(0.027)
Consumer credit	(0.077)				
Large CDs	(0.031)				
Commercial paper	(0.017)				
Security credit	(0.013)				

amount loaned always exceeds the amount borrowed by a substantial amount – called the 'trade credit discrepancy' in the flow of funds. For example, in 1983:4 trade credit lending was $667 billion while trade credit borrowing was only $569 billion. The difference is basically float. When trade credit is extended, the lender records the account receivable on his books before the borrower records the account payable. Similarly, when trade credit is paid off, the borrower erases the account payable before the lender erases the receivable. In both directions, then, lending exceeds borrowing. The trade credit discrepancy turns out to be no small matter; until very recently, it far exceeded the total volume of commercial paper, for example.

Second, while most bank deposits are excluded from any credit aggregate, an exception is made for large certificates of deposit. The reason is that there seems to be no meaningful distinction between one large bank which raises funds by selling commercial paper and another which raises funds by selling large negotiable CDs. In each case, it seems to me, the bank is borrowing on 'the credit market.' Admittedly, the distinction between small and large CDs is also somewhat tenuous; but small CDs are not traded in the capital market and thus seem closer to other bank deposits than to large CDs. This, at least, is what the Federal Reserve thinks, since it includes small CDs, but not large ones, in M2.

Third, the category called 'loans' includes bank loans other than mortgages and consumer loans (about 58 percent of the total in 1983:4), loans from nonbank financial institutions (about 17 percent), and US government loans (about 25 percent). Fourth, unincorporated businesses (including farms) are grouped with nonfinancial corporations, rather than with households.

5.2 GENERAL TRENDS AND MARKET SHARES

From the viewpoint of prevailing macroeconomic theories, the numbers in Table 5.1 prompt a few observations.

5.2.1 Market shares

First, several authors have called attention to the potentially important distinction between 'auction market' credit like bonds, commercial paper, and large CDs and 'customer market' credit (all the rest).[3] From this perspective, Table 5.1 shows that auction market credit – the 'bond market' in most macro models – has accounted for only 45 percent of total credit on average; 55 percent of credit arguably originated in customer markets.[4] If government borrowing is excluded, the dominance of customer markets is even clearer; the auction markets have provided only 22 percent of non-government borrowing on average. Thus the first stylized fact seems to be that:

> *Borrowing in customer markets, much of which is intermediated, appears to be more important than borrowing directly in auction markets.*

This at least suggests that macroeconomic theories which emphasize the 'customer' nature of credit markets may perhaps have empirical importance.

Second, while it is no surprise to find that financial institutions (not just commercial banks) are the biggest lender and that nonfinancial businesses are the biggest borrower, the substantial importance of the household sector on both sides of the credit market is worth noting. While the household sector, of course, has positive net worth on balance, it is an important net debtor in the credit market. When we examine cyclical variability in Section 5.4, the critical role of household borrowing will be even clearer.

Third, the market for trade credit, which has been virtually ignored in both theoretical and empirical research, stands out as an important source of credit – almost 8 percent of total borrowing and almost 10 percent of total lending. Despite the enormous growth of the markets for large CDs and for commercial paper in the past decade, the market for trade credit remains far larger than either of these. It is comparable in size to the markets for corporate bonds and conventional consumer credit. It would seem to me, therefore, that trade credit merits more research attention than it has received.

Fourth, we note that state and local governments (including their pension funds) and foreigners now play an almost purely intermediary role in the US credit market; their borrowing is almost equal to their lending. In both cases, this is change from their previous status as net borrowers.

And, finally, the substantial intermediary role of the federal government is worth noting. While US government borrowing accounted for 42 percent of all outstanding borrowing in early 1952, that share dwindled to below 14 percent by late 1974 and stood at 21 percent at the end of 1983. Federal lending, on the other hand, remained under 5 percent of total lending through 1965, but has since grown rapidly and now amounts to 10 percent of all lending.

5.2.2 Trends

Benjamin Friedman has called attention to the constancy of the ratio of one particular credit aggregate to nominal GNP. Friedman's aggregate (henceforth, FC, for 'Friedman credit') nets out most of the borrowing by financial intermediaries included in Table 5.1, and also excludes trade credit and the activities of foreigners. For example, in 1983:4, my broadest credit aggregate (total borrowing) was $7.10 trillion while Friedman's was only $5.24 trillion.

Figure 5.1 plots the ratio of FC to nominal GNP (FC/Y), as well as the corresponding ratios for several other credit aggregates. It can be seen that FC/Y rose considerably between 1952 and 1961, was essentially trendless between 1961 and about 1981, and has once again been rising since 1981.[5] My series on non-intermediated borrowing (described in the data appendix and called X/Y in Fig. 5.1) looks very much like FC. But my series on total borrowing (also described in the appendix) relative to GNP (B/Y) rises throughout the period.

There are two alternative views about which subperiod displays 'normal' behavior and which is unusual. Friedman's analysis suggests that constancy of FC/Y is the normal state of affairs, that is, that the income elasticity of credit is unity. On this view, the first decade of the flow of funds data represents a return to normalcy after the Depression and two wars. This seems a reasonable position. However, the recent years are troublesome for this view, since FC has grown much faster than Y. An alternative view is that there is a natural tendency for total credit (including intermediated credit) to grow faster than GNP as the financial system becomes more sophisticated and complex. On this view, the question is why the growth of B/Y was so slow during the 1960s. But while the quantitative dimensions vary, all broad credit aggregates display our second stylized fact:

Credit has grown faster than GNP during the postwar period.

Which credit markets have grown most rapidly? Table 5.2 shows that the fastest growth has been in the commercial paper and large CD markets, both of which were minuscule in the 1950s. However, while they have grown rapidly, neither market bulks large in total credit even today. The more important growth has come in the mortgage market, which increased its share of total borrowing from 19 percent to 26 percent – all in the first dozen years of the data. In fact, a remarkable feature of these data is that

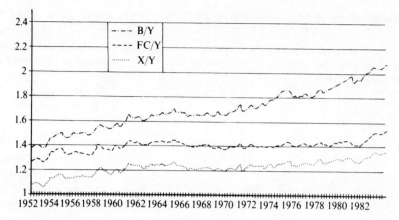

Fig. 5.1 Ratios of bank credit (*B*), Friedman credit (*FC*), and nonintermediated borrowing (*X*) to nominal GNP (*Y*).

Table 5.2 Shares in total borrowing, by market

	1953:4	1963:4	1973:4	1983:4
Bonds	0.542	0.408	0.323	0.355
excluding government	0.102	0.105	0.108	0.095
Mortgages	0.190	0.271	0.276	0.257
Loans	0.108	0.123	0.153	0.140
Trade credit	0.062	0.071	0.082	0.080
Consumer credit	0.069	0.081	0.083	0.069
Large CDs	0.011	0.020	0.051	0.050
Commercial paper	0.005	0.009	0.020	0.037
Security credit	0.012	0.016	0.012	0.013

mortgage indebtedness as a share of total borrowing grew rapidly from 1952 through 1963, and then abruptly stopped. Why this happened is an intriguing question. The share of loans has also increased, from 11 percent in 1953:4 to 14 percent in 1983:4. The only shrinking market has been the bond market, which accounted for 54 percent of all borrowing in 1953:4, but only 36 percent in 1983:4. But all of this can be accounted for by the falling ratio of government bonds to GNP. Thus, while there are some exceptions, a rough generalization seems to be that:

> *The shares of the major credit markets in total private borrowing have not changed very much since 1962.*

If we look at the behavior of shares of total borrowing and total lending by agent, rather than by market, the major facts are the diminishing importance of federal government debt in total borrowing (see Table 5.3), the increased

Table 5.3 Shares in total borrowing, by borrower

	1953:4	1963:4	1973:4	1983:4
Federal government	0.390	0.229	0.142	0.209
Nonfinancial business	0.271	0.304	0.355	0.322
Households	0.210	0.291	0.284	0.273
State/local government	0.061	0.085	0.081	0.058
Financial institutions	0.037	0.060	0.107	0.101
Foreigners	0.031	0.032	0.031	0.036

role of governments at all levels as lenders (see Table 5.4), and the increasing importance of borrowing by financial institutions (see Table 5.3).

> *During the postwar period, the government has become less important as a borrower and more important as a lender.*

5.3 THE VARIABILITY OF CREDIT AGGREGATES AND SUB-AGGREGATES

Those (like me) whose interest in credit markets derives from a suspicion that credit market fluctuations are linked to macroeconomic fluctuations will be at least as interested in the *variability* of the different credit aggregates as in their *means*. Variability was investigated in two ways. The first is based on the existence of deterministic trends in the credit data. Regressions of the form:

$$\log(C/P)_t = a + bt + ct^2 + dt^3 + u_t \tag{5.1}$$

where C is some nominal credit series, P is the GNP deflator, and t is time, were run for each credit aggregate and subaggregate. The standard errors of these regressions were taken as one measure of the basic variability of each series, and are displayed to the left of the 'slashes' in Table 5.5.

It has been argued, however, that what appear to be deterministic trends in economic time series are often illusions left by the meanderings of random walks. To look at the data in this alternative way, regressions of the form:

$$\Delta \log(C/P)_t = a + u_t \tag{5.2}$$

were also run for each credit series. The standard errors from these random walk regressions are our second measure of variability, and are displayed to the right of the 'slashes' in Table 5.5.

The first column of Table 5.5 shows that differences in variability around trend among the broad credit aggregates are unimportant. Friedman credit is the 'stablest' aggregate, but the margin is slim. As Friedman suggested, bank credit seems to be far too narrow a concept to qualify as one of the broad

Table 5.4 Shares in total lending, by lender

	1953:4	1963:4	1973:4	1983:4
Financial institutions	0.562	0.598	0.584	0.542
Households	0.202	0.158	0.141	0.143
Nonfinancial business	0.139	0.127	0.119	0.108
Federal government	0.050	0.049	0.062	0.099
State/local government	0.032	0.048	0.060	0.065
Foreigners	0.015	0.019	0.034	0.043

credit aggregates; its variability is noticeably larger than that of any of the broad aggregates. We also see that, with very few exceptions:

Broad credit aggregates fluctuate far less than their components.

This fact was also noted by Friedman and seems to suggest a considerable degree of substitutability, without saying anything about whether the substitutability comes from the supply side or the demand side.

A question which naturally arises at this point is: are these series all measuring the same thing? Table 5.6 addresses this question. It shows, below the diagonal, the correlation matrix among the residuals from equations (5.1) – the deviations from cubic trends – for the five broad aggregates plus one new one, total lending by financial institutions ('financial lending'). Above the diagonal, Table 5.6 shows the corresponding correlations among the residuals from equations (5.2) – the innovations in the random walk models. Not surprisingly, all the correlations are positive and substantial. However, the matrix nonetheless illustrates the following four points:

1. Friedman's credit aggregate is virtually the same as my series on non-intermediated borrowing ($r = 0.96$) and financial lending ($r = 0.94$) according to the deterministic trend model, but not quite so close according to the random walk model.
2. *FC* is close to, but by no means identical to, my total borrowing (or lending) series.
3. My measures of non-intermediated borrowing and total lending by financial institutions are very similar to one another.
4. As noted above, bank credit probably should not be considered one of the broad credit aggregates. Its correlations with the other aggregates are the lowest in the table.[6]

The second column of Table 5.5 shows the variability of credit issued in different markets. The markets are listed in descending order of size in 1983:4. The stablest markets are, naturally, the long-term ones – the bond market and the mortgage market – which have a natural inertia stemming from the fact that quarterly flows are so small relative to outstanding stocks.

Table 5.5 The variability of credit aggregates

Broad aggregates		By market		By borrower		By lender	
Total borrowing	0.0206/0.0070	Bonds	0.0226/0.0095	Nonfinancial business	0.0195/0.0088	Financial institutions	0.0271/0.0083
Total lending	0.0209/0.0070	Mortgages	0.0306/0.0091	Households	0.0333/0.0108	Households	0.0322/0.0166
Nonintermediated borrowing	0.0207/0.0066	Loans	0.0468/0.0184	Federal government	0.0386/0.0167	Nonfinancial business	0.0305/0.0176
Friedman credit	0.0204/0.0064	Trade credit lending	0.0368/0.0169	Financial institutions	0.0828/0.0335	Federal government	0.0340/0.0163
Bank credit	0.0313/0.0123	Trade credit borrowing	0.0499/0.0213	State/local government	0.0285/0.0125	State/local government	0.0555/0.0163
		Consumer credit	0.0461/0.0176	Foreigners	0.0615/0.0198	Foreigners	0.1386/0.0366
		Large CDs	0.1619/0.0696				
		Commercial paper	0.1260/0.0555				
		Security credit	0.1468/0.0685				

Table 5.6 Correlations among deviations from trend, broad credit aggregates

	Total borrowing	Total lending	Nonintermediated borrowing	Financial lending	Friedman credit	Bank credit
Total borrowing	1	0.988	0.858	0.815	0.862	0.701
Total lending	0.997	1	0.862	0.818	0.850	0.719
Nonintermediated borrowing	0.921	0.923	1	0.886	0.907	0.718
Financial lending	0.929	0.935	0.954	1	0.827	0.872
Friedman credit	0.880	0.890	0.959	0.941	1	0.638
Bank credit	0.800	0.817	0.742	0.856	0.758	1

Notes:
Correlations among deviations from cubic trend below the diagonal.
Correlations among innovations in random walk models above the diagonal.

The extremely volatile markets are the three small ones at the bottom of the list. Intermediate between these are the 'mid-sized' markets – those for loans, trade credit, and consumer credit – which seem to be of roughly comparable variability. A rough generalization is:

The smaller credit markets are more volatile than the larger ones.

The data on variability by borrower (third column of Table 5.5) hold at least one surprise – the extreme stability of borrowing by nonfinancial businesses. Using the deterministic trend model, the standard deviation of 0.0195 is the lowest in the entire table. Using the random walk model, the variability of nonfinancial business borrowing is not quite so small; but it is still one of the lowest in the table.

Business borrowing is the least volatile component of total borrowing.

This fact is potentially bad news for macro theories which stress the role of business borrowing in business cycles, such as King and Plosser (1984) and Blinder (1987).[7]

5.4 THE CYCLICALITY OF CREDIT

Of more direct interest to students of business cycles, however, is how short-run movements of real credit are related to short-run fluctuations of real GNP. Table 5.7, which follows the organization of Table 5.5, gives two ways to answer this question on the view that both real credit and real GNP have deterministic time trends. 'Correlation' is the simple correlation between the credit series and real GNP after removing a cubic time trend from each. 'Elasticity' is the coefficient, ε, in the OLS regression:

$$\log(C/P)_t = a + bt + ct^2 + dt^3 + \varepsilon \log y_t + u_t \qquad (5.3)$$

where y is real GNP. The rankings of the subaggregates by these two measures of cyclicality correspond quite well, though not perfectly.

Table 5.8 offers corresponding information based on the random walk model. 'Correlation' is the simple correlation between the innovations in equation (5.2) and the innovation in a corresponding random walk model of real GNP. 'Elasticity' is the coefficient ε in regressions of the form:

$$\Delta \log(C/P)_t = a + \varepsilon \, \Delta \log y_t + u_t \qquad (5.4)$$

In Table 5.7, the four broad aggregates (I have now dropped bank credit from the list) again look the same and are quite highly correlated with GNP ($r = 0.8$, approximately). In Table 5.8, the two broadest aggregates (total lending and total borrowing) look a bit different from the two narrower aggregates and correlations are more modest. But in both tables the short-run (i.e., cyclical) demand for credit seems to be inelastic with respect to

GNP. Or is it the supply of credit? Perhaps a more neutral way to state this observation is:

Regardless of which broad aggregate is used, credit 'velocity' is clearly procyclical.

While the broad aggregates all look alike, the cyclical behavior of the different credit markets is amazingly disparate. According to Table 5.7 (the deterministic trend model), only consumer credit dances at all tightly to the tune of the business cycle. Mortgages and other loans (I ignore security credit as empirically unimportant) are moderately cyclical. But fluctuations in the bond, commercial paper, and CD markets are not at all highly correlated with fluctuations in GNP. The random walk model (Table 5.8) sees things slightly differently. The consumer credit market remains the most cyclical, but now mortgages, loans, and trade credit are not far behind. The commercial paper and CD markets appear countercyclical in Table 5.8, whereas they did not in Table 5.7.[8] However, both methods of analysis agree that:

Fluctuations in the intermediated forms of credit are tied more closely to business cycles than are fluctuations in auction market credit.[9]

If we look across classes of borrowers, it is the household sector – which, of course, borrows mainly in the forms of mortgages and consumer credit – that stands out from the rest if we use the deterministic trend model (Table 5.7). However, according to the random walk model (Table 5.8), household and business borrowing are about equally cyclical.

These observations suggest (to me, at least) that students of business cycles should pay more attention to the role of financial intermediation and to household borrowing than has been the case.[10]

5.5 COMOVEMENTS OF COMPONENTS OF CREDIT

Another set of facts of interest to theorists pertains to how various credit subaggregates move relative to one another, rather than relative to GNP. For example, Stiglitz and I (1983) have argued that small firms may be rationed more strictly when the volume of bank loans (henceforth L) contracts, leading to real effects. But this would not happen to any great degree if the small firms were simply extended trade credit (henceforth T) by the big firms, who in turn borrowed in the commercial paper (P) market. If this story has much empirical validity, we ought to find that L is negatively correlated with T and P. As will be seen shortly, this is not the case.

Movements in credit aggregates may be positively or negatively correlated because they respond in the same or opposite direction to business cycles, or for reasons unrelated to the cycle. Thus, there are two ways to measure covariation – with the cycle left in and with the cycle taken out. I present both in Tables 5.9 and 5.10, which look across the seven markets (security credit is

Table 5.7 The cyclicality of credit aggregates: deterministic trend model

Broad aggregates	Correlation[a]	Elasticity[b]	By market	Correlation	Elasticity
Total borrowing	0.77	0.65	Bonds	0.29	0.27
Total lending	0.78	0.67	Mortgages	0.64	0.80
Nonintermediated			Loans	0.57	1.09
borrowing	0.78	0.66			
Friedman credit	0.79	0.65	Trade credit		
			borrowing	0.12	0.25
			Trade credit		
			lending	0.44	0.66
			Consumer credit	0.80	1.52
			Large CDs	0.08	0.55
			Commercial paper	0.13	0.69
			Security credit	0.61	3.56

By borrower	Correlation	Elasticity	By lender	Correlation	Elasticity
Nonfinancial			Financial		
business	0.48	0.39	institutions	0.78	0.87
Households	0.81	1.10	Households	0.06	0.08
Federal			Nonfinancial		
government	0.34	0.53	business	0.48	0.60
Financial			Federal		
institutions	0.30	1.03	government	0.50	0.71
State/local			State/local		
government	0.19	0.22	government	0.59	1.35
Foreigners	0.45	1.13	Foreigners	−0.30	−0.31

Notes:

[a] Correlations between residuals from regressions of the form $\ln (C/P)_t = a + bt + ct^2 + dt^3 + u_t$, where C/P is the real value of the credit aggregate or subaggregate.

[b] Estimated value of ε in regressions of the form $\ln (C/P)_t = a + bt + ct^2 + dt^3 + \varepsilon \ln y_t + u_t$, where y_t is real GNP.

ignored). In Table 5.9, a cubic time trend was always removed from the log of each series, as in equation (5.1). The correlations reported *below* the diagonal are computed from the resulting detrended data. The correlations reported *above* the diagonal remove the effect of real GNP in addition, as in equation (5.3). In Table 5.10, the entries *below* the diagonal are correlations among the error terms in equation (5.2). The entries *above* the diagonal are correlations among the error terms in equation (5.4).

Table 5.8 The cyclicality of credit aggregates: random walk model

Broad aggregates	Correlation[a]	Elasticity[b]	By market	Correlation	Elasticity
Total borrowing	0.48	0.32	Bonds	0.10	0.09
Total lending	0.48	0.32	Mortgages	0.36	0.31
Nonintermediated			Loans	0.39	0.69
borrowing	0.40	0.25			
Friedman credit	0.42	0.26	Trade credit		
			borrowing	0.38	0.77
			Trade credit		
			lending	0.42	0.68
			Consumer credit	0.47	0.78
			Large CDs	−0.09	−0.62
			Commercial		
			paper	−0.26	−1.36
			Security credit	0.11	0.74

By borrower	Correlation	Elasticity	By lender	Correlation	Elasticity
Nonfinancial			Financial		
business	0.43	0.35	institutions	0.38	0.30
Households	0.43	0.44	Households	0.08	0.13
Federal			Nonfinancial		
government	0.07	0.12	business	0.50	0.84
Financial			Federal		
institutions	0.12	0.37	government	0.16	0.24
State/local			State/local		
government	0.10	0.12	government	0.14	0.22
Foreigners	0.16	0.31	Foreigners	−0.06	−0.20

Notes:
[a] Correlation between residuals from regressions of the form $\Delta \ln(C/P)_t = a + u_t$, where C/P is the real value of the aggregate or subaggregate.
[b] Estimated value of e in regressions of the form $\Delta \ln(C/P)_t = a + e\Delta \ln Y_t + u_t$, where y_t is real GNP.

Virtually every number in each matrix tells a story, and the interested reader is invited to peruse the numbers. I will mention just two. First, contrary to the scenario sketched two paragraphs ago, loans are not negatively correlated with trade credit and commercial paper; in fact, these correlations are positive regardless of the 'detrending' procedure and of whether the business cycle is left in or taken out. And many of them are substantially positive.[11]

Table 5.9 Correlations among credit subaggregates, by market: deterministic trend model

	Bonds	Mortgages	Loans	Trade credit lending	Consumer credit	Large CDs	Commercial paper
Bonds		0.13	−0.61	−0.60	0.11	−0.05	−0.33
Mortgages	0.28		0.05	−0.00	0.52	0.53	−0.24
Loans	−0.32	0.40		0.27	0.19	0.21	0.45
Trade credit lending	−0.39	0.28	0.45		0.18	−0.26	0.13
Consumer credit	0.30	0.75	0.55	0.44		0.17	−0.09
Large CDs	−0.02	0.46	0.22	−0.20	0.17		−0.10
Commercial paper	−0.26	−0.10	0.44	0.17	0.06	−0.09	

Notes:
Below diagonal: cycle 'in.'
Above diagonal: cycle 'out.'

Table 5.10 Correlations among credit subaggregates, by market: the random Walk model

	Bonds	Mortgages	Loans	Trade credit lending	Consumer credit	Large CDs	Commercial paper
Bonds		0.05	−0.31	−0.23	0.08	−0.07	−0.28
Mortgages	0.08		0.19	0.25	0.63	0.17	0.03
Loans	−0.24	0.31		0.42	0.30	0.03	0.13
Trade credit lending	−0.17	0.36	0.51		0.05	−0.07	0.25
Consumer credit	0.12	0.69	0.43	0.24		−0.01	−0.12
Large CDs	−0.07	0.12	−0.01	−0.11	−0.05		0.01
Commercial paper	−0.30	−0.07	0.02	0.11	−0.22	0.04	

Notes:
Below diagonal: cycle 'in.'
Above diagonal: cycle 'out.'

Second, when the business cycle is left in (below the diagonal), the largest correlation coefficient in either Table 5.9 or Table 5.10 is that between mortgage debt and consumer credit, which are highly positively correlated ($r = 0.75$ or $r = 0.63$). Part of this correlation is due to the fact that both are quite cyclical, as can be seen by comparing the above-diagonal correlation ($r = 0.52$) with the below-diagonal correlation ($r = 0.75$) in Table 5.9. But even after the cycle is taken out (above the diagonal), these two series remain highly correlated. An interesting question is whether this is a demand-side phenomenon (when consumers borrow to buy a house they also borrow to buy durable goods) or a supply-side phenomenon (when banks ease credit availability both types of borrowing rise). The latter interpretation is suggested by the fact that loans also display positive correlations with both mortgages and consumer credit.

It is also of interest to divide credit market activity by borrower rather than by type of instrument. This is done in Tables 5.11 and 5.12, which have the same basic format as Tables 5.9 and 5.10. When this is done, negative correlations are a crude indicator of 'crowding out' in that more borrowing by one type of agent (relative to trend) leads to less borrowing by another. A casual inspection indicates that there are more positive than negative correlations. If we restrict attention to the four major borrowers (by ignoring the last two rows and the last two columns), and leave the cycle in, we find two negative correlations in Table 5.11 and three in Table 5.12. All five of these involve the federal government. By this crude *mutatis mutandis* measure, it appears that federal borrowing crowds out borrowing by financial institutions and, especially, by nonfinancial businesses. Thus:

A crude look at the data suggests that federal government borrowing may crowd out mainly business borrowing.

When the cycle is taken out of the data (above the diagonal), the strength of this 'crowding out' effect looks quite impressive ($r = -0.77$) in Table 5.11.

It is interesting to contrast the correlations with and without the cyclical element. There are 15 correlations in each table, and every one that changes when the common business cycle element is removed from the data (moving from below the diagonal to above it) moves in the negative direction. Negative correlations become more negative and positive correlations become less positive. Changes are particularly marked in Table 5.11 (the deterministic trend model). This suggests an economic message. We saw in Tables 5.7 and 5.8 that almost every type of borrowing is procyclical (though to different degrees); so the cycle imparts a positive covariance to any two components of total borrowing. When this cyclical element is removed, crowding out (i.e., negative covariance) becomes more apparent. Thus:

Over business cycles, most types of borrowing tend to rise and fall together. But fluctuations in government borrowing for other reasons may crowd out private (especially business) borrowing.

5.6 CONCLUSIONS

In sum, this brief tour through the data seems to point to the following facts which should be of interest to those doing research on credit:

Table 5.11 Correlations among credit subaggregates, by borrower: deterministic trend model

	Nonfinancial business	Households	Federal government	Financial institutions	State/local government	Foreigners
Nonfinancial business		0.05	−0.77	0.27	0.18	−0.46
Households	0.42		0.22	0.41	−0.16	0.59
Federal government	−0.47	0.39		−0.29	−0.08	0.48
Financial institutions	0.37	0.48	−0.16		0.26	0.06
State/local government	0.25	0.06	−0.01	0.30		−0.53
Foreigners	−0.14	0.67	0.55	0.19	−0.38	

Notes:
Below diagonal: cycle 'in'.
Above diagonal: cycle 'out'.

Table 5.12 Correlations among credit subaggregates, by borrower: random walk model

	Nonfinancial business	Households	Federal government	Financial institutions	State/local government	Foreigners
Nonfinancial business		0.44	−0.28	0.29	0.18	−0.03
Households	0.54		−0.08	0.33	0.56	0.00
Federal government	−0.22	−0.04		−0.12	−0.19	−0.01
Financial institutions	0.31	0.35	−0.11		0.12	0.05
State/local government	0.20	0.55	−0.18	0.13		0.02
Foreigners	0.04	0.07	−0.00	0.07	0.04	

Notes:
Below diagonal: cycle 'in'.
Above diagonal: cycle 'out'.

1. Credit extended in customer markets – where prices seem to be sticky and where informational and screening issues and quantity rationing may be important – is more important than credit extended in auction markets, especially where cyclical fluctuations are concerned.
2. Intermediated credit is far more cyclical than is nonintermediated credit, at least in terms of contemporaneous correlation.
3. Household borrowing may be more volatile and more sensitive to the business cycle than is business borrowing.
4. Crowding out seems not to be a business cycle issue; and it is business borrowing, not household borrowing, that seems to get crowded out by government borrowing.
5. While credit has grown faster than GNP, the relative sizes of the major private credit markets have changed only modestly.
6. Trade credit merits more attention from researchers than it has received.

5.7 NOTES

1. See, however, the last part of Bernanke (1983), a series of papers by B. Friedman, and S. R. King (1986).
2. However, agency holdings of Treasury securities (and *vice versa*) were netted out.
3. See Blinder and Stiglitz (1983), Blinder (1987), and Okun (1981).
4. The proper classification of mortgages is debatable. They clearly *originate* in customer markets but, in recent years, are *traded* in secondary auction markets.
5. The period emphasized by Friedman was 1960–80.
6. King's (1986) empirical results unfortunately are restricted to bank credit.
7. Consistent with this, King (1986) finds that 'other' bank loans correlate better with GNP than do commercial and industrial loans.
8. It is not clear how to classify trade credit. Trade credit borrowing is not very cyclical; but the trade credit discrepancy (float) is, which makes trade credit lending much more cyclical than trade credit borrowing.
9. This statement applies only to contemporaneous correlations.
10. King's (1986) results cited in note 7 seem to agree with this.
11. If we use trade credit borrowing rather than trade credit lending, the correlation is much weaker.

5.8 REFERENCES

Bernanke, B. (1983) 'Non-monetary effects of the financial collapse in the propagation of the great depression,' *American Economic Review*, vol. 73 (June), pp. 257–76.

Blinder, A. S. (1987) 'Credit rationing and effective supply failures,' *Economic Journal* (June), Chapter 3 in this volume.

Blinder, A. S. and J. Stiglitz (1983) 'Money, credit constraints, and economic activity,' *American Economic Review*, vol. 73 (May), Chapter 2 in this volume.

Friedman, B. (1983) 'The roles of money and credit in macroeconomic analysis,' in J. Tobin (ed.) *Macroeconomics, Prices and Quantities*, Washington: Brookings.

Friedman, B. (1983) 'Debt and economic activity in the United States,' in B. Friedman (ed.) *The Changing Roles of Debt and Equity in Financing US Capital Formation*, Chicago: University of Chicago Press.

King, R. G. and Plosser, C. I. (1984) 'Money, credit and prices in a real business cycle,' *American Economic Review*, vol. 74 (June).

King, S. R. (1986) 'Monetary transmission: through bank loans, or bank liabilities?", *Journal of Money, Credit and Banking* (August),

Okun, A. M. (1981) *Prices and Quantities*, Washington: Brookings.

APPENDIX 5.1 · DEFINITIONS OF CREDIT AGGREGATES

TOTAL BORROWING AND TOTAL LENDING

Total borrowing represents all borrowing transacted domestically. This includes domestic and foreign borrowers, financial and nonfinancial borrowers, and private and Federal, state, and local government borrowers.

Borrowing is defined to include all credit market instruments, as they are defined in the Federal Reserve Board's flow of funds accounts, that is, bonds, commercial paper, banker's acceptances, mortgages, consumer credit, and loans. It also includes security credit, trade credit and large time deposits.

Federal government borrowing includes borrowing by government agencies and mortgage pools, but excludes holdings of Federal or agency debt by the Federal government or by agencies. Similarly excluded are state and local debt holdings by state and local governments or pension funds. In both cases it was felt that such cases of simultaneous borrowing and lending by what amounts to a single entity should not be counted.

Total lending is identical to total borrowing except that it is larger by the difference between trade credit and trade debt, the 'trade credit discrepancy' described in the text.

NONINTERMEDIATED BORROWING

Nonintermediated borrowing is derived by excluding from total borrowing that portion which is used to fund lending. Subtracted from total Federal borrowing is total Federal lending, from total state and local borrowing is state and local lending, and from nonfinancial business borrowing is total nonfinancial business lending. All financial borrowing is excluded. Household and foreign borrowing are left unchanged.

6 · CREDIT, MONEY, AND AGGREGATE DEMAND

Most standard models of aggregate demand, such as the textbook *IS/LM* model, treat bank assets and bank liabilities asymmetrically. Money, the bank liability, is given a special role in the determination of aggregate demand. In contrast, bank loans are lumped together with other debt instruments in a 'bond market,' which is then conveniently suppressed by Walras's Law.

Much recent research provides reasons to question this imbalance. A growing theoretical literature, based on models with asymmetric information, stresses the importance of intermediaries in the provision of credit and the special nature of bank loans. Empirically, the instability of econometric money demand equations has been accompanied by new interest in the credit–GNP relationship (see especially the work of Benjamin Friedman).

We have developed several models of aggregate demand which allow roles for both money and 'credit' (bank loans). We present a particularly simple one, a variant of the textbook *IS/LM* model, in this paper.

Though it has a simple graphical representation like *IS/LM*, this model permits us to pose a richer array of questions than does the traditional money-only framework.

6.1 THE MODEL

The *LM* curve is a portfolio-balance condition for a two-asset world: asset holders choose between money and bonds. Tacitly, loans and other forms of customer-market credit are viewed as perfect substitutes for auction-market credit ("bonds"), and financial markets clear only by price. Models with a distinct role for credit arise when either of these assumptions is abandoned.

Following Tobin (1970) and Brunner and Meltzer (1972), we choose to abandon the perfect substitutability assumption and ignore credit rationing.[1] Our model has three assets: money, bonds, and loans. Only the loan market needs explanation. We assume that both borrowers and lenders choose

Written with Ben S. Bernanke, Princeton University, Princeton, NJ 08544. We are grateful to the NSF for supporting this research.

between bonds and loans according to the interest rates on the two credit instruments. If ρ is the interest rate on loans and i is the interest rate on bonds, then loan demand is: $L^d = L(\rho, i, y)$. The dependence on GNP (y) captures the transactions demand for credit, which might arise, for example, from working capital or liquidity considerations.

To understand the genesis of loan supply, consider a simplified bank balance sheet (which ignores net worth) with assets: reserves, R; bonds, B^b, loans, L^s; and liabilities: deposits, D. Since reserves consist of required reserves, τD, plus excess reserves, E, the banks' adding-up constraint is: $B^b + L^s + E = D(1 - \tau)$. Assuming that desired portfolio proportions depend on rates of return on the available assets (zero for excess reserves), we have $L^s = \lambda (\rho, i)D(1 - \tau)$, with similar equations for the shares of B^b and E. Thus the condition for clearing the loan market is:

$$L(\rho, i, y) = \lambda (\rho, i) D (1-\tau) \tag{6.1}$$

The money market is described by a conventional LM curve. Suppose banks hold excess reserves equal to $\varepsilon(i)D(1-\tau)$.[2] Then the supply of deposits (we ignore cash) is equal to bank reserves, R, times the money multiplier, $m(i) = [\varepsilon(i)(1-\tau) +\tau]^{-1}$. The demand for deposits arises from the transactions motive and depends on the interest rate, income, and total wealth, which is constant and therefore suppressed: $D(i, y)$. Equating the two gives:

$$D(i, y) = m(i)R \tag{6.2}$$

Implicitly, $D(i, y)$ and $L(\rho, i, y)$ define the nonbank public's demand function for bonds since money demand plus bond demand minus loan demand must equal total financial wealth.

The remaining market is the goods market, which we summarize in a conventional IS curve, written generically as:[3]

$$y = Y(i, \rho) \tag{6.3}$$

6.2 GRAPHICAL REPRESENTATION

Use (6.2) to replace $D(1 - \tau)$ on the right-hand side of (6.1) by $(1 - \tau)m(i)R$. Then (6.1) can be solved for ρ as a function of i, y, and R:[4]

$$\rho = \phi\left(i, y, R\right) \tag{6.4}$$

Finally, substitute (6.4) into (6.3) to get:

$$y = Y(i, \phi(i, y, R)) \tag{6.5}$$

which, in deference to Patinkin (1956), we call the CC curve (for 'commodities and credit'). It is easy to see that the CC curve is negatively sloped like an IS curve, and for much the same reasons. However, it is shifted by monetary policy (R) and by credit-market shocks that affect either the $L(\cdot)$ or $\lambda(\cdot)$ functions, while the IS curve is not. The CC and LM curves are shown together in Fig. 6.1.

Our CC curve reduces to the IS curve if loans and bonds are assumed to be perfect substitutes either to borrowers ($L\rho \to -\infty$) or to lenders ($\lambda\rho \to \infty$), or if commodity demand is insensitive to the loan rate ($Y\rho = 0$) – which would make the loan market irrelevant to IS/LM. This clarifies the special assumptions implicit in the money-only view.

The opposite extreme, or credit-only view, would arise if money and bonds were perfect substitutes ($D_i \to -\infty$), which would make the LM curve horizontal. Keynes's explanation for the liquidity trap is, of course, well known. We think of high substitutability as more likely to arise from financial innovations which create new money substitutes. However, even with a liquidity trap, monetary policy still matters because it influences the CC curve.

Now let us turn to the intermediate cases represented by Fig. 6.1.

6.3 COMPARATIVE STATICS[5]

Most conventional shocks work in our model just as they do in IS/LM. For example, an expenditure shock shifts the CC curve along a fixed LM curve, and a money-demand shock shifts the LM curve along a fixed CC curve. The effects are familiar and need not be discussed. The only noteworthy difference is that a rise in bank reserves might conceivably raise the rate of interest in the credit model. Graphically, the ambiguity arises because an increase in R shifts both the CC and LM curves outward. Economically, the credit channel makes monetary policy more expansionary than in IS/LM and therefore raises the transactions demand for money by more than in the conventional model.

Greater interest attaches to issues that elude the IS/LM model. An upward shift in the credit supply function, $\lambda(\cdot)$ (which might correspond, for example, to a decrease in the perceived riskiness of loans) shifts the CC curve outward along a fixed LM curve, thereby raising i and y. The interest rate on loans ρ, falls, however. An upward shift in the credit demand function, $L(\cdot)$, which might correspond to a greater need for working capital, has precisely the opposite effects.

We find it difficult to think of or identify major shocks to credit demand, that is, sharp increases or decreases in the demand for loans at given interest rates and GNP. But shocks to credit supply are easy to conceptualize and to

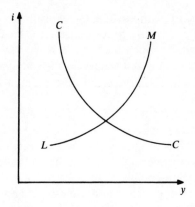

Fig. 6.1 Graphical representation of the credit model.

find in actual history. For example, Bernanke's (1983) explanation for the length of the Great Depression can be thought of as a downward shock to credit supply stemming from the increased riskiness of loans and banks' concern for liquidity in the face of possible runs. According to the model, such a shock should reduce credit, GNP, and the interest rate on government bonds while raising the interest rate on loans. Another notable example with the same predicted effects is the credit controls of March–July 1980. In this instance 'tight money' should, and apparently did, reduce interest rates on government bonds.

6.4 IMPLICATIONS FOR MONETARY POLICY

We turn next to the traditional target and indicator issues of monetary policy. The so-called monetary indicator problem arises if the central bank sees its impact on aggregate demand only with a lag but sees its impacts on financial-sector variables like interest rates, money, and credit more promptly. What does our model say about the suitability of money or of credit as indicators?

Table 6.1 shows the qualitative responses of GNP, money, credit, and bond interest rates to a wide variety of shocks, assuming that bank reserves is the policy instrument. Columns 1 and 2 display a conclusion familiar from *IS*/*LM*: money is a good qualitative indicator of future GNP movements except when money demand shocks are empirically important. Columns 1 and 3 offer the corresponding conclusion for credit: credit is a good qualitative indicator except when there are important shocks to credit demand. If money demand shocks were indeed more important than credit demand shocks in the 1980s, credit would have been a better indicator than money.

What about the target question, that is, about the choice between stabilizing money versus stabilizing credit? Rather than try to conduct a complete

Table 6.1 Effects of shocks on observable variables

Rise in:	(1) Income	(2) Money	(3) Credit	(4) Interest rate[a]
bank reserves	+	+	+	−
money demand	−	+	−	+
credit supply	+	+	+	+
credit demand	−	−	+	−
commodity demand	+	+	+	+

Note:
[a]On bonds.

Poole-style (1970) analysis, we simply ask whether policymakers would respond 'correctly' (i.e., in a stabilizing way) to various shocks if they were targeting money or targeting credit.

Consider first an expansionary *IS* shock. Table 6.1 (line 5) shows that both money and credit would rise if bank reserves were unchanged. Hence a central bank trying to stabilize either money or credit would contract bank reserves, which is the correct stabilizing response. Either policy works, at least qualitatively. A similar analysis applies to shocks to the supply of credit or to the money multiplier.

But suppose the demand for money increases (line 2), which sends a contractionary impulse to GNP. Since this shock raises M, a monetarist central bank would contract reserves in an effort to stabilize money, which would destabilize GNP. This, of course, is the familiar Achilles heel of monetarism. Notice, however, that this same shock would make credit contract. So a central bank trying to stabilize credit would expand reserves. In this case, a credit-based policy is superior to a money-based policy.

The opposite is true, however, when there are credit-demand shocks. Line 4 tells us that a contractionary (for GNP) credit-demand shock lowers the money supply but raises credit. Hence a monetarist central bank would turn expansionary, as it should, while a creditist central bank would turn contractionary, which it should not.

We therefore reach a conclusion similar to that reached in discussing indicators: If money-demand shocks are more important than credit-demand shocks, then a policy of targeting credit is probably better than a policy of targeting money.

6.5 EMPIRICAL EVIDENCE

The foregoing discussion suggests that the case for credit turns on whether credit demand is, or is becoming, relatively more stable than money demand. We conclude with some evidence that this is true, at least since 1979.[6]

Table 6.2 Simple correlations of growth rates of GNP with growth rates of financial aggregates, 1973–85[a,b]

Period	With money	With credit
1953:1–1973:4	0.51, 0.37	0.17, 0.11
1974:1–1979:3	0.50, 0.54	0.50, 0.51
1979:4–1985:4	0.11, 0.34	0.38, 0.47

Notes:
[a]Growth rates are first differences of natural logarithms.
[b]Correlations in nominal terms come first; correlations in real terms come second.

Table 6.2 shows the simple correlations between GNP growth and growth of the two financial aggregates during three periods. Money was obviously much more highly correlated with income than was credit during the period of stable money demand, 1953–73. But the two financial aggregates were on a more equal footing during 1974:1–1979:3. Further changes came during the period of unstable money demand, 1979:4–1985:4; money–GNP correlations dropped sharply while money–credit correlations fell only slightly, giving a clear edge to credit.[7]

More direct evidence on the relative magnitudes of money-demand and credit-demand shocks was obtained by comparing the residuals from estimated structural money-demand and credit-demand functions like $D(\cdot)$ and $L(\cdot)$ in our model. We used the logarithmic partial adjustment model, with adjustment in nominal terms, which we are not eager to defend but which was designed to fit money demand. Hence, our procedure seems clearly biased toward finding relatively larger credit shocks than money shocks.

Unsurprisingly, estimates for the entire 1953–85 period rejected parameter stability across a 1973:4–1974:1 break, so we concentrated on the latter period.[8] Much to our amazement, we estimated moderately sensible money and credit demand equations for the 1974:1–1985:4 period on the first try (standard errors are in parentheses):

$$\log M = -0.06 + 0.939 \log M_{-1} - 0.222i$$
$$(0.34)\ \ (0.059)\phantom{\log M_{-1}}\ \ (0.089)$$

$$+ 0.083 \log P + 0.012 \log y$$
$$(0.052)\ \ (0.059)$$

$$SEE = 0.00811 \quad DW = 2.04$$

$$\log C = -1.75 + 0.885 \log C_{-1} - 0.424\rho$$
$$(0.63)\ \ (0.076)\phantom{\log C_{-1}}\ \ (0.285)$$

$$+ 0.514i + 0.075 \log P + 0.292 \log y$$
$$(0.389)\ \ (0.086)\ \ (0.107)$$

$$SEE = 0.00797, \quad DW = 2.44$$

Here y is real GNP, P is the GNP deflator, ρ is the bank prime rate, and i is the three-month Treasury bill rate. Although the interest rate coefficients in the credit equation are individually insignificant, they are jointly significant, have the correct signs, and are almost equal in absolute value – suggesting a specification in which the spread between ρ and i determines credit demand. Notice that the residual variances in the two equations are about equal.

Since the sample was too short to test reliably for parameter stability, we examined the residuals from the two equations over two subperiods with these results:

period	variance of money residual	variance of credit residual
1974:1 – 1979:3	0.265×10^{-4}	0.687×10^{-4}
1979:4 – 1985:4	0.888×10^{-4}	0.435×10^{-4}

The differences are striking. By this crude measure, the variance of money-demand shocks was much smaller than that of credit-demand shocks during the first subperiod but much larger during the second.

The evidence thus supports the idea that money-demand shocks became much more important relative to credit-demand shocks in the 1980s. But that does not mean we should start ignoring money and focusing on credit. After all, it is perfectly conceivable that the relative sizes of money-demand and credit-demand shocks will revert once again to what they were earlier. Rather, the message of this paper is that a more symmetric treatment of money and credit is feasible and appears warranted.

6.6 NOTES

1. Blinder (1987) offers a model in which there is rationing and no substitute for bank credit.
2. For simplicity, we assume that only i, not ρ, influences the demand for excess reserves.
3. The interest rates in (6.3) should be real rates. But a model of aggregate demand takes both the price level and inflation as given; so we take the expected inflation rate to be constant and suppress it.
4. ρ is an increasing function of i as long as the interest elasticity of the money multiplier is not too large.
5. Most comparative statics results require no assumptions other than the ones we have already made. But, in a few cases, we encounter theoretical ambiguities that can be resolved by invoking certain elasticity assumptions spelled out in a longer version of this chapter. If output is fixed on the supply side, y would be replaced by P in Fig. 6.1 and in the text discussion that follows.
6. In what follows, 'money' is M1, 'credit' is an aggregate invented by one of us: the sum of intermediated borrowing by households and businesses (derived from flow of funds data). For details and analysis of the latter, see Blinder (1985).

7. Similar findings emerged when we controlled for many variables via a vector-autoregression (VAR) and looked at correlations between VAR residuals.
8. Estimation was by instrumental variables. Instruments were current, once, and twice lagged logs of real government purchases, real exports, bank reserves, and a supply shock variable which is a weighted average of the relative prices of energy and agricultural products.

6.7 REFERENCES

Bernanke, B. S. (1983) 'Nonmonetary effects of the financial crisis in the propagation of the Great Depression,' *American Economic Review* (June), vol. 73, pp. 257–76.

Blinder, A. S. (1985) 'The stylized facts about credit aggregates,' mimeo., Princeton University (June).

Blinder, A. S. (1987) 'Credit rationing and effective supply failures,' *Economic Journal*, (June), vol. 97, pp. 327–52. Chapter 3 in this volume.

Brunner, K. and Meltzer, A. H. (1972) 'Money, debt, and economic activity,' *Journal of Political Economy*, (September/October), vol. 80, pp. 951–77.

Patinkin, D. (1956) *Money, Interest, and Prices*, New York: Harper and Row.

Poole, W. (1970) 'Optimal choice of monetary policy instruments in a simple stochastic macro model,' *Quarterly Journal of Economics* (May) vol. 2, pp. 197–216.

Tobin, J. (1970) 'A general equilibrium approach to monetary theory,' *Journal of Money, Credit and Banking*, (November), vol. 2, pp. 461–72.

7 · KEYNES AFTER LUCAS

The extraordinary achievement of the classical theory was to overcome the beliefs of the 'natural man' and, at the same time, to be wrong. John Maynard Keynes

I come here neither to praise Keynes nor to bury him, but to ruminate about where Keynesian economics is going in view of what it has been through. The last 10–15 years have been a period of intellectual ferment in macroeconomics. Old beliefs have been questioned, old models discarded. Many creative and imaginative – some might say fanciful – new ideas have come to the fore. Many clever people have toiled long hours in the macro vineyards seeking to develop new, more critique-resistant strains of theory and econometrics. Many new techniques have been added to our toolkit. To be the very model of a modern macroeconomist today, your technical baggage must be much heavier than was true a decade or two ago. Yet do we know much more today than we did then about how the macroeconomy really works? I am not convinced.

Marx said that thesis and antithesis lead to synthesis. But, as we know, Marx was not always right. There is today a strong consensus that there is no macroeconomic consensus. So, if you came to hear the new post-Lucas consensus, you will be disappointed. Instead, I want to talk about resource allocation within our subdiscipline. I want to ask whether or not the prodigious amounts of labor and capital devoted to macroeconomic research since 1972 have been allocated correctly. Or has there instead been a colossal market failure? There are those, I know, who will assert that macroeconomic research must be efficient since the market is competitive, there are no government regulations, no distorting taxes, and macroeconomists rationally pursue their own self-interest. I remind them that both externalities and rational speculative bubbles can exist, and proceed.

7.1 THE KEYNESIAN CONSENSUS AS OF 1972

This section summarizes the Keynesian consensus as it existed in 1972, before Lucas and company mounted their spirited attack:[1] an *IS/LM* model plus an

Thanks go to Ben Bernanke, Steve Goldfeld and Bob Gordon for comments on an earlier draft and to Lori Grunin for research assistance.

expectations-augmented Phillips curve, with expectations modeled as adaptive. Since the model is so familiar, I will be brief.

7.1.1 IS and LM

Private aggregate demand came from a consumption function based on the work of M. Friedman (1957) or Ando and Modigliani (1963) and an investment function based on the work of Jorgenson (1963). While expectations of future variables play important roles in the theories underlying both functions, simple-minded empirical proxies for these expectations were accepted without much question in applied work.[2] The financial sector was summarized in an *LM* curve of the sort estimated by Goldfeld (1973) which, in turn, was loosely based (such looseness was tolerated in those days!) on the Baumol–Tobin model of money demand.

7.1.2 Predetermined price level

Thinking that the ghost of Pigou had been laid to rest, few macroeconomists thought it necessary to defend the notion that labor and goods markets do not clear each 'period' – even if the period was as long as a year. The macroeconomic servo-mechanism was thought to work much more slowly than this. Hence, it was natural to think of prices and wages as predetermined, which left *IS* and *LM* together to determine output in the short run.

7.1.3 The Phillips curve

The price level evolved according to an expectations-augmented Phillips curve:

$$\dot{p} = E(\dot{p}) + f(y - y^*) \tag{7.1}$$

where $\dot{p}$ is the inflation rate, y is (the log of) real output and y^* is the natural rate of output. I choose 1972 as my starting point because by then the vertical-in-the-long-run view of the Phillips curve, originally promoted by Phelps (1968) and M. Friedman (1968), had won the day.[3] Causation in equation (7.1) was supposed to flow from GNP gaps to inflation. Most economists gave (7.1) a disequilibrium, price-adjustment interpretation, following Lipsey (1960), although the Phelps–Friedman model could be interpreted as a market-clearing model subject to an informational lag. It was also taken as axiomatic that recessions were economic maladies; the idea that Okun gaps might be Pareto-optimal would have been thought eccentric.

7.1.4 Modeling expectations

The expected rate of inflation needed in (7.1) – which also entered the model as the difference between the *IS* curve's real interest rate and the *LM* curve's nominal rate – was typically modeled as adaptive, or in some other distributed lag form. The idea that expectations lagged behind reality was rarely questioned and was, of course, central to the Phelps–Friedman Phillips curve mechanism.

7.1.5 View of policy

Fiscal and monetary policies were typically viewed as exogenous (a word we thought meaningful in those days) and episodic, not the sort of thing that was suitable for forecasting by time series techniques developed for stationary stochastic processes. Despite this, there was some empirical literature on policy reaction functions, especially for monetary policy, and a well-developed approach to optimal policy in the Tinbergen–Theil framework.[4] No one paid much attention to the ideas that the economy might react differently to anticipated versus unanticipated policy changes or that changes in the nature of policy might change the 'structural' equations of the model.

7.1.6 Econometric models

Finally, all of the above elements plus a hideous number of other details (some of them quite important) were embodied in highly complex, large-scale macroeconometric models which were estimated and identified by what I will call, as a shorthand, Cowles Commission techniques. No one will accuse me of understatement if I say that the theoretical structures of these models were not very tight.

7.2 THE CONSENSUS CRUMBLES: CAN ANYBODY SPARE A PARADIGM?

The insurgents that sacked the Keynesian temple in the 1970s raised objections to every item on this list. But I think it fair to say that IS/LM was spared the heavy artillery, which was aimed at the other items. In the new classical view, prices moved quickly to clear markets; expectations about inflation, policy 'rules,' and everything else were rational; the Phillips curve offered no exploitable tradeoff; and existing econometric models were useless, or worse.

7.2.1 The Phillips curve

Lucas's (1976) original paper, of course, made the Phillips curve one of the central examples of his critique of econometric policy evaluation. And Lucas and Sargent (1978) used the alleged collapse of the Phillips curve, which they characterized as 'econometric failure on a grand scale' (1978, p. 57), as the major piece of empirical evidence in their premature obituary for Keynesian economics. The Lucas supply function turned the Phillips curve on its head. When Lucas (1973) changed equation (7.1) to:

$$y - y^* = g(\dot{p} - E(\dot{p})) \tag{7.2}$$

he gave it a market-clearing interpretation similar to Phelps–Friedman, and he meant the causation to run from expectational errors to GNP gaps. On the surface, the difference between (7.1) and (7.2) hardly looks revolutionary. Lucas's more important point was that neither the $g(.)$ function nor the distributed lag proxies typically used to model $E(\dot{p})$ were likely to be stable; they would, instead, change whenever the time-series behavior of inflation changed. His suggested answer was to model expectations as 'rational', that is, as consistent with the structure of the model.

7.2.2 Rational expectations

It took a while, and some help from Fischer (1977) and Phelps and Taylor (1977), for the profession to get clear that rational expectations (RE) is an assumption about behavior which may be right or wrong but which is logically disconnected from the hypothesis that prices move instantly to clear markets. It is more from the latter than from the former that the new classical economics (NCE) derives its distinctive implications.

Separating those two ideas helped spread the RE gospel, since formal econometric tests of the joint hypothesis of RE and market clearing almost always rejected it.[5] Most economists had a strong suspicion that the market-clearing hypothesis was the weak link in the partnership. Many, especially in the United States, eagerly embraced rational expectations as the natural accompaniment to utility maximization and profit maximization, without bothering to ask for evidence. Fischer (1986, p. 13) probably speaks for many when he states unequivocally that 'rational expectations is the right initial hypothesis.' This attitude, it seems to me, would not have appealed to Keynes, who wrote (1936, pp. 161–2):

> . . . a large proportion of our positive activities depend on spontaneous optimism rather than on a mathematical expectation . . . Only a little more than an expedition to the South Pole, is it based on an exact calculation of benefits to come. Thus if animal spirits are dimmed and the spontaneous optimism falters, leaving us to depend on nothing but a mathematical expectation, enterprise will fade and die. . .

7.2.3 Market clearing

The separation of RE from market clearing probably doomed the latter because the hypothesis of instantaneous market clearing was wildly at variance with events that were unfolding as the RE revolution took hold. For example, since rational expectations implies that $\dot{p} - E(\dot{p})$ is white noise, equation (7.2) implies that output vibrates randomly around the natural rate. (More on this below.) Yet 1973–5 witnessed the deepest recession since the 1930s, 1981–2 eclipsed that standard, and, as this is written, unemployment has yet to return to the natural rate. How and why the market-clearing approach caught on in this environment will, I venture to guess, be a source of consternation and amazement to economists of the twenty-first century – much as modern physicians marvel at the eighteenth century belief in the curative effects of bleeding. It might have prompted Keynes, were he still alive, to add the prefix 'neo' to the adjective 'classical' and say (Keynes (1936, p. 16)):

> The classical theorists resemble Euclidean geometers in a non-Euclidean world who, discovering that in experience straight lines apparently parallel often meet, rebuke the lines for not keeping straight – as the only remedy for the unfortunate collisions which are occurring.

7.2.4 Optimizing behavior

Closely connected to the puzzling popularity of market-clearing models was a revival – I might almost say a fundamentalist revival – of the search for microfoundations for macroeconomic models. That is always a worthy cause; but the NCE school pushed it to incredible extremes. It became *de rigueur* to derive everything from neoclassical first principles; all behavioral functions had to come from first-order conditions to simplistic optimization problems solved by representative agents. Realism was sacrificed to rigor, as internal consistency replaced consistency with observations as the principal criterion by which models were judged. Old ideas like corner solutions, heterogeneity, aggregation problems, and coordination failures were forgotten. New ideas that were spewing forth from the new microeconomics of imperfect information – which suggested many reasons why prices might not be able to clear markets – were ignored.

7.2.5 Econometric models

The neoclassical revival, in concert with the Lucas critique, stripped large-scale econometric models of any academic respectability they ever had. These ugly, crassly empirical creatures, with their tenuous theoretical structures, looked pitiably old-fashioned at a time when styles were turning toward smaller, cuter, more tightly theoretical models. Lucas argued that the big models, which either treated expectations as adaptive or ignored them entirely, could not be used to analyze policy. That robbed them of their main purpose. Instead of tools for investigation, the models became butts of jokes.

That was a shame, because only vector autoregressions (VARs) were offered in their place,[6] and most economists (though not Sims (1982)), thought VARs useless for policy analysis.

7.2.6 View of policy

The Lucasian revolution also sought to change the standard view of government policy. Instead of seeing policy as exogenous and episodic, rational expectationists preferred to think of the government as following 'policy rules' that were stable enough to be known (up to random error) by consumers and firms. And they took it as axiomatic that optimizing private agents would change their behavior whenever the policy rule changed. Some went even further to suggest that, since the government was already optimizing (would that it were so!), it could not change its behavior at all.[7]

Several new issues became prominent. One was the difference between anticipated and unanticipated policy changes, especially for monetary policy. In one of the few empirical salvos fired by the new classical counter-revolutionaries, Barro (1977) claimed to have found support for the idea that only unanticipated money growth can move real output. Another new issue was the so-called time consistency problem: when would the government want to stick to a pre-announced rule and when would it want to renege?[8]

7.2.7 Persistence

While criticizing the Keynesian answers to everything, the new macroeconomic paradigm created an intellectual puzzle where none existed before: why do economic fluctuations persist? Keynesians thought distributed-lag consumption, investment, and money demand functions; accelerator mechanisms in inventories, fixed investment, and consumer durables; gradual adjustment of prices and wages; and lags in expectations were more than enough to explain persistence. But all of these were banished by the new orthodoxy. Instead, we had equation (7.2), which insisted that GNP gaps had to be white noise if expectations were rational. Of course, Lucas (1973) knew this to be untrue and so had appended the lagged GNP gap to (7.2) without much theoretical justification. Subsequently, explaining persistence became a minor growth industry. Sargent (1979) appealed to adjustment costs, Lucas (1975) to fixed capital, Blinder and Fischer (1981) to inventories, Taylor (1980) to staggered contracts, Kydland and Prescott (1982) to technological lags. Each of these innovations, it seems to me, made the basic model look somewhat more Keynesian. And, once their implications were thought through, most provided a potential channel through which anticipated money might have real effects *via* changes in real interest rates.[9]

7.3 ELEMENTS OF A RENAISSANCE

In this fiftieth birthday year [1986], Keynesian economics appears to be moving out of the dark ages into a renaissance. It has been victorious by default, I think, because the new classical economics failed miserably to meet the criterion for a Kuhnian paradigm change. Not only did it fail to explain any empirical phenomenon that baffled Keynesian analysts (and there were several), but it created anomalies (like persistence) where Keynesian economics offered coherent explanations.

7.3.1 Phillips curve

As noted, the Phillips curve bore the brunt of the RE/NCE attack. But we now know that, once suitably modified to include 'supply shocks,' this empirical regularity stands up remarkably well.[10] Indeed, its stability through the 1970s and 1980s is amazing in view of the troubles encountered by money demand, investment, and other functions.

7.3.2 Lucas critique

Similarly, the Lucas critique, which at first was misinterpreted as a directive to throw the baby out with the bath water, has been put into perspective. While Lucas's conceptual point is valuable and indubitably correct, so are the well-known points that heteroskedastic or serially correlated disturbances lead to inefficient estimates and that simultaneity leads to inconsistent estimates. But we also understand that small amounts of serial correlation lead to small inefficiencies and that minor simultaneity leads to only minor inconsistencies; so suspected violations of the Gauss–Markov theorem do not stop applied econometrics in its tracks. In the same spirit, the realization is now dawning that the Lucas critique need not be a show stopper.[11] Indeed, evidence that it is typically important in applied work is lacking.

7.3.3 Rational expectations

The hypothesis that expectations are rational, that is, consistent with the model, seems to have had more enduring success, and rightly so. Certainly, the previous unthinking loyalty to adaptive expectations is gone forever. Economists will, forevermore, worry about possible direct effects of policy on expectations. But, even here, there has been significant backsliding. Taylor (1975), B. Friedman (1979), and before them Muth (1960) outlined circumstances under which adaptive expectations might be exactly or approximately rational. Frydman and Phelps (1984), among others, have pointed to a fundamental difficulty with the assumption that expectations are model-consistent when people's beliefs may differ – a difficulty well appreciated by

Keynes.[12] And it has become increasingly well-known that matching sub-jective probability distributions to objective ones is no trivial matter when the objective distribution may not be stationary, nor even exist, because the events being forecast are not repetitive. For example, who would like to tell me the probability distribution of the real price of crude oil, or of the federal budget deficit, in the year 2000?

7.3.4 Market clearing

The old-fashioned idea that goods and labor markets do not clear in-stantaneously is staging a strong comeback. How could it be otherwise, given the overwhelming evidence in its favor? Since economists are rarely moved by evidence that assaults the naked eye, it is important that rigorous econometric studies that test disequilibrium against equilibrium models on time series data almost always favor disequilibrium.[13] It is also important that new developments in micro theory show how imperfect information gives rise to moral hazard and adverse selection problems that may keep prices, interest rates, and wages from performing their traditional role of clearing markets – even in the long run.

7.3.5 View of policy

Barro's (1977) 'demonstration' that only unanticipated money has real effects did not hold up to the intense scrutiny it received. It was shown (a) to depend on an unreasonable identifying assumption that fiscal policy affects monetary policy but does not directly affect real GNP, (b) to depend on truncating the lag structure (Mishkin (1982)), and (c) to be dominated by a 'Keynesian' alternative model (Gordon (1982)). However, the general notion that anticipated and unanticipated policy changes may have different effects seems both useful and enduring.[14] The importance of other aspects of the RE view of policy – such as time consistency and the idea of conceptualizing stabilization policy as a rule or 'regime' rather than as something exogenous and episodic – remain controversial.

7.4 THE FORGOTTEN AGENDA

Despite some important new ideas, the NCE counterrevolution does not seem to me to mark a major step forward from the Keynesian tradition it supplanted. The attempted revival of market clearing was quixotic, in the worst sense of that word. The attack on the Phillips curve was scurrilous and without empirical foundation. Although the basic idea that expectations are not purely mechanical is certainly important, the wholesale adoption of rational expectations was dubious, even though the hypothesis is doubtless of considerable use in some places (such as financial markets). The renewed search for microfoundations was welcome, but the insistence on neoclassical purity probably did macroeconomics little good. Finally, the Lucas critique, while conceptually correct, is of unproven empirical significance.

To my mind, that does not add up to a major improvement over the macroeconomics of 1972. Does that mean we had it all right in 1972? Hardly. It may mean, instead, that the RE/NCE revolution concentrated its fire in the wrong directions, that our macroeconomic research resources have been misallocated. I want to close this paper by suggesting that that was indeed the case – that the most serious flaws in 1972 Keynesianism were not prominent on the NCE hit list.

I begin with a brief mention of an obvious flaw. Vintage 1972 macroeconomics – whether it was Keynesian or monetarist – was all about demand fluctuations, a term then thought to be synonymous with economic fluctuations. The 1970s and 1980s destroyed this narrow-minded focus forever. We now know that Marshall's celebrated scissors also comes in a giant economy size. Economic fluctuations can, and sometimes do, emanate from the supply side – from oil shocks, food shocks, and the like. Much theoretical and empirical work has been done on supply shocks in the last dozen years; there was no misallocation here.[15] This work will have a lasting and salutary effect on macroeconomics. But it is basically orthogonal to the debate between Keynesians and new classicals.

My main point, however, is different. It is that macroeconomics might be in better shape today if, instead of arguing interminably about clearing markets, the rationality of expectations, the Phillips curve, and the Lucas critique, economists had devoted more time to improving the theoretical and empirical foundations of *IS/LM*.

7.4.1 The LM curve

The Hicks–Hansen *LM* curve was barely touched by the insurgents; most NCE models accepted this equation without question. Indeed, they often whittled it down to the quantity theory of money. But, of course, the demand function for money was crumbling in our hands all the while. The first velocity debacle, which prompted Goldfeld's (1976) well-known search for the 'missing money,' was dwarfed in size and reversed in sign by the second velocity debacle – which may still be in progress. It is the demand for money, not the Phillips curve, that evidenced 'econometric failure on a grand scale.' And the reason seems to lie in institutional change, not in the Lucas critique.[16]

Keynesian economics now needs to pick up the pieces. The apparent disappearance of the demand function for M1 does not, as is sometimes thought, strip the economy of its nominal anchor nor render central bank policy impotent. It means, instead, that the theoretical and empirical foundations of the *LM* curve may need to be reexamined and perhaps broadened beyond the narrow confines of 'money.' One possible route is to distinguish between the underlying demand for transactions services and the derived demand for any particular monetary aggregate, recognizing that the latter may change whenever the menu of available monetary assets changes, just as the demand for coal changed when oil was discovered.[17] Another possibility is to remember the 'bond market' that Keynes surpressed and to explore the notion that alternative financial variables, such as credit, may be the main channels through which financial events impact on the real economy.[18] And there may be yet better ideas.

7.4.2 The IS curve

The Lucas critique cast a dark shadow over the Jorgensonian practise of extrapolating current variables (like relative prices, interest rates, and tax rules) into the future and set in motion a search for an alternative investment model that coped better with unobservable expectations. Since the stock market is supposed to discount future expectations in just the right way, this led to a revival of the Q-theory of investment, originally due to Tobin (1969).[19] And that, in turn, led to a dead end because of the absurd volatility of the stock market (Shiller (1981)) and the failure of empirical Q models to explain the data.[20] I do not purport to know where the investment function is going, but it needs to go somewhere. I note in passing that the simple accelerator model that was known and loved in the early 1970s – perhaps beefed up by rational expectations – seems to be making a strong come-back.[21] Here the wave of the future may be the wave of the past.

The application of RE, rather than the adaptive expectations assumed by M. Friedman (1957), to the permanent income hypothesis (PIH) of consumption was a useful idea that remains controversial. We have learned several things since Hall (1978) first suggested that only 'surprises' in income cause consumption to change. First, current income is, by far, the major determinant of current spending – just as Keynes had asserted. That is not necessarily inconsistent with RE/PIH notions because innovations in income are mostly permanent, but it does shift the emphasis away from long-run average income and back to current income. Second, liquidity constraints of one sort or another probably play some role in the consumption function, which is, of course, another Keynesian idea.[22] Third, the 'excess sensitivity' results of Flavin (1981) and others notwithstanding, there do seem to be some gains to decomposing income and wealth into anticipated and unanticipated components (Blinder and Deaton (1985)).

However, at a more fundamental level, the RE revolution, in pointing consumption theorists toward ever tighter theoretical formulations of the PIH, may have pointed in the wrong direction. Specifically, accumulating evidence suggests that the life-cycle PIH model, which looks so good in time series, may be quite wrong. I am referring here both to the indirect evidence that life-cycle accumulation may be small relative to inherited wealth[23] and to a variety of studies on longitudinal data which fail to detect the patterns predicted by life cycle theory.[24] These issues have not been fully sorted out yet, but it may be that entirely new approaches to the consumption function are called for. If so, it seems unlikely to me that stricter adherence to narrow-minded conceptions of maximizing behavior will play major roles in the rehabilitation of the consumption function. But perhaps my expectations are not rational.

7.5 IN CONCLUSION

By the early 1950s, the Keynesian revolution was consolidated. The next 20 years or so were a productive time in which Keynesian ideas were developed further, modified in places, and given empirical content. New features, like the Phillips curve, were grafted on; and the entire apparatus was built into giant 'realistic' models of the economy. Much, but not all, of that development stopped in the 1970s as macroeconomics turned introspective and nihilistic.

Some of the fundamental questions raised were good ones (why should expectations be adaptive?), others were not (does the labor market really clear every period?). But they did stop a constructive research agenda dead in its tracks. Some will say that was necessary, for the 1972 consensus was leading us astray. I am less convinced. I cannot help thinking that macro-economics would be better off today if Lucas's valid questions about how expectations were handled in theoretical and empirical models had redirected the Keynesian research agenda rather than derailed it. It may now be time to get the train back on the tracks.

7.6 NOTES

1. Actually, one of Lucas's important papers on rational expectations (1972) was written before 1972. But that paper was neither very well known nor even well understood.
2. However, Eisner's (1969) insightful piece on the 1968 surcharge was an example of what later became known as the Lucas critique.
3. See, for example, Gordon (1972).
4. Goldfeld and Blinder (1972) provides a contemporary perspective on all of these matters, plus many references.
5. For a discussion of this, see Rotemberg (1984).
6. I refer here to econometric methods for dealing with complete models. The 'deep parameters' methodology, while useful for dealing with specific equations, never offered much hope for dealing with complete models.
7. See Sargent (1984) and my comment following.

8. Kydland and Prescott (1977).
9. This is a major point of Blinder and Fischer (1981), and is pointed out for the Lucas (1975) model by Fischer (1979). Real interest rate effects are not emphasized in the other papers, but are implicitly present.
10. Among many references that could be cited, see Gordon (1977, 1985), Ando and Kennickell (1983), Perry (1983), B. Friedman (1983), Blanchard (1984), and Fischer (1984).
11. See, for example, Sims (1982), Geweke (1985), and Blinder (1986), reprinted here as Chapter 9.
12. See the famous statement likening the stock market to a beauty contest in The General Theory (1936, p.156).
13. See Altonji and Ashenfelter (1980), Altonji (1982), Brown (1982), Rosen and Quandt (1978, 1986), and Romer (1981), among others.
14. See, among the many references that could be cited, Turnovsky and Miller (1984).
15. See Bruno and Sachs (1985) and many of the references cited there.
16. See Gordon (1984), among others. Of course, it can be argued that the institutional changes were induced by previous (inflationary) policies. In addition, Lucas-style reasoning may not be entirely irrelevant to the breakdown in the money demand function. See Walsh (1984).
17. See Spindt (1984), or Baba, Hendry, and Starr (1985) for examples. The empirical importance of this idea is still subject to dispute.
18. See, among others, Bernanke (1986), Blinder and Stiglitz (1983), reprinted here as Chapter 2, and Blinder (1985), reprinted here as Chapter 3.
19. See Abel (1980), Blanchard (1980), and Summers (1981).
20. That is the opinion, for example, of Abel and Blanchard (1986), both of whom were early Q enthusiasts.
21. See Clark (1979), and Abel and Blanchard (1986).
22. Hall and Mishkin (1982), Hayashi (1985).
23. Kotlikoff and Summers (1981). See also Modigliani's (1984) critique.
24. Blinder, Gordon, and Wise (1983), Kurz (1981), Mirer (1979).

7.7 REFERENCES

Abel, A. B. (1980) 'Empirical investment equations: an integrative framework,' in K. Brunner and A. H. Metzler (eds) On the State of Macro-Economics, Carnegie-Rochester Conference Series on Public Policy, vol. 12, Amsterdam: North-Holland.

Abel, A. B. and Blanchard, O. (1986) 'Investment and sales: an empirical study,' Econometrica, vol. 51 (February), pp. 249–73.

Altonji, J. G. (1982) 'The intertemporal substitution model of labor market fluctuations: an empirical analysis,' Review of Economic Studies, vol. 49 pp. 783–824.

Altonji, J. G. and Ashenfelter, O. (1980) 'Wage movements and the labor market equilibrium hypothesis.' Economica, vol. 47, pp. 217–95.

Ando, A. F. and Kennickell, A. (1983) '"Failure" of Keynesian economics and "direct" effects of money supply: a fact or a fiction.' mimeo, University of Pennsylvania.

Ando, A. F. and Modigliani, F. (1963) 'The 'life cycle' hypothesis of saving: aggregate implications and tests.' American Economic Review, vol. 53 (January), pp. 55–84.

Baba, Y., Hendry, D. F. and Starr, R. M. (1985) 'US money demand, 1960–1984.' mimeo.

Barro, R. J. (1977) 'Unanticipated money growth and unemployment in the United States,' *American Economic Review*, vol. 67, pp. 101–15.

Bernanke, B. S. (1983) 'Nonmonetary effects of the financial crisis in the propagation of the Great Depression,' *American Economic Review*, vol. 73, pp. 257–76.

Bernanke, B. S. (1986) 'Alternative explanations of the money-income correlation,' unpublished paper.

Blanchard, O. J. (1980) 'The monetary mechanism in the light of rational expectations,' in S. Fischer (ed.) *Rational Expectations and Economic Policy*, Chicago: University of Chicago Press.

Blanchard, O. J. (1984) 'The Lucas critique and the Volcker deflation,' *American Economic Review*, vol. 74 (May) pp. 211–15.

Blinder, A. S. (1985) 'Credit rationing and effective supply failures,' NBER Working Paper 1619.

Blinder, A. S. (1986) 'A sceptical note on the new econometrics,' in M. H. Peston and R. E. Quandt (eds) *Prices, Competition and Equilibrium*, Oxford: Philip Allan.

Blinder, A. S. and Deaton, A. (1985) 'The time series consumption function revisited,' *Brookings Papers on Economic Activity*, pp. 465–511.

Blinder, A. S. and Fischer, S. (1981) 'Inventories, rational expectations, and the business cycle,' *Journal of Monetary Economics*, vol. 8, pp. 277–304.

Blinder, A. S., Gordon, R. and Wise, D. (1983) 'Social security, bequests, and the life-cycle theory of savings: cross-sectional tests,' in R. Hemming and F. Modigliani (eds) *The Determinants of National Savings and Wealth*, International Economic Association.

Blinder, A. S. and Stiglitz, J. E. (1983) 'Money, credit constraints, and economic activity,' *American Economic Review*, vol. 73, pp. 297–302, included here as Chapter 2.

Brown, J. (1982) 'How close to an auction is the labor market? Employee risk aversion, income uncertainty, and optimal labor contracts,' *Research in Labor Economics*, vol. 5, pp. 189–235.

Bruno, M. and Sachs, J. D. (1985) *The Economics of Worldwide Stagflation*, Cambridge: Harvard University Press.

Clark, P. K. (1979) 'Investment in the 1970s: theory, performance and prediction.' *Brookings Papers on Economic Activity*, pp. 73–113.

Eisner, R. (1969) 'Fiscal and monetary policy reconsidered,' *American Economic Review*, vol. 59, pp. 897–905.

Fischer, S. (1977) 'Long term contracts, rational expectations, and the optimal money supply rule,' *Journal of Political Economy*, vol. 67, pp. 191–205.

Fischer, S. (1979) 'Anticipations and the nonneutrality of money,' *Journal of Political Economy*, vol. 87, pp. 225–52.

Fischer, S. (1984) 'Contracts, credibility, and disinflation,' NBER Working Paper # 1339.

Fischer, S. (1986) '1944, 1963 and 1985: Modiglianiesque macro models,' NBER Working Paper # 1797.

Flavin, M. A. (1981) 'The adjustment of consumption to changing expectations about future income,' *Journal of Political Economy*, vol. 89, pp. 974–1009.

Friedman, B. M. (1983) 'Recent perspectives in and on macroeconomics,' NBER Working Paper 1208.

Friedman B. M. (1979) 'Optimal expectations and the extreme information assumptions of rational expectations' macromodels,' *Journal of Monetary Economics*, vol. 5, pp. 23–41.

Friedman, M. (1957) *A Theory of the Consumption Function*, Princeton: Princeton University Press.

Friedman, M. (1968) 'The role of monetary policy,' *American Economic Review*, vol. 58, pp. 1–17.

Frydman, R. and Phelps, E. (1984) *Individual Forecasting and Aggregate Outcomes: 'Rational Expectations' Examined.* Cambridge: Cambridge University Press.

Geweke, J. (1985) 'Macroeconomic modelling and the theory of the representative agent,' *American Economic Review*, vol. 75, pp. 205–10.

Goldfeld, S. M. (1973) 'The demand for money revisited,' *Brookings Papers on Economic Activity*, pp. 577–646.

Goldfeld, S. M. (1976) 'The case of the missing money,' *Brookings Papers on Economic Activity*, pp. 683–730.

Goldfeld, S. M. and Blinder, A. S. (1972) 'Some implications of endogenous stabilization policy,' *Brookings Papers on Economic Activity*, pp. 585–640.

Gordon, R. J. (1972) 'Wage-price controls and the shifting Phillips curve,' *Brookings Papers on Economic Activity*, pp. 385–421.

Gordon, R. J. (1977) 'Can the inflation of the 1970s be explained?' *Brookings Papers on Economic Activity*, pp. 253–77.

Gordon, R. J. (1982) 'Price inertia and policy ineffectiveness in the United States, 1890–1980,' *Journal of Political Economy*, vol. 90, pp. 1087–117.

Gordon, R. J. (1984) 'The short-run demand for money: a reconsideration,' *Journal of Money, Credit, and Banking* vol. 16 (November) pp. 403–34.

Gordon, R. J. (1985) 'Understanding inflation in the 1980s,' *Brookings Papers on Economic Activity*, pp. 263–99.

Hall, R E. (1978) 'Stochastic implications of the life cycle-permanent income hypothesis: theory and evidence,' *Journal of Political Economy*, vol. 86, pp. 971–87.

Hall, R. E. and Mishkin, F. S. (1982) 'The sensitivity of consumption to transitory income–estimates from panel data on households,' *Econometrica*, vol. 50, pp. 461–8.

Hayashi, F. (1985) 'The effect of liquidity constraints on consumption: a cross-sectional analysis,' *Quarterly Journal of Economics*, vol. 50 (February) pp. 183–206.

Jorgenson, D. W. (1963) 'Capital theory and investment behavior,' *American Economic Review*, vol. 53, pp. 247–59.

Keynes, J. M. (1936) *The General Theory of Employment, Interest, and Money*, New York: Harcourt, Brace and World.

Kotlikoff, L. J. and Summers, L. H. (1981) 'The role of intergenerational transfers in aggregate capital accumulation,' *Journal of Political Economy*, vol. 89, pp. 706–32.

Kotlikoff, L. J. (1985) 'The contribution of intergenerational transfers to total wealth,' unpublished paper.

Kurz, M. (1981) 'The life-cycle hypothesis and the effects of social security and private pensions on family savings,' mimeo, Stanford University.

Kydland, F. E. and Prescott, E. C. (1977) 'Rules rather than discretion–the inconsistency of optimal plans.' *Journal of Political Economy*, Vol. 85, pp. 473–91.

Kydland, F. E. and Prescott, E. C. (1982) 'Time to build and aggregate fluctuations,' *Econometrica*, vol. 50, pp. 1345–70.

Lipsey, R. G. (1960) 'The relation between unemployment and the change of money wage rates in the United Kingdom, 1862–1957–A further analysis,' *Economica*, vol. 27, pp. 1–31.

Lucas, R. E. Jr (1972) 'Econometric testing of the natural rate hypothesis,' in Otto Eckstein (ed.) *The Econometrics of Price Determination*, Washington: Board of Governors of the Federal Reserve Systems.

Lucas, R. E. Jr (1973) 'Some international evidence on output–inflation tradeoffs,' *American Economic Review*, vol. 63, pp. 326–44.

Lucas, R. E. Jr (1975) 'An equilibrium model of the business cycle,' *Journal of Political Economy*, vol. 83, pp. 1113–44.

Lucas, R. E. Jr (1976) 'Econometric policy evaluation: a critique,' in K. Brunner and A. H. Meltzer (eds) *The Phillips Curve and Labor Markets*, Carnegie-Rochester Conferences on Public Policy, vol. 1, Amsterdam: North-Holland.

Lucas, R. E. Jr and Sargent, T. (1978) 'After Keynesian macroeconomics,' in *After the Phillips Curve: Persistence of High Inflation and High Unemployment*, Conference Series # 19, Federal Reserve Bank of Boston.

Mirer, T. W. (1979) 'The wealth–age relation among the aged,' *American Economic Review*, vol. 69, pp. 43–54.

Mishkin, F. S. (1982) 'Does anticipated monetary policy matter? An econometric investigation,' *Journal of Political Economy*, vol. 90, pp. 22–51.

Modigliani, F. (1984) 'Measuring the contribution of intergenerational transfers to total wealth: conceptual issues and empirical findings,' paper presented at a seminar on Modeling the Accumulation and Distribution of Personal Wealth, Paris, September 10–11, 1984.

Muth, J. F. (1960) 'Optimal properties of exponentially weighted forecasts,' *Journal of the American Statistical Association*, vol. 55, pp. 299–306.

Perry, G. L. (1983) 'What have we learned about disinflation?' *Brookings Papers on Economic Activity*, pp. 587–602.

Phelps, E. S. (1968) 'Money-wage dynamics and labor market equilibrium,' *Journal of Political Economy*, vol. 76, pp. 678–711.

Phelps, E. S. and Taylor, J. B. (1977) 'Stabilizing powers of monetary policy under rational expectations,' *Journal of Political Economy*, vol. 85, pp.163–90.

Quandt, R. E. and Rosen, H. S. (1986) 'Unemployment, disequilibrium and the short-run Phillips curve: An econometric approach,' mimeo, Princeton University.

Romer, D. (1981) 'Rosen and Quandt's disequilibrium model of the labor market: a revision,' *Review of Economics and Statistics*, vol. 63, pp. 145–6.

Rosen, H. S. and Quandt, R. E. (1978) 'Estimation of a disequilibrium aggregate labor market,' *Review of Economics and Statistics*, vol. 60, pp. 371–9.

Rotemberg, J. J. (1984) 'Interpreting some statistical failures of some rational expectations macroeconomic models,' *American Economic Review*, vol. 74, pp. 188–93.

Sargent, T. J. (1979) *Macroeconomic Theory*, New York: Academic Press.

Sargent, T. J. (1984) 'Autoregressions, expectations and advice,' *American Economic Review*, vol. 74, pp. 408–15.

Shiller, R. J. (1981) "Do stock prices move too much to be justified by subsequent changes in dividends?" *American Economic Review*, vol. 71, pp. 421–36.

Sims, C. A. (1982) 'Policy analysis with econometric models,' *Brookings Papers on Economic Activity*, pp. 107–52.

Spindt, P. (1984) 'Money is what money does: monetary aggregation and the equation of exchange,' mimeo.

Summers, L. H. (1981) 'Taxation and corporate investment: a q-theory approach,' *Brookings Papers on Economic Activity*, pp. 67–127.

Taylor, J. B. (1975) 'Monetary policy during a transition to rational expectations,' *Journal of Political Economy*, vol. 83, pp. 1009–21.

Taylor, J. B. (1980) 'Aggregate dynamics and staggered contracts,' *Journal of Political Economy*, vol. 88, pp. 1–23.

Tobin, J. (1969) 'A general equilibrium approach to monetary theory,' *Journal of Money, Credit and Banking*, vol. 1, pp. 15–29.

Turnovsky, S. J. and Miller, M. H. (1984) 'The effects of government expenditure on the term structure of interest rates,' *Journal of Money, Credit and Banking*, vol. 16, pp. 16–33.

Walsh, C. E. (1984) 'Interest rate volatility and monetary policy,' *Journal of Money Credit and Banking*, vol. 16, pp.133–50.

8 · KEYNES, LUCAS, AND SCIENTIFIC PROGRESS

In one of those marvelous coincidences of intellectual history, Bob Lucas was born the year after the publication of Keynes's *General Theory*. For the first 35 years of their mutual lives, the two apparently coexisted in harmony. But their relationship has been tumultuous ever since. Lucas has frequently criticized Keynesian economics as poor science; and it is precisely in that spirit that I want to address the debate today.

We all know the old joke about the professor who uses the same exam questions year after year, but changes the answers. That joke encapsulates all too well what has happened to macroeconomics these last 15 years and seems to reflect poorly on economics as a science. Or does it? On second thought, the best answers to scientific questions *do* change as new observations are made, as new experiments are run, and as better theories are developed. The issue is whether the answers to important questions in macroeconomics have changed for good scientific reasons or for other reasons.

The joke provides the framework for my talk. I will pose eight exam questions; and for each one I will summarize the answers given by Keynes, by Lucas and his followers, and by modern Keynesians. I pick only questions that are answered differently by Keynesians and Lucasians and that are central to contemporary macroeconomic debates. The focus is on whether the Keynesian or new classical answers have greater claim to being 'scientific.' Each student must answer every question.

8.1 ARE EXPECTATIONS RATIONAL?

Keynes, though no stranger to probability theory, was nonetheless unequivocal in his denial that expectations are what we now call rational (1936, pp. 161–2):

Prepared for the meetings of the American Economic Association, New Orleans, 29 December 1986. I am grateful for stimulating discussions or correspondence with Ben Bernanke, Andrew Caplin, Mark Gertler, Stephen Goldfeld, David Romer, Andrei Shleifer, Robert Solow, and Lawrence Summers. But none of them, except probably Solow, agrees with all the highly opinionated opinions expressed herein.

> . . . a large proportion of our positive activities depend on spontaneous opti-
> mism rather than on a mathematical expectation. . . Only a little more than an
> expedition to the South Pole, is it based on an exact calculation of benefits to
> come. Thus if animal spirits are dimmed and the spontaneous optimism falters,
> leaving us to depend on nothing but a mathematical expectation, enterprise will
> fade and die. . .

That attitude left a big loose end in *The General Theory*. Business investment
is supposedly driven by 'the state of long-term expectations,' but expectations are not pinned down by the theory, leaving substantial room for
gyrations in macroeconomic activity driven by autonomous changes in
animal spirits. That hardly constitutes a tight scientific theory; but Keynes
was probably happy to leave the loose end loose. Modern 'sunspot theorists'
have tightened up the argument considerably, in ways that Keynes might
have found congenial.

Lucas, of course, changes the answer to yes. Was this change motivated by
empirical evidence that subjective expectations match the conditional expectations generated by models – or even that actual expectations are unbiased and efficient? No. Indeed, Prescott (1977, p. 30) has boldly asserted
that 'surveys cannot be used to test the rational expectations hypothesis.'
Rather, economists are supposed to convert to rational expectations (RE)
because of the unloveliness of the *ad hoc* expectational mechanisms that
preceded it[1] and because RE is more consistent with their (unverified) world
view that people always optimize at all margins. As Sargent (1982, p. 382) put
it: 'Research in rational expectations. . . has a momentum of its own. . .
that. . . stems from the logical structure of rational expectations as a
modeling strategy.' The momentum, you will note, does not stem from
empirics. I leave it to you to decide whether these criteria are more like those
that led physicists to dump Newton in favor of Einstein or those that led
artists to abandon Manet to follow Picasso.

Modern Keynesians are split on this question. To some, the theoretical
appeal of RE and the general idea that expectations should respond to policy
changes are sufficient reason to conclude that 'rational expectations is the
right initial hypothesis' (Fischer (1986), p. 13). Others harbor doubts. I think
the weight of the evidence – both from directly observed expectations and
from indirect statistical tests of rationality (usually in conjunction with some
other hypothesis) – is overwhelmingly against the RE hypothesis. (Lovell
provides a convenient recent summary of some of this evidence.) Furthermore, RE is not without theoretical difficulties. We all know that RE models
often have multiple equilibria. More fundamentally, RE is theoretically
coherent only in the context of a single agreed-upon model. In an economy in
which different people hold different views of the world, the very notion lacks
clarity. For example, if Paul Volcker announces today that on New Year's
Day he will raise M1 by 20 percent, I imagine Lucas and I will make different
revisions in our expectations for, say, real GNP in 1987. Whose expectations

are 'rational?' A volume of essays put together by Frydman and Phelps (1984) explores the serious theoretical problems that heterogeneous beliefs pose for RE. They *are* serious.

As scientists, then, I think we should be hesitant to embrace RE.

8.2 IS THERE INVOLUNTARY UNEMPLOYMENT?

Keynes said, nay screamed, yes. Lucas not only says no, but questions whether the phrase has meaning. In his words (1986, p. 38), 'To explain why people allocate time to . . . unemployment we need to know why they prefer it to all other activities.' Notice the words *allocate* and *prefer*. In his view, the unemployed are engaged in intelligent search or purposeful intertemporal substitution. He scoffs at the Keynesian tradition which, 'by dogmatically insisting that unemployment be classified as "involuntary" . . . simply cut itself off from serious thinking about the actual options unemployed people are faced with' (1986, p. 47).

This is a tough question to adjudicate on scientific grounds since the issue is largely definitional and, as Lewis Carroll pointed out, everyone is entitled to his own definitions. In Lucas's view, a person laid off from a job can, presumably, shine shoes in a railroad station or sell apples on a street corner. If he is not doing any of these things, he must be *choosing* not to do so. Both statements like this and reactions to them tend to be polemical. I guess dogmatism is in the ear of the beholder.

However, a few pertinent facts should leaven the ideological debate. First, when the unemployment rate rises, it is layoffs, not quits, that are rising while consumption falls rather than rises – all of which is bad news for search theory. Second, real wage movements are close to a random walk – which is bad news for the intertemporal substitution approach. Third, unemployment is heavily concentrated among the long-term unemployed; in 1985, for example, people who were jobless for 27 weeks or more constituted 54 percent of all unemployment and the expected duration of a completed spell of unemployment was 31 weeks (see Summers (1986)). Can that be intertemporal substitution? Fourth, unemployed workers normally accept their first job offer, and those who are looking for work spend an average of only four hours per week on search activity (see Clark and Summers (1979)). That hardly suggests a predominant role for search in explaining unemployment.

8.3 DO WAGE MOVEMENTS QUICKLY CLEAR THE LABOR MARKET?

Keynes certainly thought not, for such reasons as trade union aggressiveness, custom and inertia, and outright stubbornness. Lucas answers yes – though perhaps only in a broad sense. He has, for example, cited approvingly the competitive contract equilibrium approach of Hansen (1985) in which workers have 100 percent unemployment insurance and, because of indivisibilities, are chosen randomly to work either, say, 40 hours a week or zero – meaning, of course, that unemployed workers have higher utility than employed ones. In Lucas's opinion (1986, p. 48), there is 'no reason to believe' that competitive models of labor markets that treat unemployment like leisure commit 'a serious strategic error.'

No reason? I think the preponderance of the evidence says otherwise. Unemployment insurance replaces only about 40 percent of lost earnings. Lately, only about one-third of the unemployed collect it. Where is the evidence that the unemployed are happier than the employed? Most economists think Lucas's distinguished predecessor at the University of Chicago had it right when he wrote, 'Under any conceivable institutional arrangements, and certainly those that now prevail in the United States, there is only a limited amount of flexibility in prices and wages' (Friedman (1968), p. 13). And it is hard, for me at least, to look at what has gone on in the United States – not to mention in Europe – since 1974 and see clearing labor markets. That the market-clearing approach caught on in this environment is testimony to Bob Lucas's keen intellect and profound influence, not to economists' respect for facts.

More than just casual empiricism supports this view; numerous formal econometric studies reject the market-clearing hypothesis against some sort of disequilibrium alternative. Unfortunately, it is usually spot-market clearing that is rejected. Equilibrium contracting models in which the wage plays little or no short-run allocative role are difficult to formulate econometrically, much less to reject. Indeed, it is hard to know what observations could contradict such models; theory just leaves too many open possibilities.[2]

Nonetheless, certain observations are worth making. For one, both Kreuger and Summers (1986) and Dickens and Katz (1986) have pointed to interindustry wage differentials that are persistent across both time and space – differentials which are not easily squared with market clearing. Theoretically, Stiglitz and others have stressed that the wage rate may not be able to clear the labor market in a world of imperfect information – not even in the long run. Of course, that efficiency wage models can be built does not imply that they describe reality. But it does mean that market clearing models have no particular claim to the theoretical high ground.

In sum, the scientific basis for modeling labor markets – or goods markets for that matter – as continuously clearing escapes me.

8.4 IS THE NATURAL RATE OF UNEMPLOYMENT A STRONG ATTRACTOR FOR THE ACTUAL RATE OF UNEMPLOYMENT?

Keynes thought not. Indeed, in his revolutionary zeal, Keynes spoke loosely (loose) talk was a problem for Keynes) of an 'unemployment equilibrium'–which would seem to deny the natural rate any attractive force at all. Lucas answers in the affirmative

Modern Keynesians have long had trouble with the master's notion that the economy could equilibrate below full employment; they prefer to think of unemployment as a long-lasting disequilibrium. In the United States, at least, the validity of the natural rate hypothesis has not been at issue for a long time. The argument, instead, is over whether the speed of convergence to the natural rate is rapid or glacial.

On this, the American evidence is unequivocal and the European evidence is overwhelming. The US civilian unemployment rate peaked at 8.9 percent in May 1975 and then took almost three years to get back down to 6 percent. It then peaked again at 10.7 percent in November–December 1982; now, four years later, it has yet to fall below 6.7 percent for even a single month. Some will argue that 7 percent is now the natural rate, without worrying much about how it grew so high. My view is that a theory that allows the natural rate to trundle along after the actual rate is not a natural rate theory at all.

In Europe, the evidence is far more compelling. Unemployment rates rose more or less steadily from 1974 to 1985 – from 3 percent to over 13 percent in the UK, from 2.8 percent to 10.5 percent in France, and from 1.6 percent to 8 percent in West Germany. Some young men in these countries have *never* held a job and may never be productive workers. Facts like these prompted Blanchard and Summers (1986) to seek models which explicitly reject the natural rate hypothesis in favor of hysteresis. And recent econometric work by Campbell and Mankiw (1986) suggests hysteresis in postwar US real GNP as well.[3]. It may well be that Keynesians caved in too readily to the natural rate hypothesis.

8.5 IS THERE A RELIABLE SHORT-RUN PHILLIPS CURVE?

Keynes, of course, did not answer this question; the Phillips curve came later. I include it on the exam because Lucas and Sargent (1978) made it central to their attack on Keynesian economics. The alleged failure of the Phillips curve was their main piece of evidence (1978, p. 49) that empirical Keynesian models 'were wildly incorrect, and that the doctrine on which they were based is fundamentally flawed.' (Please notice the adverbs.)

This charge was repeated so often and with such certitude that it became part of the conventional wisdom. Unfortunately, it is, to coin a phrase, wildly incorrect. The fact is that, the Lucas critique notwithstanding, the Phillips curve, once modified to allow for supply shocks (any one of several variables will do), has been one of the best-behaved empirical regularities in macroeconomics – much better behaved, in fact, than we had any right to expect. A long list of studies supports this conclusion.[4] Nonetheless, Lucas (1986, p. 12) continues to speak of the Phillips curve as an econometric basket case.

Let me anticipate the obvious objection that saving the Phillips curve after the fact by adding a supply variable does not absolve it of its *ex ante* forecasting errors. It is true that, while Bob Gordon's latest Phillips curves fit the data well, his pre-1972 equations do less well. And they did not predict the rise and fall of OPEC. But there is no sense in which new classical models either anticipated the error or pointed to the solution; like Keynesian models, they were designed to analyze demand shocks. Events in the 1970s and 1980s demonstrated to Keynesian and new classical economists alike that Marshall's celebrated scissors also comes in a giant economy size. It is a debater's tactic, and a poor one at that, to claim that supply shocks are outside the purview of Keynesian economics.

8.6 DOES A CHANGE IN THE MONEY SUPPLY HAVE REAL EFFECTS?

Keynes and the Keynesians answered yes, without bothering to distinguish between anticipated and unanticipated changes. Lucas and the Lucasians answer that money has real effects only if it is misperceived. In their view, a properly perceived injection of money is like a currency reform.

Here, again, the weight of the econometric evidence (though certainly not all of it) suggests that Keynes had the right answer after all. Gordon (1982), Mishkin (1982) and others refuted Barro's (1977) alleged empirical demonstration that only unanticipated money has real effects. Boschen and Grossman (1982) showed that perceived changes in money are not neutral.

8.7 DOES SOCIAL WELFARE RISE WHEN BUSINESS CYCLES ARE LIMITED?

Keynes tacitly, but unequivocally, answered yes. If asked for proof, he probably would have chuckled with the condescension of the British upper crust – which is hardly a scientific attitude.

Lucas is carefully agnostic, but clearly leans toward the answer no. He has long been sympathetic to the idea that successful stabilization policies that smooth business cycles may actually decrease welfare. Prescott is less circumspect. Without bothering to draw any distinction between modeling a conclusion and proving it, he asserts (1986, p. 31) that 'costly efforts at stabilization are likely to be counterproductive' because 'economic fluctuations are optimal responses to uncertainty in the rate of technological change.' Clearly, Harberger triangles look bigger and Okun gaps smaller near lakes than near oceans. Is Prescott's attitude more scientific than Keynes's?

I think it is worth taking a moment to explain why Lucas believes that the potential gains from stabilization policy are so small. The postwar standard deviation of log quarterly consumption around trend is about 0.013. Lucas asks an infinitely-lived consumer living under perfect capital markets how much he would be willing to give up to reduce this small standard deviation to zero. Unsurprisingly, the answer comes back: not much. So Lucas (1986, p. 75) concludes that 'the post-war business cycle is just not a very important problem in terms of individual welfare.' That is a stunning assertion, especially when juxtaposed against the conventional wisdom that governments rise and fall on the vicissitudes of the business cycle.

Lucas's conclusion, it seems to me, ignores a few pertinent facts. First, the cycle is not mainly in consumer expenditures, much less in consumption. Indeed, there is virtually no cycle at all in spending on nondurables and services. Are large swings in consumer durables, in inventories, and in fixed investment all socially costless? Don't these ups and downs impose serious adjustment costs and dislocations on society?

Second, Lucas's calculation assumes that cyclical fluctuations take place around an unchanged trend, with booms as likely as recessions. But what if recessions leave permanent scars on either labor or capital or productivity? What if there is hysteresis, so the natural rate hypothesis fails? What if there is a systematic tendency for output to be too low on average? Then the Keynesian goal of filling in troughs without shaving off peaks starts to make sense.

Third, Lucas ignores a variety of psychological, sociological, and physiological costs which many people feel are important. Against Lucas's benign view of the cycle compare the opinion of Martin Luther King, who wrote that, 'In our society, it is murder, psychologically, to deprive a man of a job or an income. You are in substance saying to that man that he has no right to exist.'[5] The truth, I think, lies somewhere between Dr Lucas and Dr King.

Finally, it is important to remember that cyclical losses are not distributed uniformly, as Lucas assumes; instead, most people lose little while a minority suffers much. Let me illustrate with some simple calculations. Suppose everyone has log utility and consumes $3000 per quarter. Let a severe recession reduce consumption 4 percent. Utility falls 4.1 percent, which is no big deal, especially since every down is matched by a subsequent up. This is Lucas's world.

Now change utility to the Stone–Geary form: $U = \log(C - \$1500)$. Here a 4 percent drop in consumption reduces utility by 8.3 percent. That seems a bigger deal. Finally, let the cycle instead reduce the consumption of 10 percent of the population by 40 percent while the other 90 percent loses nothing. (Note that I am allowing very generous unemployment insurance here.) With the Stone-Geary utility function, mean utility declines 16.1 percent. Now we're talking real utils.

Lucas will, of course, counter that any such problem is best dealt with by better unemployment insurance, not by stabilization policies that interfere with free-market allocations. The same logic says that fire and theft insurance – where moral hazard problems are certainly less severe – obviate the need for fire and police departments. Isn't prevention better than insurance?[6]

However, Lucas's challenge to the Keynesian presumption that smaller cycles are better cycles needs to be addressed scientifically. And, since we can't observe cyclical fluctuations in utility, that requires the use of theory. The relevant theory is, I think, just beginning to be developed in the burgeoning literature on monopolistic competition and aggregate demand externalities.[7] It would be foolish to say that a definitive answer is in hand; but some good answers may be on the horizon.

8.8 MUST MACROECONOMICS BE BUILT UP FROM NEOCLASSICAL FIRST PRINCIPLES?

Keynes answered no. A practical man living in a complex world, he would not close his eyes to apparent deviations from narrow-minded concepts of optimizing behavior–nor even to gross deviations from rationality. He believed in modeling behavior as it was. Witness his defense of money illusion in labor supply (1936, p. 9):

> Now ordinary experience tells us. . . that a situation where labor stipulates. . . for a money-wage rather than a real wage, so far from being a mere possibility, is the normal case. . . It is sometimes said that it would be illogical for labour to resist a reduction of money-wages but not to resist a reduction of real wages. . . But, whether logical or illogical, experience shows that this is how labour in fact behaves.

8.8.1 Caveat theoria!

Lucas and other new classicists take a different view. They emphasize the importance of building up macroeconomic relationships from sound microfoundations, by which they mean the solutions to dynamic, stochastic games. Lapses from what Lucas (1986, p. 77) called 'the only "engine for the discovery of truth"' are one of the chief grounds on which Keynesianism is branded unscientific.

Now, neither side is hostile either to first principles or to factual accuracy. We all agree that the ideal macro theory would be built up logically from first principles and would explain the data well. But we also agree that such a theory is a long way off. The issue is how religiously we must adhere to frictionless neoclassical optimizing principles until that glorious day arrives. Here the devoutness of American economists distinguishes us from our colleagues in other lands. But which attitude leads to better science? Is it better to start deductively from axioms or inductively from facts? When the time comes to choose between internal consistency and consistency with observations, which side should we take? Must we be restricted to micro-foundations that preclude the colossal market failures that created macro-economics as a subdiscipline?

Here followers of Keynes and followers of Lucas often part company. Like Keynes, modern Keynesians are inclined to began by 'taking things as they are;' rigorous optimizing explanations for what they observe (such as nominal wage contracts) can come later. The important thing is to make sure our models are congruent with the facts. Lucasians, it seems to me, reverse the sequence. They want to begin with fully articulated, tractable models and worry later about realism and descriptive accuracy.

This is a judgement call; but I judge the Keynesian approach more scientific. First, good science need not always be built up from solid micro-foundations. Thermodynamics and chemistry, for example, have done pretty well without much micro theory. Boyle's Law applies directly to aggregates, much like the marginal propensity to consume. And the microfoundations of medicine are often very poor; yet much of it works. Empirical regularities that are formulated and tested directly at the macro level *do* have a place in science.

Second, it is far from clear that the particular first principles selected by new classical economists deserve to come first. Why don't people know the money supply or the price level within very small margins of error? Who imposed a cash-in-advance constraint? Why should price move to equate supply and demand in markets with asymmetric information? Why, Keynes might ask, are these postulates more acceptable as first principles than nominal wage contracting?

Third, the model of man as a strongly rational maximizer is not the only option open to theorists. Simon and others have developed theories of 'bounded rationality' and Akerlof and Yellen are working on theories of 'near rationality.' Even within the strict optimizing framework, neoclassical tangencies are not the only, nor even the most likely, alternative. Bar-Ilan and I have suggested (1986) that pervasive lumpy transactions costs lead to 'the optimality of usually doing nothing,' meaning that it rarely pays to change your decision variable, even if it is not set at the frictionless 'optimal' value. In a word, near rationality is full rationality. It is continuous opti-mization that would be irrational.

Direct empirical evidence on individual behavior is difficult – some would say impossible – to come by. But what little we know from experiments by psychologists like Kahneman and Tversky and others does not suggest that *Homo sapiens* behaves like *Homo economicus*.[8] (Perhaps that is why they have different names.) Inconsistent choices are common. People put too much weight on what has happened to them and to their friends and too little on statistical evidence. Framing of the question matters. The Neumann–Morgenstern axioms are routinely violated. It is remarkable how little impact this evidence has had on modern economics. Is that scientific detachment or religious zealotry?

So I have come to the end of my exam with the conclusions you might have guessed at the outset: that when Professor Lucas changed the answers given by Mr Keynes, he was mostly turning better answers into worse ones; that modern Keynesian economics, though far from flawless, has a better claim to being 'scientific' than does new classical economics.

8.9 NOTES

1. Incidentally, Keynes seemed to believe in adaptive expectations for what he called 'short-term' expectations. See *The General Theory*, pp. 50–1.
2. Stiglitz (1986) provides a nice comprehensive summary.
3. Cochrane (1986), using nonparametric methods, argues that real GNP is much less persistent than Campbell and Mankiw say. But Campbell and Mankiw show that Cochrane's apparently contradictory results stem mainly from including prewar, and especially pre-1929, data. Apparently, real GNP was far less persistent before 1929.
4. Among the many references that could be cited, see Gordon (1977, 1985), Ando and Kennickell (1983), Perry (1983), B. Friedman (1983), Blanchard (1984), and Fischer (1984). There are others.
5. See King (1983), p. 45.
6. My rhetorical question presupposes that business cycles are not Pareto optimal. My postjudices show through here.
7. Ball and Romer (1987) is particularly germane here.
8. A recent fascinating source is Kahneman, Knetsch and Thaler (1986), which also has many references.

8.10 REFERENCES

Akerlof, G. and Yellen, J. L. (1985) 'Can small deviations from rationality make significant differences to economic equilibria?', *American Economic Review* (September), vol. 75, no. 4, pp. 708–20.

Ando, A. and Kennickell, A. (1983) ' "Failure" of Keynesian economics and "direct" effects of money supply: a fact or a fiction,' mimeo, University of Pennsylvania (March).

Ball, L. and Romer, D. (1987) 'Are prices too sticky?' *National Bureau of Economic Research* (February), working paper 2171.

Bar-Ilan, A. and Blinder, A. S. (1986) 'On the optimality of usually doing nothing with an application to consumer durables,' mimeo (December).

Barro, R. J. (1977) 'Unanticipated money growth and unemployment in the United States,' *American Economic Review*, vol. 67, no. 2, pp. 101–15.

Blanchard, O. J. (1984) 'The Lucas critique and the Volcker deflation,' *American Economic Review*, vol. 74 (May), pp. 211–15.

Blanchard, O. J. and Summers, L. H. (1986) 'Hysteresis and the European unemployment problem,' *NBER Macroeconomics Annual 1986*. pp. 15–78.

Boschen, J. F. and Grossman, H. I. (1982) 'Tests of equilibrium macroeconomics using contemporaneous monetary data,' *Journal of Monetary Economics* (November), vol. 10, no. 3, pp. 309–34.

Campbell, J. Y. and Mankiw, N. G. (1986) 'Are output fluctuations transitory?', mimeo, Princeton University (September).

Clark, K. B. and Summers, L. H. (1979) 'Labor market dynamics and unemployment: a reconsideration,' *Brookings Papers on Economic Activity 1*.

Cochrane, J. H. (1986) 'How big is the random walk in GNP?', unpublished paper, University of Chicago (April).

Dickens, W. T. and Katz, L. (1986) 'Interindustry wage differences and theories of wage determination,' mimeo (August).

Fischer, S. (1984) 'Contracts, credibility, and disinflation,' National Bureau of Economic Research, working paper # 1339 (April).

Fischer, S. (1986) '1944, 1963 and 1985: Modiglianiesque macro models,' National Bureau of Economic Research, working paper # 1797 (January).

Friedman, B. M. (1983) 'Recent perspectives in and on macroeconomics,' National Bureau of Economic Research, working paper # 1208 (September).

Friedman, M. (1968) 'The role of monetary policy,' *American Economic Review*, vol. 78, no.1, pp. 1–17.

Frydman, R. and Phelps, E. (1984) *Individual Forecasting and Aggregate Outcomes: 'Rational Expectations' Examined*. Cambridge: Cambridge University Press.

Gordon, R. J. (1977) 'Can the inflation of the 1970s be explained?', *Brookings Papers on Economic Activity 1*, pp. 253–77.

Gordon, R. J. (1982) 'Price inertia and policy ineffectiveness in the United States, 1890–1980,' *Journal of Political Economy*, vol. 90, no. 6, pp. 1087–117.

Gordon, R. J. (1985) 'Understanding inflation in the 1980s,' *Brookings Papers on Economic Activity 1*, pp. 263–99.

Hansen, G. D. (1985) 'Indivisible labor and the business cycle,' *Journal of Monetary Economics* (November), vol. 16, no. 3, pp. 309–27.

Kahneman, D., Knetsch, J. L. and Thaler, R. (1986) 'Fairness as a constraint on profit seeking: entitlements in the market,' *American Economic Review* (September), vol. 76, no. 4, pp. 728–41.

Keynes, J. M. (1936) *The General Theory of Employment, Interest, and Money*, New York: Harcourt, Brace and World.

King, C. S. (1983) *The Words of Martin Luther King, Jr.*, New York: Newmarket Press.

Krueger, A. B. and Summers, L. H. (1986) 'Efficiency wages and the wage structure,' National Bureau of Economic Research, working paper # 1952 (June).

Lovell, M. C. (1986) 'Tests of the rational expectations hypothesis,' *American Economic Review* (March), vol. 76, no. 1, pp. 110–24.

Lucas, R. E. and Sargent, T. (1978) 'After Keynesian macroeconomics,' in *After the Phillips Curve: Persistence of High Inflation and High Unemployment*, Conference Series # 19. Federal Reserve Bank of Boston.

Lucas, R. E. Jr (1986) 'Models of business cycles,' paper prepared for the Yrjo Jahnsson Lectures, Helsinki, Finland, March 1986, mimeo.

Mishkin, F. S. (1982) 'Does anticipated monetary policy matter? An econometric investigation,' *Journal of Political Economy*, vol. 90, no. 1, pp. 22–51.

Muth, J. F. (1985) 'Short run forecasts of business activity,' mimeo, Indiana University (March).

Perry, G. L. (1983) 'What have we learned about disinflation?', *Brookings Papers on Economic Activity 2*, pp. 587–602.

Prescott, E. (1977) 'Should control theory be used for economic stabilization?', in K. Brunner and A. Meltzer (eds) *Optimal Policies, Control Theory, and Technological Exports*, vol. 7, Carnegie-Rochester Conferences on Public Policy, *Journal of Monetary Economics*, suppl., pp. 13–38.

Prescott, E. (1986) 'Theory ahead of business cycle measurement,' Federal Reserve Bank of Minneapolis Research Department Staff Report 102 (February).

Sargent, T. J. (1982) 'Beyond demand and supply curves in macroeconomics,' *American Economic Review Papers and Proceedings* (May), vol. 72, pp. 382–9.

Stiglitz, J. E. (1986) 'Theories of wage ridigity,' in J. Butkiewicz *et al.* (eds) *Keynes' Economic Legacy*: Contemporary Economic Themes, New York: Praeger, pp. 153–206.

Summers, L. H. (1986) 'Why is the unemployment rate so very high near full employment?' *Brookings Papers on Economic Activity*, vol. 2, pp. 339–6.

9 · A SKEPTICAL NOTE ON THE NEW ECONOMETRICS

In an important paper published in 1976, Robert E. Lucas Jr offered an insightful and stunning critique of what were then standard econometric practises. The critique took the profession by storm, and econometricians – or at least macro-econometricians – have been struggling with the problem of how to reconstruct econometrics ever since.[1] In this brief paper, I argue that one of the major approaches that has been developed for dealing with the Lucas critique may introduce errors of its own into econometric estimates – errors that may well be more serious in practice than those pointed out by Lucas.

9.1 THE OLD ECONOMETRICS AND THE LUCAS CRITIQUE

I begin with an example that characterizes the way in which econometrics worked before Lucas, and illustrates why Lucas (correctly) claimed that this way might lead to error.

Consider the problem of estimating a supply curve and a demand curve for a single market, as depicted in Fig. 9.1. Econometricians used to conceptualise the inference problem as follows. For each time period we have a pair of observations on price and quantity, (p_t, x_t), which we interpret as the intersection of the demand curve D and the supply curve S (point E). If there are one or more shift variables that affect the demand curve but not the supply curve, and one or more shift variables that affect the supply curve but not the demand curve, then standard procedures can be used to estimate the slopes of these two curves.

Why, apart from the general quest for knowledge, would we want to estimate such parameters? There are many possible reasons. One which seems germane to the issue raised by Lucas is that the government might be considering regulating the supply of the commodity, and would like to

I am grateful to Ray Fair, Mark Machina, Frederic Mishkin, Richard Quandt, Harvey Rosen, Kenneth Small, Robert Solow, Lawrence Summers, and John Taylor for useful suggestions, and to the National Science Foundation for financial support. The research reported here is part of the NBER's research programme in Economic Fluctuations. Any opinions expressed are those of the author and not those of the National Bureau of Economic Research.

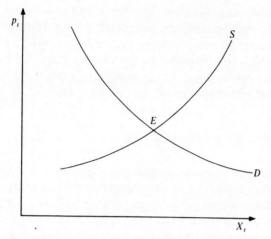

p_t

S

E

D

X_t

Fig. 9.1 A conventional supply–demand diagram.

estimate the changes in price and quantity that would result. The standard procedure in the 'old econometrics' would be to estimate the parameters of the demand curve (say, by two-stage least squares) and then use these estimates to predict behavior. Essentially, this amounts to extrapolating past patterns of behavior into the future.

Enter the Lucas critique. Lucas argued, quite correctly, that the supply and/or demand curves observed in the past might change if there were a change in the economic environment (e.g. in government policy). For example, suppose a demand curve had been estimated on data from a period during which the government set the price (p_t) exogenously, and the econometric estimate was:

$$x_t = a - bp_t + cy_t \qquad (9.1)$$

where y_t is income. But suppose the estimate of b really combined the true demand slope and an expectational parameter. For example, suppose the 'true' demand curve was:

$$x_t = \alpha - \beta_1 p_t + \beta_2(_t p_{t+1}) + \gamma y_t + \varepsilon_t \qquad (9.2)$$

where $_t p_{t+1}$ denotes the (rational) expectation of the next period's price. If prices during the period of observation had followed the stochastic process:

$$p_t = A + \rho p_{t-1} + \omega_t \qquad (9.3)$$

where ω_t is a white noise error term, then the (rational) expected future price would have been $A + \rho p_t$, leading to the observed demand rule:

$$x_t = \alpha + \beta_2 A - (\beta_1 - \rho\beta_2)p_t + \gamma y_t + \varepsilon_t \qquad (9.4)$$

Comparing (9.4) with (9.1), we see that a and b are really estimates of $\alpha + \beta_2 A$ and $\beta_1 - \rho\beta_2$ respectively, and therefore should change if the stochastic process generating prices change. The upshot of this observation is that the estimates of a and b derived from the historical data might be inappropriate if the policy rule changed. Put differently, extrapolations of past demand behavior might systematically err.

9.2 THE NEW ECONOMETRICS

Several approaches have been suggested for dealing with the Lucas critique. One is to introduce directly observed expectational variables into our equations, rather than using standard observable variables to 'proxy' expectations (as, for example, p_t proxied in part for $_t p_{t+1}$). It is in this spirit that several scholars have suggested estimating investment spending as a function of 'Tobin's q' rather than as a function of directly observed variables such as interest rates and tax parameters.[2] I take this to be the best possible approach where it is feasible. Unfortunately, most expectational variables are not directly observed.

A second approach is to impose, in estimation, the cross-equation constraints suggested by rational expectations.[3] For example, we could try to estimate jointly equations (9.2) and (9.3), taking account of the fact that $_t p_{t+1} = A + \rho p_t$.

A third approach, and the one I want to take issue with here, is to go 'beyond demand and supply curves' (in Sargent's (1982) words) and try to estimate the taste and technology parameters which, according to neoclassical equilibrium theory, underlie them.[4]

As I interpret this third approach, the suggestion is no longer to think of our data as coming from Fig. 9.1's supply and demand curves, but rather as coming from Fig. 9.2, where I depict an indifference curve for the representative consumer and a transformation curve for the representative firm. Here we see the consumer's and the producer's choices. between two goods, x_1 (which is the numeraire) and x_2; the relative price, p_t, appears as the slope of the tangent line at point E. Whereas in the old econometrics we would have taken data on x_{2t} and p_t and tried to estimate the slopes of the supply and demand curves, the new econometrics tries to use these same data to estimate the slopes of the indifference and transformation curves – the 'taste and technology parameters.'

The program of the new econometrics is beyond reproach *in principle*. The issue is whether or not we can really expect to carry it out successfully. What are some of the pitfalls of which we must beware? To be specific, I will focus on one particular class of reasons to show why the methods advocated by Hansen and Sargent (1980) and others may err systematically – and by gross amounts.

The reasons are quite simple and general: much of the time series data we get on prices and quantities may not reflect neoclassical equilibria of the sort depicted in Fig. 9.2. Two instances seem to me to be of great empirical importance. First, many of the price–quantity combinations we observe may reflect disequilibria rather than equilibria. It is by now well known that imposing the (false) hypothesis of equilibrium in such cases may, but need not always, lead to grievous errors.[5] Second, many of the equilibria attained by even rational and well-informed optimising agents may be corners rather than nice tangencies such as point E in Fig. 9.2. The next section illustrates this problem with a specific example, and suggests that the errors introduced by forcing the data into the Procrustean bed of Fig. 9.2 might be enormous.

9.3 AN EXAMPLE

Consider a consumer allocating his total income, y, between two goods. x_1 is the numeraire and is infinitely divisible. x_2 has a price of p, but consumers can only choose between buying it ($x_2 = 1$) or not buying it ($x_2 = 0$). There are many examples of goods that x_2 might represent, and I think the general phenomenon is very important. For many goods, the primary reason for a downward-sloping market demand curve may be that more people drop out of the market as the price rises, not that each individual consumer reduces his purchases. (Think, for example, of books, furniture, cars, houses, movie tickets.)[6] Another important application might be labor supply, with x_2 interpreted as the fraction of time devoted to leisure and p interpreted as the real wage.

The consumer's 'budget constraint' is:

$$x_1 + px_2 = y \tag{9.5}$$

but his only real choice is between ($x_2 = 0$, $x_1 = y$) and ($x_2 = 1$, $x_1 = y - p$). (I assume $y > p$ to make this problem meaningful.)

To create a simple example, assume that every consumer has a Stone–Geary utility function:

$$U(x_1, x_2) = \log(1 + x_1) + \alpha \log(1 + x_2) \tag{9.6}$$

where α is a taste parameter that differs across individuals. The consumer's optimisation problem is easily solved, but *not* by calculus. If he buys x_2, his utility is:

$$\log(1 + y - p) + \alpha\log(2)$$

whereas if he does not buy x_2, his utility is:

$$\log(1 + y)$$

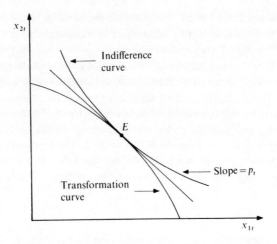

Fig. 9.2 Competitive equilibrium with a representative consumer and a representative firm.

He therefore will buy x_2 if and only if:

$$\alpha > \frac{\log(1+y) - \log(1+y-p)}{\log(2)} \tag{9.7}$$

To generate a downward-sloping market demand curve from the individual demand curves that are step functions, define the right-hand side of (9.7) as α^*, which depends on y and p. To keep the example simple, assume that y is the same for everyone, and let $f(\alpha)$ be the density function of the taste parameter α. Then market demand is:

$$X_2(p, y) = \int_{\alpha*(y, p)}^{\infty} f(\alpha)d\alpha = 1 - F[\alpha^*(y, p)] \tag{9.8}$$

where $F(\cdot)$ is the cumulative distribution function corresponding to $f(\cdot)$. Notice that the price and income derivatives of the demand function are:

$$\frac{\partial X_2}{\partial p} = -f(\alpha^*)\frac{\partial \alpha^*}{\partial p} = \frac{-f(\alpha^*)}{(1+y-p)\log(2)} < 0$$

$$\frac{\partial X_2}{\partial y} = -f(\alpha^*)\frac{\partial \alpha^*}{\partial y} = \frac{p\,f(\alpha^*)}{\log(2)(1+y)(1+y-p)} > 0$$

where I have used the definition of $\alpha^*(p, y)$ in taking the derivatives. The market demand function is thus well behaved: it is increasing in income and decreasing in price.

What would an econometrician practising the new econometrics do in this case? So as not to becloud the issue, assume that he gets the utility function exactly right.[7] His only error, I assume, is that he mistakenly interprets the market demand curve as a blowup of the individual demand curve of a *representative consumer,* not realising that x_2 is available only in discrete amounts. That is, he erroneously interprets the price and quantity data as reflecting tangencies between indifference curves and budget lines as in Fig. 9.2.

The hypothetical representative consumer would then maximize:

$$\log(1 + X_1) + a \log(1 + X_2)$$

subject to budget constraint (9.5), yielding the following demand curve for X_2:

$$X_2 = \frac{a}{1+a}\left(\frac{1+y}{p}\right) - \frac{1}{1+a} \tag{9.9}$$

Following the program suggested by Sargent and others, he would then use data on y, p and X_2 along with equation (9.9) to infer the value of the taste parameter, a. What would he get? It is convenient to define a synthetic variable:

$$Z_t = \frac{1 + y_t}{p_t} \tag{9.10}$$

Then equation (9.9) can be written as the simple linear regression:

$$X_{2t} + 1 = A(Z_t + 1) \tag{9.9'}$$

where $A \equiv a/(1+a)$. The ordinary least squares estimator of this single parameter has probability limit:

$$\text{plim } \hat{A} = \frac{\text{cov}(X_2, Z)}{\sigma_z^2} \tag{9.11}$$

Let us assume that the true model is as indicated earlier, and that it holds without error. A computationally convenient case arises when the taste parameter α has the following exponential density:

$$f(\alpha) = \lambda e^{-\lambda \alpha} \quad \alpha \geqslant 0$$

with $\lambda = \log 2$. (So the mean of α is $1/(\log 2) \approx 1.44$.) In this case, it turns out that the true demand curve, equation (9.8), has the simple form:

$$X_{2t} = 1 - \frac{1}{Z_t} \tag{9.8'}$$

where Z_t is defined in equation (9.10). From equation (9.8'), the covariance needed for equation (9.11) is seen to be:

$$\text{cov}(X_2, Z) = \overline{Z} E\left(\frac{1}{Z}\right) - 1$$

which is necessarily positive by Jensen's inequality. To take this calculation further, use the second-order Taylor series approximation for $1/Z$ around the point $Z = \bar{Z}$, namely:

$$\frac{1}{Z} \approx \frac{1}{\bar{Z}} - \frac{1}{(\bar{Z})^2}(Z - \bar{Z}) + \frac{1}{(\bar{Z})^3}(Z - \bar{Z})^2$$

Taking expectations gives:

$$E\left(\frac{1}{Z}\right) \approx \frac{1}{\bar{Z}}\left[1 + \left(\frac{\sigma_z}{\bar{Z}}\right)^2\right]$$

so that equation (9.11) becomes simply:

$$\text{plim } \hat{A} = \frac{1}{(\bar{Z})^2} \tag{9.11'}$$

This would be the estimated 'slope' of the demand curve with respect to Z derived by the procedures of the new econometrics. It is to be compared with the true slope which, according to equation (9.8') is:

$$\frac{\partial X_2}{\partial Z} = \frac{1}{Z^2} \tag{9.12}$$

At the mean Z (which is *not* the mean y and p) these slopes are equal. But at a value of Z that is, say, twice the mean – which is not at all unusual in time series data – the estimated slope would be four times too large. Huge errors seem likely.

Notice also that the econometric procedures based on the false assumption of interior maxima badly distort the shape of the true demand function. For example, the estimated demand curve would be thought to be linear in income and convex in price:

$$\frac{\partial^2 X_2}{\partial y^2} = 0; \quad \frac{\partial^2 X_2}{\partial p^2} = 2\hat{A}(1+y)p^{-3} > 0$$

whereas in fact the true demand curve is concave in income and linear in price:

$$\frac{\partial^2 X_2}{\partial y^2} = -2p(1+y)^{-3} < 0, \quad \frac{\partial^2 X_2}{\partial p^2} = 0$$

Figure 9.3 charts the actual and estimated demand curves as a function of Z in the case of $\bar{Z} = 2$ (which corresponds to $A = 1/4$).

In this example, which I do not believe is contrived in any sense except, of course, its reliance on discrete choice, the potential errors in pursuing the new econometrics are enormous. It would take a lot of persuasion – and some evidence – to convince me that the problem isolated by Lucas typically leads to errors of this magnitude.

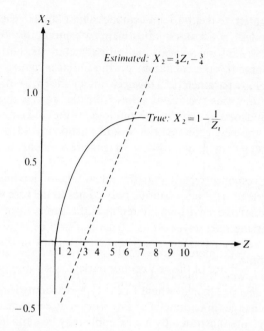

Fig. 9.3 Graphical representation of actual and estimated demand curves.

Two responses can be made to this example. The first notes that my example is just a case of specification error, and everyone knows that misspecification can lead to bad estimates. For instance, if the econometrician had understood the discrete nature of the choice problem, he would have estimated (9.8′) instead of (9.9) and would not have made a mistake.

Naturally, this is so. I presume that maximum likelihood estimation of *the correct* model always leads to the best estimates; the trick is to find the correct model. My point is that the particular procedures advocated by the new econometricians invariably view the data as being generated by *interior* solutions to optimization problems solved by *representative* individuals and firms. My example shows that, if this view of the world is wrong, huge errors can result. I claim further that discrete choice and differences in tastes are pervasive phenomena, so the example is not some pathological case but is illustrative of a wide class of problems.

Two examples are worth mentioning in this context. (I am sure there are many others.) The first has to do with taste parameters. Christensen, Jorgenson and Lau (1975) used a very flexible functional form, but still rejected the hypothesis that the aggregate data could have been generated as the solution to a utility maximization problem. The second involves technology parameters. Blinder (1981) showed that the (S, s) model of inventory behavior can be aggregated to lead to an equation that looks just like a stock adjustment model. In the stock adjustment interpretation of the equation, which can be derived from a linear-quadratic structure similar to that used by Hansen and Sargent,[8] the coefficient on the initial inventory stock reflects certain 'technology parameters.' However, under the (S, s) interpretation of the same equation, this coefficient arises from the aggregation process and has nothing whatsoever to do with technology. If the (S, s) model is true, the procedures of the new econometrics would mistakenly 'identify' the 'technology parameters' of a quadratic cost function when, in fact, no such function exists.

The second response recalls that the advantage of having an estimator which is immune to the Lucas critique only comes to the fore when there is a regime change. If the environment remains the same, even reduced-form parameters passing themselves off as 'structural' will be invariant. But only taste and technology parameters will remain invariant in the face of large changes in regime.

I have two answers to this. First, it seems to me that we rarely experience major, abrupt regime changes where Lucas-type reasoning leads us to expect sudden, large changes in parameters.[9] For workaday econometrics, the kinds of estimation errors illustrated by my example may be quite large relative to those introduced by ignoring the Lucas critique.

Second, let us use the example to examine the chief selling point of the new econometrics: that it can handle regime changes better because it yields estimates of taste and technology parameters. In the example, the taste parameters are summarized by an exponential distribution of the taste parameter α, whose mean is $1/\log 2 \approx 1.44$. The new econometric procedures would yield a single taste parameter: the 'a' in the utility function of the representative consumer, which it would use to predict behavior following a change of regime.

Since the point estimate of $A = a/(1+a)$ has $(\bar{Z})^{-2}$ as its probability limit, the plim of a is:

$$\text{plim } a = \frac{1}{(\bar{Z})^2 - 1}$$

Depending on the precise value of $\bar{Z}$, this may or may not bear much resemblance to the mean value of α in the population. For example, in the $\bar{Z} = 2$ case depicted in Fig. 9.3, plim $a = 1/3$, which is less than one quarter of the true population mean!

There is thus no reason to think that the 'taste and technology parameters' derived from the new econometrics will be good guides to what actually happens following a regime change (unless, of course, we really get the model right).

9.4 CONCLUSION

This short paper should not be misinterpreted as a brief against rational expectations, nor even against imposing the cross-equation constraints delivered by rational expectations in applied econometric work. The criticisms of the old econometrics made by Lucas, Sargent and others are not wrong; they are absolutely correct.

The paper *is*, however, a brief against the view that there is any one 'right way' to do econometrics. In statistical work with dirty data, there is no room for purity and no such thing as a free lunch. The applied econometrician who single-mindedly devotes his energies to coping with the Lucas critique is likely to be blind-sided by another problem.

Saying this in no way denies the validity of the Lucas critique, but merely points out that it may not always be of great empirical importance. In my view, the critique should take its place as one among many serious problems that confront the applied econometrician – on a par, perhaps, with violations of the assumptions of the Gauss – Markov theorem. The realization, for example, that least squares bias can always be present has not stopped applied econometrics in its tracks (though it has given cause for humility). Perhaps the Lucas critique should be treated in the same way.

This broader perspective dictates that we follow a more pragmatic, case-by-case approach in which we recognize that other problems may be more important than the Lucas critique in particular cases. Certainly, there is no *a priori* reason to suppose that the best econometric estimates are those that are most immune to the Lucas critique if the procedures employed to deal with the critique introduce errors of their own.

Specifically, the example in this paper suggests that the new econometrics – which views the world as composed of concave consumers and concave firms that compute mathematical expectations and meet atomistically in blissful equilibrium along separating hyperplanes – is potentially fraught with error. Using these techniques to go "beyond supply and demand curves" to the taste and technology parameters that presumably underlie them may be a high-risk strategy. And in many cases we may conclude that, the Lucas critique notwithstanding, extrapolating supply and demand curves based on past behavior is the best technique we have for predicting the future.

9.5 NOTES

1. The Lucas critique is just as applicable to microeconomics as to macroeconomics. However, it seems that mostly macro-econometricians have worried about it.
2. See Abel (1980), Blanchard (1980), or Summers (1981).

3. For an example, see Taylor (1979).
4. It should be pointed out that the three approaches are by no means mutually exclusive.
5. See Rosen and Quandt (1978) for an example.
6. Clearly, the length of the period is critical here. If we take the lifetime as the time unit, discrete purchases are probably not terribly important for most commodities. But the data we work with are generally monthly, quarterly or annual. Over these time periods, discrete choice is probably quite important. Some of the relevant theory is displayed in Novshek and Sonnenschein (1979).
7. This, of course, is an unwarranted assumption, and suggests an additional source of error. But getting the functional form right is *always* a problem in *any* style of econometric work.
8. See Blinder (1982).
9. Sims (1982) shares this view.

9.6 REFERENCES

Abel, A. B. (1980) 'Empirical investment equations: an integrative framework,' in K. Brunner and A. H. Meltzer (eds) *On the State of Macroeconomics*, Carnegie–Rochester Conference Series, vol. 12, Amsterdam: North-Holland.

Blanchard, O. J. (1980) 'The monetary mechanism in the light of rational expectations,' in S. Fischer (ed.) *Rational Expectations and Economic Policy*, Chicago: University of Chicago Press.

Blinder, A. S. (1981) 'Retail inventory behavior and business fluctuations,' *Brookings Papers on Economic Activity*, vol. 2, pp. 443–505.

Blinder, A. S. (1982) 'Inventories and sticky prices: more on the microfoundations of macroeconomics,' *American Economic Review* (June), vol. 72, pp. 334–48.

Christensen, L. R., Jorgenson, D. W. and Lau, L. J. (1975) 'Transcendental logarithmic utility functions,' *American Economic Review* (June), vol. 65, pp. 367–83.

Hansen, L. P. and Sargent, T. J. (1980) 'Formulating and estimating dynamic linear rational expectations models,' *Journal of Economic Dynamics and Control*, vol. 2.

Lucas, R. E. Jr (1976) 'Econometric policy evaluation: a critique,' *Journal of Monetary Economics* (January (supplement)), vol. 2, pp. 19–46.

Novshek, W. and Sonnenschein, H. (1979) 'Marginal consumers and neoclassical demand theory,' *Journal of Political Economy* (December), vol. 87, no. 6, pp. 1368–76.

Rosen, H. S. and Quandt, R. E. (1978) 'Estimation of a disequilibrium aggregate labor market,' *The Review of Economics and Statistics* (August), vol. LX, no. 3, pp. 371–9.

Sargent, T. J. (1982) 'Beyond demand and supply curves in macroeconomics,' *American Economic Review*, vol. 72 (May).

Sims, C. (1982) 'Policy analysis with econometric models,' *Brookings Papers on Economic Activity*, vol. 1.

Summers, L. H. (1981) 'Taxation and corporate investment: a *q*-theory approach,' *Brookings Papers on Economic Activity*, vol. 1, pp. 67–127.

Taylor, J. B. (1979) 'Estimation and control of a macroeconomic model with rational expectations,' *Econometrica*, vol. 47.

10 · THE CHALLENGE OF HIGH UNEMPLOYMENT

The Ely Lecture is an occasion to indulge in big think, to eschew equations and 'speak prose' – a respite from the daily grind of vector autoregressions, Euler equations, and phase diagrams. I intend to take full advantage of this privilege tonight. Judging by past Ely Lectures, it is also an occasion either to celebrate the profession (or one's own contributions to it) or to chide it. Some combination of flaws in my character and flaws in our discipline incline me toward the latter.

My topic is the challenge of high unemployment, one which both policy-makers and economists have failed to meet. The challenge to policy-makers is to reduce unemployment. About this, I will be brief and to the point. The challenge to economists is to explain high unemployment and understand its implications for things economic. Here I will dwell longer.

10.1 THE CHALLENGE TO POLICY-MAKERS

The failure to provide productive employment for all those willing and able to work has long been one of the major weaknesses of market capitalism. Since the mid-1970s, it has been shamefully debilitating. If one picture is worth a thousand words, Fig. 10.1 will help shorten the lecture. It shows unemployment rates in the United States and the European OECD countries in two different periods: 1961–74 and 1975–85. The contrast is stark.

The costs summarized in this graph are enormous for the United States and colossal for Europe. And the corresponding Okun gaps, wide as they are, understate the full costs. A high-pressure economy provides opportunities, facilitates structural change, encourages inventiveness and innovation, opens doors for society's underdogs, and yields a fiscal dividend that can be spent, among other things, on public charity. All these promote the social cohesion and economic progress that make democratic mixed capitalism such a wonderful system when it works well. A low-pressure economy slams the

Department of Economics, Princeton University, Princeton, NJ 08544. I am grateful to Will Baumol, Ben Bernanke, Avinash Dixit, Bob Eisner, Steve Goldfeld, Bob Gordon, Dan Hamermesh, David Romer, Harvey Rosen, Bob Solow, and Larry Summers for helpful comments.

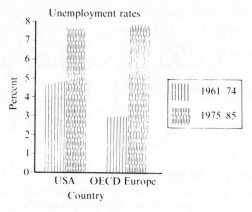

Fig. 10.1 The rise in unemployment since 1971.

doors shut, breeds a bunker mentality that resists change, stifles productivity growth, and fosters both inequality and mean-spirited public policy. All this makes reducing high unemployment a political, economic, and moral challenge of the highest order.

To make the point in extreme form, think about the US economy during the Second World War, when unemployment virtually vanished, the economy flexed its muscles, and the United States truly became a land of opportunity. Among the remarkable features of this period was a 16 percent rise in real consumer spending between 1939 and 1944 despite the wholesale redirection of economic activity toward war production. Now imagine that there was no war and all those soldiers and equipment went abroad to work, not to fight, sending home no goods, just remittances. But leave in your minds all the rationing and other nasty Harberger triangles caused by the shortage economy. Ask yourself whether the utility of the representative American would have been higher under these hypothetical conditions or under the actual conditions of 1939 – or, abstracting from secular growth, even 1987 for that matter. My suggested answer, you can tell, is yes.

A debater's point, you say, for wartime unemployment rates were absurdly and unsustainably low. Probably so. But remember that just 14 years ago the unemployment rates (using US concepts) were 3.2 percent in the United Kingdom, 2.7 percent in France, and 0.7 percent in Germany. These are surely not unimaginable worlds. And think of the social dividend that would be reaped if those countries got unemployment even halfway back to where it was in 1973. Or think about the present-day United States. While many people see today's 6 percent national unemployment rate as 'full employment,' the unemployment rate is more like 3–4 percent in Massachusetts and New Jersey. Those two states and parts of others do show clear signs of labor scarcity: *Help Wanted* signs are everywhere and wages are rising faster than the national average. For all I know, there may even be people whose marginal utility of leisure exceeds their wage. But there are no signs of chaos, and shortages of goods and services are rare. The local economies are, as a matter of fact, doing quite well, thank you. Wouldn't it be nice if the whole country were in such good shape? Aren't we wasting something precious if it could be?

Yet in the United States and, especially, in Europe, those in authority often accept high unemployment with an air of resignation, as if it stemmed from acts of nature rather than from acts of man. This is an attitude conducive to paralysis; and so we wind up with an excess supply of excess supply.

The European and American experiences differ both quantitatively and qualitatively. While there is much we do not know about the details, the broad outlines of the origins of high European unemployment are familiar enough. Intransigent trade unions and well-intentioned but unintelligent governments have erected a web of microeconomic barriers to full employment that both make labor more expensive and transform wages from variable into fixed costs. These include (with different weights in different countries) high minimum wages, excessive severance pay, heavy fixed costs of employment, restrictions on hiring and firing, support for the closed union shop, meaningless licensing requirements, heavy-handed workplace rules, and impediments to geographic mobility.[1] There is nothing at all 'natural' about unemployment that results from such misguided micro policies, and economists rightly oppose them.

But there is also an important macro component to the slack we see in Europe today. And in the United States, which has avoided the horror stories of European labor markets, restrictive policy is virtually the whole story behind the Great Recession of the 1980s. Put plainly, governments here and abroad have used high unemployment to exorcise the inflationary demon.

Unfortunately, economists are terribly divided on the relative importance of the micro and macro explanations for high unemployment. Some think macro policy played a major role in the drama; others assign it only a bit part. This internal schism, I am afraid, contributes to the policy paralysis—which brings me to the role of economists, beginning with macro-economists.

10.2 THE CHALLENGE TO MACROECONOMISTS

Every science has its game playing and puzzle solving. It's harmless, good clean fun, helps sharpen the mind, and occasionally turns up something spectacularly useful. Economics is no exception, nor should it be. But I want to suggest that contemporary academic economists have taken a good thing too far, pushed the game-playing aspects beyond the region of even positive marginal returns, and disengaged themselves from the practical policy concerns that affect the lives of millions. We will not contribute much toward alleviating unemployment while we fiddle around with theories of Pareto optimal recessions – an avocation that might be called Nero-classical economics.

It wasn't always that way. A century ago, Alfred Marshall concluded the inaugural lecture for his Chair at Cambridge with these words:

> It will be my most cherished ambition . . . to increase the numbers of those whom Cambridge, the great mother of strong men, sends out into the world with cool heads but warm hearts, willing to give some at least of their best powers to grappling with the social suffering around them.[2]

Even after translating the soppy Victorian prose into the modern vernacular, Marshall's sentiments are frightfully out of touch with the realities of contemporary academia, where a stubborn fixation on the real world is apt to be considered boorish, if not downright anti-intellectual.

Yet is Marshall's ideal really foolishly romantic? Isn't it better than Nero's? Didn't Keynes have a point when he longed for the day when economists would be as useful as dentists? Greater concentration on real, rather than imagined, problems need not make economics less scientific. Why, for example, are so many scientists now working on AIDS and cancer? Yes, I know that part of the answer is the one Willy Sutton gave when asked why he robbed banks: 'That's where the money is.' But another part of the answer is: 'That's where the suffering is.' It's a good answer, too.

Don't get me wrong. I am not suggesting that we all forsake mathematics for social work. Being a do-gooder may not be the best way to do good; nor should that be the sole concern of a scientist. Nor am I suggesting more top-notch, policy-oriented research will banish the scourge of high unemployment. Vested interests, ideological cant, and sheer ignorance surely hold more sway over policy than does economic science. I am suggesting something far more modest: that a major redirection of the work of hundreds of economists might conceivably raise the quality of national economic policy from, say, 3 to 4 on a scale of 10. Hell, Keynes did more than that by himself.

As I see it, the challenge of unemployment to macroeconomists is fourfold: to define involuntary unemployment, to explain it theoretically, to give the theory empirical content, and then to devise policies to reduce it.

10.2.1 First challenge: define it

Some economists, you know, lean toward the tautological view that anything done without literal compulsion must of necessity be voluntary. Others detect elements of involuntarism whenever constraints become too constraining. It may be that *involuntary unemployment* is like pornography: it's hard to define, but you know it when you see it.

Actually, defining involuntary unemployment is no trick at all in the mythical case of homogeneous labor. If labor supplied exceeds labor demanded at the going wage, the difference is literally and unambiguously involuntary. This simplistic view of the world identifies involuntary unemployment with wages that will not fall – a point to which I will return. But with heterogeneous labor the simple definition no longer works, and the whole concept gets slippery. What wage do we mean? Which types of labor?

In the Keynesian oral tradition, the term 'involuntary unemployment' signifies two major ideas. The first is that there are identifiably bad times, called recessions or depressions, when the unemployment rate rises and signs of economic distress are apparent. The second, and more controversial, is that unemployment tends to be too high on average. Pursuing the analogy to pornography, perhaps we should treat the term involuntary unemployment as synonymous with 'pornographic unemployment': joblessness without redeeming social value.

This suggests an operational definition. Ask the following simple question of job losers and job leavers: would you willingly take your previous job back on the terms now available in the market? If the answer is yes, the person is involuntarily (or pornographically) unemployed. This seems a straightforward test whenever there is a well-defined previous job, but it cannot be readily applied to new entrants or reentrants.[3] Fortunately, job losers and job leavers constitute 60–70 percent of total measured unemployment in the United States and about 75–80 percent of the rise in unemployment during recessions.[4] So conceptual difficulties with new entrants and reentrants are of minor practical importance. We can probably get an excellent indication of *changes* in involuntary unemployment by looking only at job losers.

The definition helps distinguish involuntary (or socially useless) unemployment from voluntary (or socially useful) unemployment. People who are enjoying leisure rather than working at what they perceive as unusually low wages would not be considered involuntarily unemployed since they presumably would not take their old jobs back on the previous terms. But few of the unemployed seem to be doing that, and the facts that real wages are (a) close to a random walk[5] and (b) not very cyclical[6] cast serious doubt on the empirical importance of intertemporal substitution in labor supply. Similarly, people who are actively pursuing productive job search are not uselessly unemployed. Certainly, there are such people; but probably not many. We know, for example, that the average job seeker spends only a few hours a week on search and rarely rejects a job offer.[7]

The mention of search brings up the second challenge: explaining high unemployment theoretically.

10.2.2 Second challenge: explain it theoretically

In my view, one main reason for our lack of progress in explaining high unemployment is that academic economists have spent too much time and energy debating whether involuntary (or pornographic) unemployment exists and too little theorizing why. Furthermore, too much of our theoretical debate has taken place within the confining structures of homogeneous labor, where the question reduces to whether and why 'the wage rate' is sticky. That is a reasonable question; but it is not the *only* question.

Once we force ourselves to think seriously about the *heterogeneity* of labor, the very concept of wage rigidity loses precision. For example, is it the *average level* of wages or the structure of *relative* wages that is sticky? Instead of sterile debates about why rational people would leave unexploited Harberger triangles lying on the table, we start thinking about things like relative status and coordination failures. These are important issues. I suspect they may be central to understanding high unemployment. But they simply cannot arise in a homogeneous labor market.

Let me illustrate by pursuing the tantalizing question raised by search theory: why doesn't an unemployed person take the first job she finds while continuing to look for a better one? As a stylized example, why don't unemployed steelworkers go to work at McDonald's? And, if they do not, should we consider their unemployment voluntary?

The traditional search-theoretic answer is straightforward and almost certainly wrong. It holds that search is so much more efficient off the job than on the job that the efficiency gains from searching while unemployed outweigh the lost income. No evidence supports this hypothesis. We know that people can search better on the job in some labor markets. Even in markets where search is best done while unemployed, it is hard to believe that a few hours of search activity per week interfere unduly with holding a job – unless geographical relocation is necessary.

An alternative explanation posits the existence of substantial transactions costs from taking and leaving an interim job. On this view, the dislodged steelworker rationally refuses the job at McDonald's because his in-and-out costs exceed the value of the wages he could earn during a few weeks spent flipping hamburgers. This explanation is logically coherent and even believable for people who anticipate an extremely short spell of unemployment.[8] But most unemployment is accounted for by long spells. For example, 54 percent of all unemployment in 1984 was accounted for by those unemployed for 27 weeks or more.[9] And besides, it is hard to see how the in-and-out costs of taking a short-term job could possibly amount to much more than one day's time. That can hardly explain voluntarily forsaking several weeks' wages.

Another possibility is that workers who lose 'good' jobs worry about being stigmatized by taking 'bad' jobs. I could make this explanation sound less like pop sociology and more like modern economics by gussying it up with words like signalling, asymmetric information, and adverse selection. I could even say it with algebra – but not right after dinner. In whatever guise, the idea is simply that unemployed steelworkers do not want potential employers thinking of them as hamburger flippers. To those willing to venture beyond the confines of neoclassical economics, this is an appealing notion. But there is one big problem. An unemployed steelworker can lose the stigma and keep the income by taking the McDonald's job, omitting it from his résumé, and telling prospective employers that he is unemployed.

So let me suggest an alternative hypothesis based on a very old idea, one which all social scientists but economists find compelling and for which Robert Frank (1985), in particular, has argued eloquently: that people care deeply about their relative status in society. To be more precise, suppose utility depends not just on the *level* of income but also on one's *position in the income distribution*. Suppose further, and this is the critical leap, that you retain the relative status attached to your old job until you take a new one. Thus an unemployed steelworker remains a steelworker – both in his mind and in the minds of others – until he takes a new job; then his status changes. If concern about status is high enough and the gap between the available wage and unemployment compensation is low enough, the individual may prefer unemployment as a steelworker to employment on an inferior job.

Direct empirical evidence on this hypothesis is difficult to come by, though Frank has offered evidence for the importance of relative status in a wide variety of contexts, some of them even biological.[10] So, once again, a thought experiment may help. Suppose a plant closing costs a steelworker his job. After two weeks of puttering around the house, he walks past the local McDonald's and sees a *Help Wanted* sign. Does he walk in and take the job? I think not. Now *why* not? Is it because it would interfere with his job search? Not likely. Is it because he doesn't want personnel directors at other steel mills to think of him as a fast-food worker? Perhaps. But how would they know? I suggest that it may really be because he doesn't want his friends and neighbors – and, especially, doesn't want *himself* – to see him in that low-status position.[11]

Though based on concern for social status rather on coordination failures, this idea is reminiscent of an old Keynesian saw: that workers resist wage reductions because they are concerned that other wages will not follow suit. To hone and quantify our intuition, consider the following simple example that applies to either case.

Utility for individual i depends on his own real income and on the ratio of his own wage to some comparison wage, w_i/w_j. Using Cobb–Douglas utility for convenience, utility while employed is:

$$U = (w_i/w_j)^\alpha w_i^{1-\alpha} \equiv U_0$$

Now suppose the worker loses his job and must choose between accepting a job paying λw_i ($\lambda < 1$) or remaining unemployed and receiving income $b w_i$ ($b < \lambda$) from unemployment insurance, home production, or whatever. If he takes the job, utility is:

$$U = \left(\frac{\lambda w_i}{w_j}\right)^\alpha (\lambda w_i)^{1-\alpha} = \lambda U_0 \tag{10.1}$$

If he turns it down, he gets:

$$U = \left(\frac{w_i}{w_j}\right)^\alpha (bw_i)^{1-\alpha} = b^{1-\alpha} U_0 \tag{10.2}$$

Thus he will prefer unemployment to the low-paying job if and only if:

$$b^{1-\alpha} > \lambda \tag{10.3}$$

When there is no concern for relative status, ($\alpha = 0$), only income matters and the bad job is preferred to unemployment as long as $b < \lambda$. But as α gets bigger, the left-hand side of (10.3) gets larger and the possibility that the worker might refuse the job grows. A convenient way to look at this is to ask how large b (the replacement rate) must be to induce the worker to turn down a job that offers a wage of λw_i. Table 10.1 tabulates the answer for various combinations of λ and α. For example, if $\alpha = 0.2$, the worker will turn down a job paying half his previous wage if his replacement rate is above 42 percent. The gap between 50 and 42 percent may not be exciting. But if α is as large as $1/2$, the critical replacement rate drops to 25 percent – meaning that the worker prefers unemployment and a 75 percent drop in income to a job paying half his previous wage.

Precisely the same comparison arises in the Keynesian case of uncoordinated wage cutting. If workers assume that those earning w_j will not take a wage cut, they expect to receive (10.1) if they accept a $100(1 - \lambda)$ percent wage cut, and (10.2) if they refuse and lose their jobs. Condition (10.3) is thus the condition for preferring a layoff to a wage cut when you do not expect other wages to fall. It turns out also to be the condition for refusing the wage cut when you *do* expect other wages to fall, for if you take a cut and retain your job, you get $\lambda^{1-\alpha} U_0$, while if you refuse and lose your job, you get $(w_i/\lambda w_j)^\alpha$ $(bw_i)^{1-\alpha} = b^{1-\alpha}\lambda^{-\alpha} U_0$. The latter exceeds the former if and only if (10.3) holds.

Perusing Table 10.1 makes it clear that the value of α is of great moment. If α is small, concern for social status cannot take us very far in explaining unemployment. If α is large, it becomes a powerful explanator. To 'estimate' α, I again ask you to introspect. Imagine that in one case your university raises *only your salary* by 10 percent, while in another it gives k percent *to everyone*. How large must k be for these two events to give you the same satisfaction? Table 10.2 shows some answers for several values of α and raises of different sizes. For example, if $\alpha = 0.2$, a 10 percent raise given just to you is as good as a 12.7 percent raise across the board. Each of you can make your own judgment, but this strikes me as less concern with relative status than most real people have. Similarly, the $\alpha = 0.8$ column strikes me as much more. Personal introspection tells me that α is between 0.2 and 0.5. For example, if $\alpha = 1/3$, a 10 percent raise for me only makes me just as happy as a 15.4 percent raise for everyone in my university. That strikes me as roughly correct.

Table 10.1 Replacement rate needed to turn down job

	$\alpha=0$	$\alpha=0.2$	$\alpha=0.5$	$\alpha=0.8$
$\lambda=0.90$	0.90	0.88	0.81	0.59
$\lambda=0.80$	0.80	0.76	0.64	0.33
$\lambda=0.70$	0.70	0.64	0.49	0.17
$\lambda=0.50$	0.50	0.42	0.25	0.03
$\lambda=0.30$	0.30	0.22	0.09	0.002

Table 10.2 Utility equivalent raises

$\alpha=0.2$		$\alpha=0.5$		$\alpha=0.8$	
(1)	(2)	(1)	(2)	(1)	(2)
5	6.3	5	10.3	5	27.6
10	12.7	10	21	10	61.1
15	19.1	15	32.3	15	101
20	25.6	20	44	20	149

Note:
Shown in percent. Columns (1) denote 'just for you,' and Columns (2) denote 'for everyone.'

This much concern with relative status is enough to matter. For example, the entry that would appear in Table 10.1 for $\alpha=1/3$ and $\lambda=0.5$ is 0.35, meaning that I would rather accept unemployment and a 65 percent drop in income than take a job at half my present wage.

Now what I have just presented is an idea, not a model. It has been said that an economist is someone who sees that something works in practice and wonders if it also works in theory. I will not be so obtuse as to try to build a theoretical model incorporating this idea at this late hour. But the dim outlines of such a model are already implicit in an important paper by Ball and Romer (1987b). Working with prices of goods rather than wages of labor, they show that a large real rigidity coupled with a small fixed cost of changing nominal prices can explain large nonneutralities of money. By analogy, I conjecture that it is possible to show that monetary shocks have large effects on employment when workers care about relative wages and firms have small fixed costs of changing nominal wages.

This is just one example of the possibilities that arise once we leave the mythical world of homogeneous labor – as I think we should. Happily, the latest developments in the never-ending quest for microfoundations of macroeconomics make heterogeneity an essential part of the story. I refer, in particular, to theories of unemployment based on imperfect information, efficiency wages, insider–outsider distinctions, and monopolistic competition. And I would like to see concern with relative wages and 'fairness' included on this list, maybe at the top.

Models of labor markets with imperfect information stress such things as unobservable differences in productivity and inability of management to monitor the performance of individual workers. The central message of this burgeoning literature is that wages may not be able to clear markets because they are too busy doing other things. Insider–outsider models recognize the inherent asymmetry in the positions of incumbent workers and challengers. Heterogeneity of goods is, of course, the essence of monopolistic competition models. And efficiency-wage models provide many reasons why firms might deliberately set wages above market-clearing levels – for example, to reduce turnover or to encourage greater work effort.

Each of these approaches contributes something to giving theoretical coherence to the Keynesian intuition that unemployment is often too high. However, I do not wish to oversell the results, for the welfare economics is a bit dicey. In imperfect-information and efficiency-wage models, 'too high' generally means higher than in some unattainable perfect-information equilibrium. In monopolistic competition models, output is lower than it would be under perfect competition. In these cases, policy interventions are not always called for and, if they are, may not take the form of macro stabilization policy (see Ball and Romer (1987a)). Still, I find all this a refreshing departure from the scholastic dogma of high neoclassicism.

However, these new models have so far contributed little to explaining the *changes* in unemployment that we observe in time series and that we call business cycles. Indeed, some seem ill-suited to the task. Hysteresis models may be the most promising in this regard, especially in the European context, for they show how changes in demand can essentially drag supply along – in a neat reversal of Say's Law.

Finally, these models shed little light on why nominal shocks have strong real effects, for each is fundamentally a story about relative prices or real wages. As I just indicated, one way to transform a real rigidity into a nominal rigidity is to add costs of changing nominal prices or wages. Akerlof and Yellen (1985) add fixed costs of changing prices to a model with efficiency wages.[12] Blanchard and Kiyotaki (1987), building on the insights of Mankiw (1985), do the same in a monopolistic competition model. I believe combining costs of changing money wages with a strong concern about relative wages and/or 'fairness' is a promising approach to explaining how fluctuations in demand produce fluctuations in employment.

This theoretical work is still in its infancy (some of it is still *in utero*) and is not without difficulties. While costs of changing prices certainly exist, it is hard to believe that they are large. That is why Ball and Romer's (1987b) demonstration that large monetary nonneutralities can result from the interaction of small nominal rigidities and large real rigidities is so important. However, costs of changing *quantities* also undoubtedly exist; so it is not clear that adjustment costs logically lead to rigid prices and flexible quantities. Finally, theories based on fixed costs of changing prices ('menu costs') need to be recast in a dynamic framework which recognizes that optimal strategies are likely to be variants of the (S, s) rule of inventory theory in which firms adjust prices at different times.[13]

The Keynesian promised land is not yet in sight; but we may, at long last, be emerging from the arid desert and looking over the Jordan. Let me use the license granted me on this occasion to peer beyond where we can really see and speculate briefly on the outlines of a model that is both theoretically respectable and can be explained in mixed company without embarrassment. The model I envision – but do not have – has three main ingredients.

The first is efficiency wages, so there is no tendency for labor markets to clear in the naive neoclassical sense. Large firms, most of which have market power and some fat in their cost structures, pay wages high enough to maintain a queue of qualified job seekers and to retain the workers they have. They do so because turnover is disruptive, because higher wages attract superior applicants, and, perhaps most importantly, because workers perform better when they feel they are well paid.[14] The result is excess supply and unemployment in equilibrium. I propose to call this unemployment *involuntary*, though nothing of substance rides on the name.

The second ingredient is the hypothesis that workers care deeply about relative wages. This accomplishes two things. It rationalizes firms' decisions to pay efficiency-wage premia. And it explains why a worker laid off from a 'good job' may prefer unemployment to a 'bad job,' at least for a while. The latter makes it possible for secondary labor markets to clear, or even to have excess demand, while involuntary (or socially useless) unemployment exists in primary labor markets.

Third, small costs of changing nominal wages and prices, coordination failures ('I'll cut my wage if you'll cut yours'), and notions of fairness[15] combine to prevent full adjustments to moderate shocks, whether nominal or real.

Consider what might happen in such a model if aggregate demand declines. Sales fall in many sectors of the economy, but unevenly. Although prices might drop in sectors experiencing extreme declines in demand, fixed costs keep most prices fixed. Virtually no wages fall due to firms' fully rational fears that wage cuts would lead to lower productivity, perhaps because wage cutting is widely perceived to be unfair.[16] Instead, most firms reduce output and employment.

The cyclically sensitive durable goods industries will be hit hardest by a typical downturn. It seems to be an interesting fact, which I will not attempt to explain, that they also pay very high wages.[17] Many of the workers laid off by those high-wage, cyclical industries will refuse low-status jobs in less cyclical industries, preferring to be unemployed steelworkers than employed hamburger flippers. Falling incomes lead to still lower demand for goods, in a Keynesian multiplier process. Social welfare, I submit, falls.

10.2.3 Third challenge: explain it empirically

Economics is not an art form. So we must not be content with a coherent and vaguely sensible theory of unemployment – welcome as that would be. We must give the theory empirical content, test it, and estimate its central parameters.

In a sense, macroeconomics has progressed further on the empirical front than on the theoretical front. The truth of the matter is that empirical Keynesian models equipped with Phillips curves that allow for supply shocks have done rather well lately. Furthermore, the Phillips curves has been one of the strongest links in the empirical chain. Despite frequent reports of their demise, Gordon's (1988) equations are alive and well and living near Chicago. Academic economists jettisoned the Phillips curve not because of empirical failures, but because of *a priori* theoretical objections.[18] If we keep behaving like that, we may never become as useful as dentists.

What macroeconomics needs next is to give the new generation of Keynesian microfoundations some empirical teeth. You can think of this as providing theoretical justification for the Phillips curve, if you wish. I prefer to think of it as providing empirical justification for all the theorizing.

10.2.4 Fourth challenge: devise policies to reduce it

Logically, of course, this is the last step. But Keynes did not work that way, and the world will not wait while we perfect our models.

Observation of real economies suggests that the qualitative effects of demand management policies are more or less as taught in the elementary textbooks, or at least in *most* of them. Among other things, that means there will be an inflationary price to pay if unemployment is reduced by stimulating aggregate demand. It is the drive to subdue inflation, not any lack of knowledge about how to manipulate aggregate demand, that has accounted for high unemployment these past dozen years.

The nature of the policy challenge depends sensitively on whether or not the natural rate hypothesis is valid. If it is, then we can do no more than seek to flatten the short-run Phillips curve or reduce the natural rate by labor market policies. That remark is a place to begin a lecture, not to end one, so I will not pursue it further.

More enticing possibilities emerge if the natural rate is not so natural. Suppose, for example, that the equilibrium level of unemployment is strongly affected by hysteresis. Then a boost to demand might give the economy much more than a temporary high; it might actually lower unemployment *permanently*. My Keynesian instincts tell me that the low-unemployment equilibrium must be better than the high-unemployment one.

The US data for the 1980s look pretty consistent with the natural rate hypothesis to me – with a natural rate in the 5.5–6 percent range. But there is room for doubt. However, both the evidence of the senses and econometrics shun the natural rate hypothesis for Europe,[19] where none of the microeconomic factors comes close to explaining a quadrupling of unemployment. There a dose of expansionary policy might do the world a world of good.

10.3 THE CHALLENGE TO MICROECONOMISTS

Macroeconomics has long been regarded as the poor cousin of microeconomics, and with some justification. Surely it is mainly macroeconomists who have sullied the family name. But that is not because microeconomists have dealt with unemployment better; far from it. For the most part, microeconomic analysis ignores unemployment, as if it were an institutional detail of no great import.

Working within a full-employment framework would be justifiable on division-of-labor grounds if the premise of the neoclassical synthesis had been fulfilled. But plainly it has not been. Governments have failed to maintain anything like full employment and therefore have not created the conditions under which standard micro theory applies. Alternatively, the microeconomist's fixation on full employment models might be legitimate if allocative decisions neither affected nor were affected by the overall level of employment. This might be true in some applications,[20] but there is no reason to think it holds generally. Let me illustrate with two examples.

10.3.1 International trade theory

My first example is trade theory. Virtually all economists support free trade; but a frustratingly large number of noneconomists do not. Members of our fraternity are constantly amazed at the depth and strength of protectionist sentiment, which we view as evidence of either rent-seeking behavior or low intelligence. Doubtless, some protectionists qualify under both rubrics. But I want to suggest there is more to the matter.

One reason for economists' near-unanimous support of free trade is our use of the long-run, full-employment framework for policy evaluation. In our world, workers displaced by foreign competition move into industries in which our country has a comparative advantage. That can only raise productivity; so both GNP and social welfare should rise. How, except as viewed through the distorting lenses of a special pleader, could that be bad?

But people unencumbered by advanced degrees in economics see trade policy differently. They live in real space and time, where unemployment truly exists and workers displaced by foreign competition often move into unemployment rather than into new jobs. So they reason that our GNP will fall if our markets are opened to free trade. How, except in the strange world of the economic theorist, could that be good?

The two world-views generate rather different predictions. Which is right?

Consider a concrete example. Korean firms learn how to make television sets efficiently and want to export them to the United States. The TV industry and its workers petition Congress for a strict quota to 'save jobs.' Economists scoff at the idea. According to standard trade theory, the United States can only gain by opening its borders to Korean TVs. A quota cannot save jobs; it can only trap labor in an industry in which the United States has no comparative advantage.

Though oversimplified and missing many of the qualifications a good trade theorist would want, this conclusion probably characterizes the typical economist's view of the matter. And it is also probably the right view for the long run. It might even be right for the short run, if the unemployment rate were 4 percent. But suppose Korea learns how to make TVs when the US unemployment rate is 10 percent. Who can honestly assure a displaced factory worker that she will quickly find a new job at a wage close to her present one, as she would in the world envisioned by Ricardian comparative advantage? Isn't it more likely that she will suffer a spell of joblessness, perhaps a lengthy one? Aren't these short-run costs relevant to any social decision?

I anticipate your response and I agree with it: the appropriate solution is not to erect trade barriers but to pursue a vigorous full employment policy so that displaced workers will be quickly reemployed. That is precisely my point. Conditions of full employment are necessary to validate standard propositions in trade theory. High unemployment calls many of these propositions into question. Both the positive predictions of trade theory and its normative prescriptions may be wrong. For example, Brecher (1974) showed years ago that, when unemployment results from a rigid real wage, free trade may reduce both employment and welfare. Furthermore, if unemployment were eradicated by abolishing the wage floor, patterns of trade might reverse. Those who are wary of free trade may have a valid point in the presence of unemployment, as even Adam Smith realized (see Myint (1958)). At the very least, trade adjustment assistance should perhaps become a more integral part of the advocacy of free trade.[21]

Now, I am not trying to argue for protectionism. Though *we* may all be dead in the long run, *someone* will be alive. And a nation that protects one senile industry after another winds up looking like a nursing home for state capitalism. Economists correctly seek to avoid this outcome. Besides, the mere existence of unemployment does not by itself imply that protection is better than free trade.

I *am* arguing, however, that trade theorists could do their job – the job Marshall wanted them to do – better if they paid more attention to the short run. At a minimum, it would narrow the communication gap between economists and the public. We insist on speaking in a long-run equilibrium dialect to people who live in a short-run disequilibrium world. No wonder what we say sounds Greek to them. We could, I believe, spend more time in their world without abandoning our own. And, if we did, everyone would benefit. Isn't that an unexploited Harberger triangle?

The phenomenon of unemployment, of course, is not unknown to trade theorists; and some interesting work has been done. But ask yourself what fraction of the enormous trade-theory literature deals with unemployment: 10 percent? 5 percent? Can that be an optimal allocation of resources?

10.3.2 Public finance

My second and last case in point, public finance, is a far greater offender. Once we get past the sizable literature on unemployment insurance, hardly any work in public finance even recognizes the existence of unemployment. Looking at this allocation of scholarly resources tempts me to prescribe a Pigouvian tax on full employment theorizing.

Here is what we typically tell our youth about tax incidence. An excise tax is imposed on commodity A. In consequence, the price of A rises and the quantity falls. Resources released from the A industry migrate into the B, C, D... industries, where prices therefore fall and quantities rise. In the end, labor and capital are reallocated, relative prices adjust to the tax distortion, and another deadweight loss is born – about which we teach our students to worry deeply. Chances are that neither the price level nor aggregate employment ever arises.

Ordinary people may be forgiven for wondering if something important has not been left out of the story. Will displaced workers really be quickly reemployed in other industries? Aren't they more likely to experience a transitional period of joblessness, perhaps a long one? And won't the excise tax raise the price level? Old-fashioned macroeconometric models, you'll note, share this commonsense view. Plug an excise-tax hike into the DRI or Wharton model and you'll get back increases in both prices and unemployment. (You won't get the Harberger triangle, which is a shortcoming of these models.) Maybe, just maybe, the macro models are right and the micro theorists wrong.

I am not looking to score debater's points here. My claim is that many of the most cherished results of incidence theory change fundamentally once we allow for unemployment.

Consider, for example, the simple idea that an increase in an excise tax raises the price of the commodity to consumers. In one of the few papers on public finance theory in the presence of unemployment, Dixit (1976) showed that falling employment might so depress demand that the price of the taxed commodity actually falls.

Or consider what may be the most basic theorem of public finance: the irrelevance of the side of the market on which a tax is levied. We all have had fun explaining to our beginning students why it doesn't matter whether the payroll tax is levied on employers or employees. Then why, perhaps we should wonder, do Congress, labor, and management all think the decision so momentous? Sheer lack of understanding? Maybe. But maybe not.

I submit that part of the answer is, once again, that we economists insist on thinking long-run equilibrium while everyone else lives in short-run disequilibrium. The truth of the matter is that the incidence of the payroll tax may differ dramatically in the short and long runs; and, as Hamermesh (1980) showed with an empirically based simulation model, the short run may not be so short.

To see why, let us trace through what would happen if Congress abolished the employee's share and raised the employer's share by an equal amount—a nonevent in the eyes of conventional theory. Initially, contractual wages are fixed, so both labor costs and take-home pay would rise. That, as we know, would create excess supply in labor markets, wages would fall, and so on. You can all complete the story leading to the conclusion that, in the end, nothing will have changed.

True enough. But the end is not the beginning. By blithely skipping over the adjustment period, we miss something important. Immediately after the law changes, firms are paying more and workers are receiving more; so capital bears the entire burden of the tax change—just as our mythical Congress intended. Had Congress shifted burdens in the opposite direction, labor would have lost out in the short run. So Congress's decision really does matter, at least for a while. No wonder workers and capitalists fret over where the tax is levied and are mystified by economists' indifference. We call them myopic. They call us out of touch. Both, I am afraid, are right.

Essentially this same point underlies an interesting paper by Poterba, Rotemberg, and Summers (1986) which shows that a balanced-budget shift from direct to indirect taxation will reduce employment in a Keynesian model with nominal rigidities, but not in a classical full employment model. In a similar vein, van de Klundert and Peters (1986) coax a number of fascinating results out of a disequilibrium simulation model reminiscent of Dixit's theoretical paper. They find, for example, that a sales tax given back in a lump sum reduces employment dramatically more in the Keynesian first period than in the classical steady state.

Thus the differences between the long-run equilibrium results that we know and love (and teach to our young) and the short-run disequilibrium results that people actually experience are no mere quibbles. They may be fundamental. And that may be one reason why our advice so often falls on deaf ears.

Once again, the solution is not to abandon long-run analysis. The long-run questions are important and meaningful, and here economists are often right and the public wrong. Rather, the solution is to allow some consideration of short-run employment effects to creep into and temper our analysis.

10.4   VISIONS OF SUGAR PLUMS. . .

Lest I have failed to say anything provocative so far, let me conclude by trying once again, on this third night after Christmas, to get visions of New Jersey–or, if that is impossible, Massachusetts–dancing in your heads.

America now has a remarkable swath of prosperity in its northeast quadrant. It starts around Boston, runs through most of New England and down to the New York metropolitan area, then continues through central New Jersey and Philadelphia and on into Delaware, Maryland, and Washington DC, finally ending in portions of Virginia and North Carolina. By world standards, this is a very large economy; and, within it, unemployment rates of 4 percent and below are common.

Three questions cry out for answers. First, what created the boom? Second, how have these prosperous states managed to sustain such tight labor markets without blowing the lid off inflation? Third, could the entire United States accomplish something similar?

Both New Jersey and Massachusetts moved from being basket cases to showcases in a scant eight years.[22] New Jersey's unemployment rate went from 2.7 percentage points *above* the national rate in 1976 to 2.3 points *below* in 1984. Massachusetts' unemployment rate went from 2.6 points above the national rate to 2.7 points below between 1975 and 1983. How?

The answers are not well known and are probably not simple. Obviously, it was not Keynesian demand management by the state governments. However, rapid aggregate demand growth did play an important role in Massachusetts, which benefited from strong defense spending and 'exports' of high-technology manufactures to the rest of the United States. But New Jersey's economic renaissance came while its manufacturing sector was dwindling from 33 percent of private sector employment to only 23 percent. Services, especially information services, and construction led the way.

At the national level, we understand how to stimulate demand. So the more interesting question is how New Jersey and Massachusetts have kept inflation in check despite stunningly low unemployment rates.[23]

Two hypotheses can be ruled out immediately. The first is that stingy unemployment insurance and other tight-fisted government policies lowered the natural rates of unemployment. None of this is remotely close to the truth in either state.[24] The second hypothesis is that immigration or, alternatively, the use of guest workers provided these states with large influxes of labor at more or less fixed wages. No such thing happened. In fact, population growth in Massachusetts and New Jersey has been slower, and wage growth faster, than in the rest of the country. And I can assure you that New Jersey sends more guest workers–we call them commuters–to New York than New York sends to New Jersey.

The reasons must lie elsewhere. Let me offer two speculative possibilities. The first is hysteresis. Whether because outsiders became insiders, because high employment led to high capital formation, or because rapid growth stimulated innovation, the equilibrium unemployment rates in these two states may now be far lower than they were in 1975. If that is the explanation, we are left wondering whether the entire United States might do something similar.

The second has to do with openness. Each state of the union is a small open economy with fixed exchange rates and no trade barriers *vis-à-vis* the others. It can therefore acquire the goods its citizens demand at more or less fixed prices in the huge national market. That is why textiles, shoes, refrigerators, and automobiles cost no more in New Jersey and Massachusetts than in the other 48 states. Nontraded goods, of course, are a different matter. Housing prices in the Boston and Princeton areas (indeed, in all the suburbs of New York), for example, are legendary. Were these states closed to trade with the rest of the country, their inflation rates would undoubtedly be much higher.

But what about the nation as a whole? The United States is certainly not a small economy. Nor is it as open to trade with the rest of the world as individual states are with the rest of the nation. Nor is the exchange rate fixed. So, if the national labor market tightened dramatically, we could not count on an infinitely elastic supply of imports to keep inflation as subdued as in New Jersey and Massachusetts. However, we *could* count on the world market to provide *some* moderation of inflationary pressures in tradable goods – at least as long as the rest of the world was not also in an exuberant boom. So perhaps the nation, with a balanced monetary and fiscal expansion and thorough-going free trade in goods (but not in labor), could emulate the Massachusetts and New Jersey success stories to some degree.

This is an important respect, I believe, in which free trade helps support a policy of low unemployment. And I argued earlier that low unemployment helps support free trade. That raises the tantalizing possibility of a virtuous circle in which high levels of aggregate demand create tight labor markets while open international trade moderates inflationary pressures. Now, that would truly be a grand neoclassical synthesis. But, to get there, policymakers, macroeconomists, and microeconomists all must rise to meet the challenge of high unemployment.

To do so effectively, we must leave the rubble of academic Star Wars behind us. We must stop arguing over easy questions with known answers (like whether socially useless unemployment exists), and start worrying about difficult questions with unknown answers (like which of the theoretical explanations for unemployment are empirically important). Macroeconomics these last 15 years has accomplished far too little that would make Alfred Marshall proud. It is time we gave that grand old man his due.

10.5 NOTES

1. Among the many possible references that could be cited, see the special 1986 supplement of *Economica* or Gennard (1985).
2. A. Marshall (1925) 'The present position of economics,' in A. C. Pigou (ed.) *Memorials to Alfred Marshall*, London: Macmillan, p. 174 (original in 1885). I thank Avinash Dixit for finding this quotation.
3. Clark and Summers (1979) have argued persuasively that many reentrants are really job losers. The definition also applies to such people.
4. Data on unemployment by reason are available only for the last four recessions. In those recessions, job losers and leavers accounted for 70, 73, 93, and 80 percent of the peak-to-trough rise in the unemployment rate (using NBER cycle dates). The vast majority of this was from job losers. A regression of the job loser rate on time, a constant, and the overall unemployment rate (monthly data, January 1967 to February 1987) produces a coefficient of 0.75 on the latter.
5. See Altonji and Ashenfelter (1980).
6. See Geary and Kennan (1982) and Bils (1985).
7. Clark and Summers (1979, pp. 54–5). Only 10 percent of unemployed people in the special 1976 job-search survey reported rejecting a job offer.
8. In such cases, intertemporal substitution is also an attractive explanation.
9. See Summers (1986), Table 5, page 353.
10. Interviews conducted by Jean Baldwin Grossman (1980) found that most firms adjusted above–minimum wages promptly after the statutory increase in the minimum wage in January 1979.
11. As evidence for this, labor economists have found that high previous wages lead to high reservation wages. See, for example, Kiefer and Neumann (1979).
12. Akerlof and Yellen actually assume what they call 'near rationality.' This is equivalent to rationality in the presence of fixed costs.
13. Caplin and Spulber (1987) illustrate the idea; but their analysis pertains only to steady states with constant s and S. In reality, s and S will undoubtedly be time varying. See, for example, the analysis in my 1981 article, or Bar-Ilan and myself (1988).
14. See Akerlof (1982) and Akerlof and Yellen (1987).
15. Kahneman, Knetsch, and Thaler (1986).
16. Kahneman, Knetsch, and Thaler (1986), also Kaufman (1984).
17. In port, the high wages are compensation for the volatile employment. But I doubt that this is the whole story, for if low-wage, stable jobs were just as desirable as high-wage, variable ones, why would there always be queues of prospective workers at the high-wage firms?
18. Blinder (1986), also Blanchard (1987).
19. See Blanchard and Summers (1986).
20. For example, some micro policies are too small to have meaningful macro effects (for example, airline deregulation). Another possibility is that central bank policy fixes real GNP.
21. Riordan and Staiger (1987) show that trade adjustment assistance is welfare improving if terms of trade shocks are large enough. In their model, the unemployment results from informational asymmetries.
22. On Massachusetts, see Ferguson and Ladd (1986) and Bradbury and Browne (1987). The New Jersey story has been studied much less. See the New Jersey Economic Policy Council's *Annual Report* (1986).

23. There is no CPI for New Jersey. But inflation rates in both the Philadelphia and New York City areas have been slightly *below* the national average. Inflation in the Boston area has run only slightly higher than national inflation.
24. The taxpayers' revolt in Massachusetts is sometimes cited; but the timing is all wrong. Tax cuts began in 1981, but the 'miracle' occurred between 1975 and 1983.

10.6 REFERENCES

Akerlof, G. A. (1982) 'Labor contracts as partial gift exchange,' *Quarterly Journal of Economics* (November), vol. 92, pp. 543–69.

Akerlof, G. A. and Yellen, J. L. (1985) 'A near-rational model of the business cycle with wage and price inertia,' *Quarterly Journal of Economics*, suppl., pp. 823–38.

Akerlof, G. A. and Yellen, J. L. (1987) 'The fair wage/effort hypothesis and un-employment,' unpublished, University of California-Berkeley.

Altonji, J. and Ashenfelter, O. (1980) 'Wage movements and the labour market equilibrium hypothesis,' *Economica* (August), vol. 47, pp. 217–45.

Ball, L. and Romer, D. (1987a) 'Are prices too sticky?,' NBER working paper no. 2171 (February).

Ball, L. and Romer, D. (1987b) 'Real rigidities and the non-neutrality of money,' unpublished (June).

Bar-Ilan, A. and Blinder, A. S. (1988) 'Consumer durables and the optimality of usually doing nothing,' unpublished (January).

Bils, M. J. (1985) 'Real wages over the business cycle: evidence from panel data,' *Journal of Political Economy* (August), vol. 93, pp. 666–89.

Blanchard, O. J. (1987) 'Why does money affect output? A survey,' NBER working paper no. 2285 (June).

Blanchard, O. J. and Kiyotaki, N. (1987) 'Monopolistic competition and the effects of aggregate demand,' *American Economic Review* (September), vol. 77, pp. 647–66.

Blanchard, O. J. and Summers, L. H. (1986) 'Hysteresis and the European unemploy-ment problem,' NBER *Macroeconomics Annual 1986*, pp. 15–78.

Blinder, A. S. (1981) 'Retail inventory behavior and business fluctuations,' *Brookings Papers on Economic Activity*, vol. 2, pp. 443–505.

Blinder, A. S. (1986) 'Keynes after Lucas,' *Eastern Economic Journal* (July–September), vol. 12, pp. 209–16.

Bradbury, K. L. and Browne, L. E. (1987) 'The state of the New England region,' unpublished, Federal Reserve Bank of Boston (October).

Brecher, R. A. (1974) 'Minimum wage rates and the pure theory of international trade,' *Quarterly Journal of Economics* (February), vol. 88, pp. 98–116.

Caplin, A. and Spulber, D. (1987) 'Menu costs and the neutrality of money,' *Quarterly Journal of Economics* (November), vol. 102, pp. 703–25.

Clark, K. B. and Summers, L. H. (1979) 'Labor market dynamics and unemployment: a reconsideration,' *Brookings Papers on Economic Activity*, vol. 1, pp. 13–72.

Dixit, A. (1976) 'Public finance in a Keynesian temporary equilibrium,' *Journal of Economic Theory* (April), vol. 12, pp. 242–58.

Ferguson, R. F. and Ladd, H. F. (1986) 'Economic performance and economic development policy in Massachusetts,' discussion paper D86–2, Harvard Univer-sity (May).

Frank, R. H. (1985) *Choosing the Right Pond*, New York: Oxford University Press.

Geary, P. T. and Kennan, J. (1982) 'The employment–real wage relationship: an international study,' *Journal of Political Economy* (August), vol. 90, pp. 854–71.

Gennard, J. (1985) 'Job security: redundancy arrangements and practices in selected OECD countries,' Paris: OECD.

Gordon, R. J. (1988) 'The role of wages in the inflation process,' *American Economic Review Proceedings* (May), vol. 78, pp. 276–83.

Grossman, J. B. (1980) 'The response of wages to the minimum wage: theory and empirical evidence,' unpublished doctoral dissertation, MIT (May).

Hamermesh, D. S. (1980) 'Factor market dynamics and the incidence of taxes and subsidies,' *Quarterly Journal of Economics* (December), vol. 95, pp. 751–64.

Kahneman, D., Knetsch, J. L. and Thaler, R. (1986) 'Fairness as a constraint on profit seeking,' *American Economic Review* (September), vol. 76, pp. 728–41.

Kaufman, R. T. (1984) 'On wage stickiness in Britain's competitive sector,' *British Journal of Industrial Relations* (March), vol. 22, pp. 101–12.

Kiefer, N. M. and Neumann, G. R. (1979) 'An empirical job-search model, with a test of the constant reservation-wage hypothesis,' *Journal of Political Economy* (February), vol. 87, pp. 89–107.

Mankiw, N. G. (1985) 'Small menu costs and large business cycles: a macroeconomic model of monopoly,' *Quarterly Journal of Economics* (May), vol. 100, pp. 529–37.

Myint, H. (1958) 'The "classical theory" of international trade and the under-developed countries,' *Economic Journal* (June), vol. 68, pp. 317–37.

New Jersey Economic Policy Council (1986) *18th Annual Report*, Trenton (October).

Pigou, A. C. (1925) *Memorials to Alfred Marshall*, London: Macmillan.

Poterba, J. M., Rotemberg, J. J. and Summers, L. H. (1986) 'A tax-based test for nominal rigidities,' *American Economic Review* (September), vol. 76, pp. 659–75.

Riordan, M. and Staiger, R. W. (1987) 'Sectoral shocks and structural unemployment,' unpublished, Stanford University (July).

Summers, L. H. (1986) 'Why is the unemployment rate so very high near full employment?,' *Brookings Papers on Economic Activity*, vol. 2, pp. 339–96.

Van de Klundert, Th. and Peters, P. (1986) 'Tax incidence in a model with perfect foresight of agents and rationing in markets,' *Journal of Public Economics* (June), vol. 30, pp. 37–59.

11 · INDEXING THE ECONOMY THROUGH FINANCIAL INTERMEDIATION

11.1 INTRODUCTION AND SUMMARY

This paper attempts to unravel the great mystery in the economic analysis of indexing – why have so few indexed contracts arisen in market economies, except under government instigation?

Section 11.2 provides a simple theoretical model of the 'market' for indexed contracts, and points out why wage escalators and indexed financial instruments are *substitutes* in the perceptions of both workers and firms. While the model is very simple, the central point is, I think, very robust. With incomplete indexing in financial markets, real returns on assets decline with unexpected inflation. On general portfolio-diversification grounds, therefore, workers demand wage escalators as hedges against reductions in property income. Firms will be amenable to this idea because inflation reduces their real interest costs; they too find an element of insurance in escalators.[1] Where indexed bonds are more prevalent, workers have less to gain from indexing wages, and firms have more to lose. The suggestion, then, is that a scarcity of indexed bonds will create great incentives to escalate wage contracts.

Section 11.3 develops a parallel analysis of the market for indexed bonds, and reaches parallel conclusions. Workers who lack complete cost-of-living protection for their wages will be willing to pay a premium for an indexed bond or, better yet, a security whose real rate of return rises with inflation. Similarly, firms without wage escalators will gain from an inflation which erodes real labor costs, and thus would be eager to hedge these gains by issuing indexed bonds. When wage escalators are widespread, both incentives diminish. Theory thus suggests that a lack of wage escalators will encourage the use of indexed bonds.

Econometric Research Program. This proposal has gone through several drafts, and many people have contributed helpful criticisms and insights. In addition to those cited directly in the text, I wish to thank William Baumol, William Branson, Lester Chandler, Stephen Goldfeld, Edward Gramlich, Martin Hellwig, Dwight Jaffee, Burton Malkiel, and Stephen Salop. This draft has benefited from seminar presentations at MIT, Rutgers University, University of California at San Diego, University of Florida, and the Federal Reserve Bank of Philadelphia, in addition to the Carnegie-Rochester conference. William Newton provided exceptionally fine research assistance, and financial support was provided by the National Science Foundation.

Taken together, these models offer a neat explanation of a nonexistent world – one in which economies have either a great deal of wage indexing or a great deal of bond indexing. Unfortunately, the US economy and, indeed, all the advanced market economies have surprisingly little indexing of any kind. Is it because the simple models are misleading? I think not. Their basic point – that hedging against inflation is a good idea – is too obvious to be wrong.

Section 11.4, the core of the paper, offers both an hypothesis for why things may have gone awry, and a policy prescription to set things right. I suggest that risk-averse firms would be happy to link factor payments to a price index which follows closely the movements of their own output prices, but shy away from contracts linking wages and interest to some broad price index whose movement might easily outstrip their selling prices. Conversely, workers and bondholders may be unwilling to bear the substantial risks of linking their factor payments to the prices of firms for which they work or to which they lend. Instead, they prefer linkage to a broad price index more or less representative of the things they buy. These asymmetrical perceptions of the risks caused by inflation may have resulted in the absence of both kinds of linked security.

If this is the reason, then a new kind of financial intermediary can solve the problem. Let a mutual fund be established, one holding as its assets bonds linked to the output prices of a broad collection of firms. The total interest received by the fund will then resemble the return on a bond indexed to a broad price index. Such receipts give the fund the wherewithal to issue deposits linked to such an index. Both firms and bondholders, therefore, can have the type of security they want. Of course, things are not quite so simple as this; the fund would have to face several technical problems, and remedies for each are suggested in Section 11.4.

A more fundamental problem is that of verifying that firms and bond-holders would want to borrow and lend in these forms. Taking a cue from the theoretical models of Sections 11.2 and 11.3, I seek such empirical evidence by studying how rates of return on (unindexed) human and financial assets, and corporate profits, behave in inflation. The models of consumer-worker behavior suggest that there will be a substantial demand for indexed deposits if real returns to human and nonhuman capital decline with unanticipated inflation. The models of the firm suggest that businessmen will be eager to enter into contracts linking factor payments to their own industry price if the profit performance of a firm is best when prices in its industry are rising most rapidly. Section 11.5 marshals empirical evidence, some of it necessarily impressionistic rather than definitive, in support of these hypotheses.

Despite the apparent contradiction, then, the theory, the empirical evidence, and the policy prescription are all related. The theory views escalator clauses and indexed bonds as ways to hedge inflation losses; the evidence shows that such hedges are in fact needed; and the policy prescription suggests how they may be supplied through financial innovation.

11.2 THE DEMAND FOR AND SUPPLY OF WAGE ESCALATORS

The major point of this section is that the prevalence of cost-of-living escalators in wage contracts is strongly conditioned by the presence or absence of indexed bonds. Specifically, when bonds are indexed, workers will demand less wage escalation, and firms will supply less, because indexing wages is a substitute for indexing bonds for both workers and firms.

11.2.1 The demand for escalators

At first, firms are assumed to be risk neutral, and thus indifferent among wage contracts which offer the same expected real wage, $\bar{w}$. Workers, however, are risk averse, and therefore concerned with both the mean real wage and the dispersion around that mean. They must agree on a wage contract, which is a function, $w(\pi)$, stipulating how the real wage, w, depends on the rate of inflation, π. Since firms are indifferent among all functions satisfying:

$$E[w(\pi)] = \bar{w}, \text{ a constant} \tag{11.1}$$

which contract will workers select?

Suppose the worker lives and works for two periods; enjoys real consumption, c_0 and c_1, in the two periods; earns w_0 and $w(\pi)$ in the two periods; has real assets, k_0, at the start of first period; and carries over k_1 in real assets to the second period.[2] Then his two budget constraints are:

$$c_0 = k_0 + w_0 - k_1 \tag{11.2}$$

$$c_1 = (1+r)k_1 + w(\pi) \tag{11.3}$$

where r is the real rate of return on wealth. The stochastic properties of r, especially its covariance with π, depend on whether or not financial instruments are indexed.

The worker's problem is to select k_1 and the form of the $w(\cdot)$ function so as to maximize his two-period utility, which is assumed to take the following simple form:

$$J = V(c_0) + E[U(c_1)]$$

subject to (11.1)–(11.3).

Since for any choice of a $w(\cdot)$ function, savings will be adjusted optimally to keep $\partial J/\partial k_1 = 0$, I can abstract from savings choices; treat k_1 as fixed; and find the optimal wage contract by maximizing $E[U(c_1)]$, subject to (11.1) and (11.3).[3]

Remembering that c_1 is random because both π and r are, the maximand can be expressed as:

$$E[U(c_1)] = \int_a^b \int_\alpha^\beta U(c_1) \, f(\pi, r) \, d\pi \, dr$$

where $f(\pi, r)$ is the joint density function; and where the integrals are taken over the relevant limits. Writing the joint density as $f(\pi, r) = f(\pi)f(r|\pi)$, the integral can be rewritten:

$$\int_\alpha^\beta f(\pi) \int_a^b U(c_1) \, f(r|\pi) \, dr \, d\pi \equiv \int_\alpha^\beta f(\pi) g(\pi) \, d\pi$$

which is to be maximized subject to the integral constraint:

$$\int_\alpha^\beta f(\pi) w(\pi) = \bar{w}$$

This is a well-known problem in the calculus of variations which is solved by introducing the Lagrange multiplier, λ, a constant whose value depends on $\bar{w}$, and finding an extremum of the integral:

$$\int_\alpha^\beta f(\pi)[g(\pi) + \lambda w(\pi)] \, d\pi$$

The Euler equation holds that:

$$\frac{\partial}{\partial w}[g(\pi) + \lambda w] = 0$$

for all π; or that $\partial g(\pi)/\partial w = -\lambda$ for all π. Using the definitions of $g(\pi)$ and c_1, the Euler equation implies:

$$-\lambda = \int_a^b U'(c_1) \, f(r|\pi) \, dr$$

Since this must hold for all π, we can take the derivative of each side with respect to π, viz.:

$$0 = \int_a^b w'(\pi) U''(c_1) \, f(r|\pi) \, dr + \int_a^b U'(c_1) \frac{\partial f(r|\pi)}{\partial \pi} \, dr \qquad (11.4)$$

In the case of an indexed asset, the second integral in (11.4) vanishes because real returns are not conditional on the inflation rate.[4] Assuming that $U''(c_1) < 0$ and $f(r|\pi) > 0$ within the limits of integration, equation (11.4) then implies that the optimal contract has full cost-of-living escalation: $w'(\pi) = 0$ for all π.

Now consider the case of a nonindexed asset, and assume that the distribution of real returns shifts leftward when the inflation rate rises, as depicted in Fig. 11.1. Examination of the figure reveals that $F(r|\pi_2) > F(r|\pi_1)$ everywhere; that is, the relation between the two distribution functions is one of 'first degree stochastic dominance'.[5] For infinitesimal changes, the dominance relation implies $\partial F(r|\pi)/\partial \pi > 0$. The second term in (11.4) can be integrated by parts to obtain:

$$w'(\pi) \int_a^b U''(c_1) \, f(r|\pi) \, dr = k_1 \int_a^b U''(c_1) \frac{\partial F(r|\pi)}{\partial \pi} \, dr$$

The optimal wage contract can thus be characterized by the formula:

$$\frac{w'(\pi)}{w(\pi)} = \frac{k_1}{w(\pi)} \left[\frac{\displaystyle\int_a^b U''(c_1) \frac{\partial F(r|\pi)}{\partial \pi} \, dr}{\displaystyle\int_a^b U''(c_1) \, f(r|\pi) \, dr} \right] \tag{11.5}$$

Since the ratio of the two integrals must be positive, $w'(\pi)$ has the same sign as k_1.

In words, workers with positive net worth will demand more than 100 percent wage escalation; workers with zero net worth will demand precisely 100 percent escalation; and workers with negative net worth will demand less than 100 percent escalation. The intuition behind this result was provided in Section 11.1. Since inflation lowers the real return on net worth (in a stochastic sense), workers with positive net worth will use their wage contract as 'insurance' against this contingency – recouping some of their losses in real property income by gains in real labor income. Workers with negative net worth are in the opposite position; since inflation raises (algebraically) their negative property income, they are willing to incur some losses in labor income to protect themselves against the possibility that inflation will be very low.

The percentage by which wages are escalated is $1 + w'(\pi)/w(\pi)$. By (11.5) this depends on the ratio of net worth to property income, and on the ratio of the two integrals. Not much can be said in general about the integrals; while the ratio is positive, its magnitude depends on the curvature of the utility function, and on the manner in which inflation alters the probability distribution of real returns. However, there is no reason to think it will be constant, either with respect to π, or with respect to wealth.

Among workers with positive assets, the demand for escalation will be higher the higher the ratio of assets to earnings. Thus, presumably, workers near retirement will want more inflation protection than young workers. More importantly, if most workers have positive net worth, indexed assets reduce the incentive to demand indexed wages.[6]

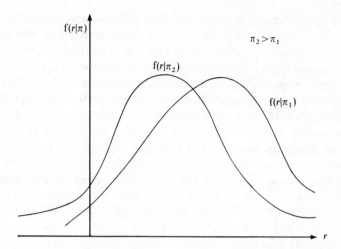

Fig. 11.1 Effect on distribution of real returns of a shift in the inflation rate.

11.2.2 The supply of escalators

Thus far I have assumed that workers can have any type of escalator they choose, so long as it is actuarially fair. But, if firms are averse to risk, they will not be so pliable at the bargaining table. In considering this complication, I simplify the problem somewhat by assuming that π, the inflation rate, is the *only* source of uncertainty; that is, r is stochastic only because of its dependence on π, as would be the case if all assets were risk-free money-fixed bonds. This enables me to adopt the results of a recent paper by Shavell (1976).

Consider a worker and a firm bargaining over the form of the wage contract, $w(\pi)$. Let $R(\pi)$ be the nonwage income of the worker, and assume that $R'(\pi) < 0$. Let $Y(\pi)$ be the net income of the firm *exclusive of wage payments*; I shall discuss the sign of $Y'(\pi)$ presently. Shavell asks: what sort of wage function would be *Pareto optimal* for the two parties? For the case in which employer and employee have the same subjective probability distribution for inflation, he shows that the contract satisfies:

$$w'(\pi) = \frac{Y'(\pi)\rho_F - R'(\pi)\rho_w}{\rho_F + \rho_w} \quad \text{for all } \pi \tag{11.6}$$

where ρ_F and ρ_w are the (positive) degrees of absolute risk aversion of the firm and worker, respectively.[7]

If firms are risk neutral ($\rho_F = 0$), (11.6) implies that the wage contract completely insures the worker against income fluctuations: $w'(\pi) + R'(\pi) = 0$. This result would have emerged from the previous analysis if inflation were the only source of uncertainty.

If firms are risk averse ($\rho_F > 0$), but their other income is unaffected by inflation [$Y'(\pi) = 0$], they will sell insurance to workers, but only on actuarially unfair terms. As a result, workers will find it optimal to buy less than complete insurance, i.e., $w'(\pi) > 0$, but $w'(\pi) + R'(\pi) < 0$.

If the firm is both risk averse and affected by inflation in ways other than through its wage payments, real wages will rise unambiguously in inflation only if $Y'(\pi) > 0$. This is the first instance of 'supply side' responses in the 'escalator market.' Firms which tend to do well in inflation [$Y'(\pi) > 0$] will be eager to give generous escalators as a form of insurance to workers – in return for lower mean wages. Conversely, and for the same reasons, firms which tend to fare poorly in inflation [$Y'(\pi) < 0$] will be reluctant to escalate wages very much, even though that implies lower mean wage costs.

What is the likely sign of $Y'(\pi)$? In Section 11.5, some indirect empirical evidence on this question is presented. It is indirect enough, however, that the issue merits some qualitative discussion. As is true of almost every question in the theory of indexing, the outcome is very different in the cases of demand-induced versus supply-induced inflations. An approximate accounting identity for $Y(\pi)$ is:

$Y(\pi) =$ real sales revenue – real materials costs – real interest payments
$\quad$ + real inventory profits – real profits taxes

Consider first a demand-pull inflation. Presumably, in such a situation, real sales revenues rise much faster than real materials costs. Real interest payments, at least on long-term debt, fall in any kind of inflation so long as bonds are not indexed. Inflation also leads to inventory revaluations, which represent genuine profits in the short run. The only negative argument is that real corporate taxes increase because inflation erodes the real value of depreciation allowances. On balance, then, it seems safe to assume that $Y'(\pi) > 0$ in demand-pull inflation; this means that firms will be eager to index wage payments. Note the role of indexed bonds in this analysis – indexing interest payments reduces $Y'(\pi)$, and thus reduces firms' willingness to index wages. To firms, as to workers, indexed bonds and indexed wages are substitutes.

Now turn to cost-push inflations, where things are quite different. Since the quantity of goods sold presumably falls in a supply side inflation, real sales receipts drop (nominal sales rise less rapidly than prices). At the same time, materials costs may rise faster than product prices. Interest payments, inventory profits, and corporate taxes behave in much the same way as under demand-pull inflation. On balance, then, it would not be surprising if $Y'(\pi) < 0$. If so, firms will be reluctant to exacerbate the burden of inflation by indexing wages; and if bonds are indexed, their resistance to wage escalation will stiffen.[8]

11.3 THE DEMAND FOR AND SUPPLY OF INDEXED BONDS

The question I address in this section is the mirror image of the question considered in Section 11.2: how does the degree of wage escalation influence the demand for and the supply of indexed bonds? The demand for indexed bonds has been treated very elegantly by Fischer (1975).[9] What follows is a highly simplified variant of Fischer's analysis which, I hope, preserves the intuitions while stripping away almost all of the mathematical complexities. I use this watered-down model to focus on the interaction of human and nonhuman capital, a point not stressed by Fischer, although it is implicit in his analysis.

11.3.1 A simple model of portfolio choice

I adopt unabashedly both mean-variance analysis and a one-period horizon in order to simplify the mathematics. Consider a worker-investor deciding how to allocate his total wealth among three assets in such a way as to maximize the expected value of his von Neumann–Morgenstern utility indicator: $U = (\bar{z}, \sigma)$, where $\bar{z}$ is the mean rate of return and σ is its standard deviation. The assets are the following:

1. Human wealth. The unique feature of human wealth is that it cannot be sold. The total amount of human wealth and, therefore, the fraction of start-of-period wealth held in human form is *given* and not subject to choice. I call this fraction a. The stochastic nature of the returns from human wealth can be parameterized in a convenient manner developed in Bodie (1975). Let H be the nominal rate of return on human wealth, and $h = H - \pi$ be the real rate of return. Express the deviation of H from its mean, $\bar{H}$, as consisting of two stochastic components, one of which is proportional to *unanticipated* inflation, $u \equiv \pi - \bar{\pi}$; the other is uncorrelated with unanticipated inflation.[10] In symbols:

$$H = \bar{H} + \alpha u + \varepsilon \tag{11.7}$$

Treating these rates of return as continuously compounded rates,[11] the interpretation of the parameter, α, is the *degree of wage escalation* – what I denoted by $1 + w'(\pi)/w(\pi)$ in Section 11.2. Subtracting π from both sides of (11.7) gives an expression for the *ex post* real rate of return on human wealth:

$$h = H - \pi = \bar{H} - \bar{\pi} + (\alpha - 1)u + \varepsilon \text{ or}$$
$$h = \bar{h} + \beta u + \varepsilon, \ \beta \equiv \alpha - 1 \tag{11.8}$$

2. Indexed bonds. This is the simplest possible type of asset with a fixed, riskless, real return denoted by r. Let b denote the fraction of total wealth held in indexed bonds.

3. Nominal bonds. I assume that nominal bonds are riskless except for inflation risk. Thus, if the nominal return is $i = R + \bar{\pi}$, the real rate of return is [12]:

$$i - \pi = R + \bar{\pi} - \pi = R - u$$

The fraction of wealth held in this form is $1 - a - b$.

Since the real rate of return on the entire portfolio is:

$$z = ah + br + (1 - a - b)(R - u)$$

$$= \{a\bar{h} + br + (1 - a - b)R\} + \{a\beta - (1 - a - b)\}u + a\varepsilon \text{ by (11.8)}$$

it follows that the mean and variance of z are:

$$\bar{z} = a\bar{h} + br + (1 - a - b)R \tag{11.9}$$

and

$$\sigma^2 = a^2 V(\varepsilon) + (1 - b - a\alpha)^2 V(u) \tag{11.10}$$

Remember that a is given, so the only choice variable is b, the fraction held in indexed bonds. The first-order condition for utility maximization is:

$$0 = \frac{dU}{db} = U_1 \frac{d\bar{z}}{db} + U_2 \frac{d\sigma}{db} \text{ or}$$

$$U_1 \cdot (r - R) = U_2 \frac{V(u)}{\sigma} (1 - b - a\alpha) \tag{11.11}$$

A major point of Fischer's (1975) paper is that $r - R$ may actually be positive, though, for reasons explained below, my guess is that it would be negative. It is simplest to start with the case, $R = r$.

The case where $R = r$

$R = r$ means that the guaranteed real rate of return on indexed bonds is equal to the *ex ante* expected real rate of nominal bonds. If this is so, (11.11) simply implies:

$$b = 1 - a\alpha \tag{11.12}$$

Complete wage indexing would make $\alpha = 1$, so that (11.12) would imply that the demand for nominal bonds is exactly zero; all financial wealth would be held in indexed bonds. This is because full wage indexing eliminates all covariances among the real returns. Since nominal bonds carry some risk, and bear no premium over indexed bonds, they are a dominated asset.

If there is literally no indexing of wages, not even tacit indexing, so that $\alpha = 0$, (11.12) states that holdings of indexed bonds equal total wealth. Since the fixed stock of human wealth is presumably very large, this implies tremendous short sales of nominal bonds. The reason is again obvious.

Human capital fares badly in inflation, as do nominal bonds, while indexed bonds are 'inflation neutral.' Selling short a volume of nominal bonds equal to one's human capital stock creates a perfect hedge, in the sense that the only remaining risk in the portfolio is the undiversifiable component of risk in human returns.

The case where there is partial indexing is intermediate between these two extremes. The central point is clear enough – the demand for indexed bonds falls as the degree of wage indexing increases.

The case where $R>r$

This tendency is muddied by introducing an expected premium for holding nominal bonds, a premium which the previous case strongly suggests would exist. If $R>r$, equation (11.11) implies that $1-b-a\alpha$ is positive.

Under full wage indexing ($\alpha=1$), then, there will be a positive demand for nominal bonds if they pay a premium. Will there be a demand for indexed bonds? One cannot say, in general, that b must be positive. For a large enough premium, the demand for indexed bonds would vanish. But this only means that the market premium would not have to be this large to induce consumers to hold nominal bonds.

For other cases, although at least one of the bonds must be held in positive amounts, we cannot establish which that will be, nor whether both are held. Of course, in the limit as the premium gets small, we can apply the results of the previous case.

The case where $R<r$

If indexed bonds pay a premium – a possibility raised by Fischer (1975) – the analysis is once again simple. Equation (11.11) states that $1-b-a\alpha<0$, which, so long as $0\leqslant a\alpha\leqslant a$, also implies that $1-b-a<0$. That is, everyone will sell nominal bonds short because short sales of nominal bonds provide a hedge against inflation-induced losses on human capital. Only more than 100 percent indexing of wages ($\alpha>1$) could possibly induce worker-investors to hold nominal bonds in positive amounts. This suggests that $R<r$ is very unlikely to obtain.

Which case is realistic?

If indexed bonds existed, one could read the answer to this question from published tables of bond yields. The OECD (1973) reports, in fact, that indexed bonds paid consistently lower interest rates during the nine years in which they coexisted with nominal bonds in France. Given the absence of indexed bonds in the United States, however, one is free to speculate.

Fischer's analysis guides the speculation. His investigation of the demand for indexed bonds concluded that the real return on indexed bonds would probably be below that on nominal bonds ($R>r$) if: (a) real returns on common stocks are negatively correlated with inflation; and, (b) real wage income is negatively correlated with inflation. Some documentation that both of these conditions have held in the postwar United States is provided in Section 11.5. I conclude that, if both types of bonds coexisted, R would exceed r.

11.3.2 The supply of indexed bonds

Will firms want to borrow on an indexed basis, given that they can probably sell such securities at real interest rates below those which they now pay on nominal bonds? If they are risk neutral, they will, for risk-neutral firms simply want to float debt at the lowest *expected real* interest cost.

But, if firms are risk averse, certain complexities arise. I can turn Shavell's analysis on its head to analyze this problem in the same way I analyzed wage contracts. If $R(\pi)$ now denotes the noninterest income of the bondholder, and $Y(\pi)$ denotes the net income of the firm *exclusive of interest payments*, equation (11.6) will again hold, with $w(\pi)$ now interpreted as the real value of debt service.

If most 'other income' of bondholders is wage income, then $R'(\pi)$ will presumably be negative, and less so the greater the prevalence of wage indexing. The previous analysis of costs and benefits to the firm can be repeated, with real wage payments replacing real interest payments. Given only partial wage escalation, this item of costs also declines in inflation. Again the situation may be that $Y'(\pi) > 0$ for demand-pull inflations, and $Y'(\pi) < 0$ for cost-push inflations.

In a word, risk-averse firms will be eager to sell indexed bonds if: (a) they are not indexing wages heavily; and, (b) they tend to do well in inflation. Risk-averse firms will be reluctant to issue indexed debt if: (a) they have large wage escalators; and, (b) they tend to suffer heavy cost increases in inflation.

11.4 THE NATIONAL INFLATION MUTUAL FUND

11.4.1 Recapitulation

The models of the previous two sections hold three main messages:

1. There are good reasons to believe that workers will demand substantial escalation in wage contracts, perhaps even more than 100 percent escalation, and that bondholders would welcome indexed bonds even if they paid lower real interest rates than nominal bonds.
2. The case for indexing is much less clear-cut for firms. But given the diversity of firms in the US economy, there must be many which could profit by indexing their debt instruments and/or escalating their wage payments.

3. Indexed bonds and escalated wages are substitutes, from the points of view of both workers and firms. Having more of one dulls the incentive to seek more of the other.

As noted in Section 11.1, the theory explains a phenomenon that, unfortunately, does not exist in the world. The models suggest that economies with substantial wage escalation should have very few indexed loan agreements, while economies with many indexed bonds should have few escalated wage contracts. In most economies, however, there is rather little indexing of any kind.

There are no indexed bonds in the United States. In addition, the notion that cost-of-living escalators are extremely widespread is a myth. The latest Bureau of Labor Statistics data show that, even after nine years of the worst inflation in modern US history, a little over half the workers covered by major collective bargaining agreements (1,000 or more employees) have any sort of cost-of-living escalator. Almost none of these contracts offers complete protection of real wages, not to mention the fanciful more than 100 percent escalation discussed in Section 11.2. Furthermore, major collective bargaining agreements cover only about 10 percent of the US labor force, and wage escalators in smaller establishments are almost nonexistent.[13]

The models do, however, suggest one possible explanation for the dearth of indexing. The really virulent inflation of the past few years has certainly come from the supply side, and has been accompanied by falling profits. For the years 1972–5, indexed bonds and highly escalated wages would not have been in the best interests of stockholders. If firms foresaw these events (or had an irrational fear of cost-push inflation which proved true!), then this could explain the absence of indexing.

But this is stretching a point. Until recently, demand-pull inflation has been the rule, not the exception. The 1966–71 inflationary period fits this pattern. The absence of indexed bonds must have another explanation. Let me suggest one.[14]

11.4.2 Asymmetries in risk and the need for an intermediary

Workers and bondholders reduce risk by linking their nominal incomes to a broad price index, more or less representative of the things they buy. But the same may not be true of firms. In a world where relative prices change rapidly, no firm is sure that the prices of the product mix it sells will move in the same way as, say, the private GNP deflator. A firm considering an indexed bond will worry – and not without reason – that its product prices will lag behind the deflator, leaving it with a burdensome level of interest payments.

The remedy for the firm is obvious. Suppose it could tie its interest payments to the prices of its own products, or at least to an index more closely tailored to its own sales. This type of indexed bond would offer a very safe way to borrow. But it would not be a safe way to lend. As viewed by consumers, such an instrument would be almost as risky as common stock, since its returns would depend on relative price fluctuations.

The outcome, then, of the operation of free markets may be that the *latent demand* for bonds indexed to a broad price index, and the *latent supply* of bonds indexed to firm-specific prices both go unsatisfied. The fact that these very real *private* risks are not *social* risks – because, on average, the selling prices of firms and the buying prices of consumers must move together[15] – motivates my proposal for a new type of financial intermediary.

Suppose a 'National Inflation Mutual Fund' (henceforth NIMF) were created and instructed to: (a) purchase bonds from firms, with the interest and principal linked to the specific price index applicable to each firm's industry; (b) issue deposits to consumers, paying a guaranteed real interest rate in terms of some broad price index. Both firms and bondholders would find the instruments far safer than the present nominal bonds. NIMF itself would be simply an intermediary. Given the right set of weights for each industry in NIMF, the fund would be literally self-insured.

11.4.3 A mutual fund of indexed bonds

While many different variants of NIMF might be designed, depending on the maturity structure of its assets and liabilities, I will concentrate – solely for concreteness – on a version in which NIMF purchases one-year bonds from firms, and simultaneously issues one-year certificates of deposit to consumers.

Let $i = 1, \ldots, n$ denote the n industries. Let the price index of each industry at the end of the year, with all prices normalized to unity at the beginning of the year, be P_i. Let $I \equiv \Sigma_i \lambda_i P_i$ be the aggregate price index at the end of the year, so that λ_i represents the weight of industry i in the index. Let r_i be the real rate of interest which industry i pays into NIMF.[16] Then if B_i is the face value of the bonds which industry i sells to NIMF at the beginning of the year, its nominal payments at the end of the year will be $(1 + r_i)B_i P_i$. Deflating by the general price index, the real payment is $(1 + r_i)B_i p_i$, where the $p_i \equiv P_i / I$ are henceforth called the 'real prices' or 'relative prices' of each industry, and are assumed to have well-behaved probability distributions.

The face value of the fund is $B = \Sigma_i B_i$. If $w_i \equiv B_i / B$ is the weight of industry i in NIMF, then total deflated receipts are:

$$\sum_i (1 + r_i) B_i p_i = \left[\sum_i (1 + r_i) w_i p_i \right] B$$

In general, this will be a random variable since all the p_i are random. Payments from NIMF to bondholders at the end of the year would be simply

$(1+r_0)BI$ in nominal terms, or $(1+r_0)B$ in real terms, where r_0 is the guaranteed real rate paid on NIMF deposits. Thus, the real profit rate of NIMF is $\Sigma_i(1+r_i)w_ip_i-(1+r_0)$. Now, by the definition of the price index, the weighted sum of random variables, $\Sigma_i\lambda_ip_i$, is equal to unity *with certainty*. So NIMF will be perfectly self-insured if, and only if, $(1+r_i)w_i=k\lambda_i$, for all i, for some constant k.

Can a fund be designed which meets this requirement? I shall argue that it can.[17] However, if equal real interest rates (r_i) are charged to all firms, there is no reason to expect open participation in NIMF to result in $w_i=\lambda_i$. Indeed, there is every reason to expect w_i to differ from λ_i in a systematic way that would threaten the solvency of NIMF.

The reason is *adverse selection*, a phenomenon which is common to all insurance schemes. To cite one prominent example, it is well known that purchasers of health insurance are sicker on average than the population as a whole. The corresponding danger for NIMF is that firms which borrow from NIMF might have lower average rates of price increase than the economy as a whole, so that the fund's income would grow more slowly than its outlays. If NIMF posted equal real borrowing rates (r_i) for each industry, this would probably happen; for if every industry could borrow at a uniform real rate, r, linked to its own price index, industry i would view the real interest factor as $(1+r)p_i$. Industries expecting small price increases $[E(p_i)<1]$ would view this as 'cheap,' while industries expecting rapid inflation $[E(p_i)>1]$ would find NIMF an expensive source of funds.

One way to cope with such adverse selection is to post a set of industry-specific interest factors satisfying $(1+r_i)E(p_i)=1+\bar{r}$ for all industries. If the price projections of firms correspond to, or deviate randomly from, the price projections made by NIMF, adverse selection would be eliminated. If the two sets of price expectations differed systematically, *firms* which expected *industry* price performance superior to NIMF projections would prefer to borrow elsewhere, while firms anticipating less inflation in their industry than NIMF projections would participate actively in the fund. If businesses are better forecasters of relative prices than NIMF, this would present another – though less serious – adverse selection problem; but it is not obvious to me that they need be better.

However, even if some degree of adverse selection occurs, it need not be fatal to NIMF. Private insurance is a thriving industry in the United States today despite actual or potential adverse selection in virtually every line of insurance. Further, in coping with adverse selection, NIMF would have an important advantage over most commercial insurers because it would not continually be presented with applications from *new industries*, with which it had no past experience. NIMF could, therefore, more readily identify industries whose real price is likely to fall than, for example, could a commercial insurance company identify which of a set of new drivers is more likely to have an accident.[18] *New firms* may, of course, seek to borrow from NIMF; but they will usually be from familiar industries. New industries are simply not born as frequently as new people.

Thus far I have enumerated two constraints on NIMF. If it is to be self-insured, it must satisfy:

$$(1 + r_i)w_i = k\lambda_i$$

and, if it is to obviate adverse selection, it must set interest rates such that:

$$(1 + r_i)E(p_i) = 1 + \bar{r}$$

These two jointly determine the required NIMF-weights since:

$$w_i = \frac{k\lambda_i}{1 + r_i} = \frac{k\lambda_i}{1 + \bar{r}} E(p_i) = \lambda_i E(p_i)$$

because k must equal $(1 + \bar{r})$ if the w_is are to sum to unity. There is no particular reason to expect the ratio of an industry's NIMF-weight to its weight in the price index to be equal to its expected relative price. Therefore, if NIMF simply posts *any* vector of interest rates and accepts all comers, it probably will not acquire the risk-free weights.

But there is a simple alternative. Suppose it has been decided that an NIMF of face value B should be established as a risk-free fund. This means that NIMF must buy bonds worth $B_i = \lambda_i E(p_i)B$ from industry, i. It can achieve this by a 'Dutch auction,' whereby the rate, r_i, that NIMF charges to industry i is set by the requirement that the firms in the industry wish to borrow precisely this amount from NIMF. Call these the 'market clearing' rates.

The perceptive reader will have noticed that I have now imposed two restrictions on the r_i: first, that they clear markets; and second, that they eliminate adverse selection. However, these requirements come to roughly the same thing because markets can only clear at rates that satisfy $(1 + r_i)E(p_i) = 1 + \bar{r}$ approximately. If NIMF's lending rates were such that $(1 + r_i)E(p_1)$ was very much less than $(1 + r_2)E(p_2)$, it would be profitable for firms in industry 1 to borrow from NIMF at interest factor $(1 + r_1)p_1$, and lend to firms in industry 2 at interest factor $(1 + r^*)p_2$, where $r_1 < r^* < r_2$. Perhaps only a small spread between $(1 + r_1)E(p_1)$ and $(1 + r_2)E(p_2)$ would induce the two firms to enter into such a contract if their price expectations were basically alike. But such operations would raise industry 1's supply of bonds to NIMF, thus increasing r_1. And, as industry 2 borrows from industry 1, instead of from NIMF, r_2 would decline. The process would continue until the gap between $(1 + r_1)E(p_1)$ and $(1 + r_2)E(p_2)$ shrunk to the point where the incentive to 'arbitrage' disappeared.[19] Thus competition automatically establishes relative interest rates which minimize adverse selection.

A similar 'no arbitrage' argument establishes that $\bar{r}$ must be at least as large as r_0; that is, the NIMF cannot – even by accident – have a structure of borrowing and lending rates that would lose money! To see why not, suppose that $r_0 > \bar{r}$. Then firms could borrow from NIMF at expected interest factors $(1 + r_i)E(p_i)$, use the funds to purchase an NIMF deposit with a guaranteed return of $1 + r_0$, and earn an expected profit. As firms sought to exploit these possibilities, $\bar{r}$ would be driven up.

How big would NIMF be? The general equilibrium of the financial markets would provide the answer. There would be a supply function of bonds to NIMF, $B^s = B^s(\bar{r}, R^f)$, where R^f is a vector of alternative rates at which firms can borrow, and where $\partial B^s / \partial \bar{r}$ is presumptively negative. And there will be a demand function for NIMF deposits, $B^d = B^d(r_0, R^c)$, where R^c is a vector of alternative rates at which consumers can lend, and where $\partial B^d / \partial r_0$ is presumptively positive. Figure 11.2 shows how the profitability of NIMF – the margin between its borrowing and lending rates – depends on its size. A very small fund, like b, will have a large profit rate, while a much larger fund, like B, will be less profitable. In the long run, competition will insure that the margin between $\bar{r}$ and r_0 is just sufficient to cover the costs of operating NIMF. However, during the transitional period, there may be monopoly profits to be reaped by some enterprising financial institution.

The real empirical question is whether or not demand and supply would be strong enough (i.e., the intersection point shown in Fig. 11.2 would be far enough to the right) to support a fund of at least the minimum viable size.

11.4.4 An NIMF miscellany

Now that general equilibrium issues have been raised, it is worth noting that NIMF would probably have side effects on both the financial and real sectors of the economy. First, the establishment of NIMF would obviously affect other financial institutions, and this would affect both vectors of 'alternative rates' mentioned above. Second, by changing the terms on which firms can borrow, NIMF would affect relative prices and resource allocation. Both of these are familiar, though complex, phenomena in general equilibrium analysis which require no further comment here.

There are many variants on the NIMF theme. In order to secure wider participation, NIMF might forswear the requirement that it be risk free, and let the weights, w_i, be determined through open participation by firms. In this case, either the return to NIMF deposits would have to be risky (a proportionate share in NIMF receipts), or some other institution (the government?) would have to underwrite the risk. As a large mutual fund investing in a diversified portfolio of securities linked to specific commodity prices, it is reasonable to suppose that most (though not all) of the risk could be

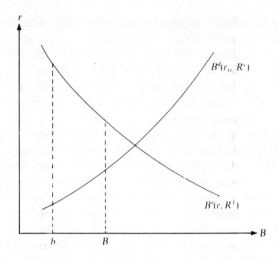

Fig. 11.2 The demand for NIMF deposits and supply of NIMF loans.

eliminated by pooling. The law of large numbers should rescue this variant of NIMF just as it rescues commercial insurers.

Another variant would be to establish an NIMF which paid interest linked to the CPI, or other index of consumer prices, rather than to the private GNP deflator used as an illustration here. I have not concentrated on such a fund here – though consumers might prefer it – as it is desirable to open partici-pation to all firms. An NIMF with deposits linked to the CPI, for example, could not lend to industries with no weight in that index. However, there is no real reason why NIMF need be monolithic. Different NIMFs could be established, each linked to a distinct price index. Indeed, this arrangement would be preferable to a single NIMF, since different households purchase different market baskets of goods and services.

With what sort of index would NIMF work best? I have used the private GNP deflator as an illustration, but the deflator for nonfarm business product might be a more likely candidate, unless farmers also borrowed from NIMF. It is arguable whether exports and imports should also be excluded on the grounds that domestic wage earners and bondholders ought not to be insulated from changes in the terms of trade.[20] In some cases (e.g., the 1973–4 oil debacle) such protection would have been most welcome.

Some readers may wonder why I propose to index loans to the *industry's* price rather than to the *firm's* price. The reason is that the latter alternative invites abuses – a kind of 'window dressing' in reverse, whereby firms, by manipulating specific commodity prices and/or sales weights, attempt to make their average price performance look worse than it really is. Industry price indices are far less subject to manipulation by firms, although some care would have to be taken in highly concentrated industries. This suggests that

NIMF should use a fairly coarse level of industrial classification. Monopoly typically disappears as industries are aggregated.

Just as industries dominated by few firms pose problems for NIMF, so do firms participating in many industries. NIMF could create for such firms a weighted average of the industry-specific price indices for those industries in which the firm does business. This assumes, however, that multi-industry firms are willing to reveal their sales weights to NIMF; it could be that some of them wish to keep this information from public view.[21] In that case, I suppose, NIMF could offer to let the firm borrow with payments linked to any of the P_i for industries in which it participates, relying on the firm to apportion its borrowing weights to its sales weights. However, even this procedure involves a (tacit) revelation by the firm of some aspects of its business and, rather than do this, some firms might simply shun participation in NIMF. I do not know how big a problem this might be in practise.

Finally, there is the question of matching the maturities of NIMF assets and liabilities. In the illustration, I assumed perfect matching, in that NIMF only borrowed and lent for precisely one year. In reality, firms might want to borrow for various durations – as they now do from banks and in the bond market. And the popularity of NIMF deposits would be enhanced greatly if the deposits were of no fixed maturity, like passbook savings accounts. It is true that, if NIMF deviates from perfect matching of maturities of assets and liabilities, it can no longer hope to be literally riskless. Like banks and all other financial intermediaries, it would be subject to random deposit out-flows. Banks and other intermediaries – even thrift institutions – manage to cope with this problem quite well. I imagine that NIMF could, too.

11.4.5 Wage escalation through NIMF

The theoretical discussion stressed the similarities between indexed bonds and wage contracts with cost-of-living escalators. Yet wages have not been mentioned in my discussion of NIMF.

If NIMF deposits were available with any starting date, or with any desired maturity, then firms could use NIMF to enter into escalated wage contracts linked to a broad price index with no risk to themselves. For example, I in wages (an uncertain nominal sum) could be paid at the end of a period by depositing $I \div (1 + r_0)$ in an NIMF account at the beginning of a period.

One objection frequently raised against any scheme for comprehensive wage indexation is that linking many, or all, money-wage rates to the same index effectively freezes the relative wage structure, thus preventing relative wage movements from accommodating shifts in demand. However, this is true of any long-term labor contract, whether or not tied to a price index. With or without indexing, relative wages are free to adjust each time a contract expires. A difference would arise only if the average duration of labor contracts were lengthened by the advent of comprehensive indexing. It is not obvious that this need occur, though it might.

Indexing wages through NIMF, rather than through conventional escalator clauses, is especially beneficial to firms when prices rise due to an external supply shock, as in 1974. In this case, workers' purchasing power is maintained, but most firms do not pay the costs of higher wages. NIMF does this instead, essentially by transferring income from firms with high P_i to firms with low P_i.[22]

11.4.6 NIMF and wage-price controls

NIMF, or indexing in general, clearly affects the trade-off between real output growth and inflation, not because it 'shifts the Phillips curve,' but because it significantly lowers the welfare costs of inflation. As such, it can be looked on as an alternative to wage-price controls.

Wage-price controls may, nevertheless, recur. It is worth asking, therefore, how the chance that controls might be reimposed affects the viability of NIMF. On the surface, the effect would seem to be devastating, since the price index, I, and some, but not all, of the P_i would be artificially held down by controls. But who would gain and who would lose?

Until controls reached the point where the prices recorded in the index seriously understated true transactions prices, consumers would be neither helped nor harmed. While their interest receipts from NIMF would be lower under controls, so would commodity prices. *Real* interest received from NIMF would be unaffected.

Redistributions among firms, however, would be substantial. But they might be in a desirable direction. The firms which suffer most from controls are, presumably, those on whom the controls are most binding, that is, those whose controlled p_i fall most short of the p_i expected before controls. But, since firms borrowing from NIMF pay an *ex post* real interest factor:

$$(1 + \bar{r}) \frac{p_i}{E(p_i)}$$

NIMF loans would ease their burdens. Conversely, firms not subject to controls would have high $p_i/E(p_i)$, since P_i would be allowed to rise while I was held down. These firms – the 'winners' from controls – would have to make larger payments into NIMF. Thus, NIMF offers a unique form of (partial) insurance against the institution of price controls.

Wage-price controls could work against NIMF – or against any indexed contract – if they include provisions for vacating contract clauses calling for index linking, as was done, for example, to some wage contracts during the 1971 wage-price freeze.[23] Investor fears that government might make it *illegal* for NIMF to pay depositors $(1 + r_0)I$ at the end of the period, even at the artificially depressed level of I, could seriously damage the attractiveness of NIMF deposits. On the other hand, if firms think that the government may mandate payments into NIMF less than the $(1 + r_i)P_i$ specified in the contract, borrowing from NIMF would be made more attractive. Whether these two forces, on balance, enhance or undermine the viability of NIMF is unclear on *a priori* grounds. However, my guess is that they would be very harmful.

11.4.7 The gulf between theory and practise

Given enough supply and demand, then, NIMF can obviate the problem of asymmetrical risks which, as I suggested, may explain the dearth of indexed contracts. But would firms and workers want to participate?

To me, it is obvious that worker-savers would be eager to subscribe, at least if the reduction in mean wage and interest payments were not too large.[24] Section 11.5 attempts to provide some reasons why NIMF would be well received by consumer-workers. The idea behind the 'evidence' is simple. Workers and savers have an incentive to participate in NIMF to the extent that (a) the real returns to human capital suffer from unanticipated inflation, and (b) the existing menu of financial instruments offers an inadequate hedge against inflation. In Section 11.5, I argue that, in the postwar United States, these have both been true.

It is a more difficult story for firms. They will be eager to link factor payments to their own prices if profits and prices tend to move together (as in demand-pull inflations), but not if profits and prices tend to move in opposite directions (as in cost-push inflations). Section 11.5 presents an initial attempt to shed some light on this question for US manufacturing corporations.

11.5 EMPIRICAL EVIDENCE ON THE NEED FOR NIMF

11.5.1 Inflation and the returns on human capital

How does unanticipated inflation affect the returns to human capital? Given the paucity of complete escalator clauses in our economy, it would be very surprising if the answer were anything but that it falls.

Before examining the data, I want to clarify one point that may be confusing. Asserting that wages fare badly in unanticipated inflation does not imply that inflation hurts labor in the long run. The indexing issue is only a live one in the short run; in the long run, everything is effectively indexed *de facto*, if not *de jure*. For the period I consider, the United States in 1948–75,[25] compensation per manhour in the private nonfarm economy rose at a compound annual rate of 5.6 percent, while productivity (output per man-hour) rose at 2.3 percent per year. The excess of wage growth over productivity growth was thus 3.3 percent per year, which slightly exceeds the average compound growth rate of the CPI (3.0 percent per year). In a word, wages kept pace with inflation in the long run.

There is no such close correspondence over shorter periods. From 1973: IV to 1974:IV, for example, compensation per manhour grew 9.7 percent, while consumer prices rose 12.1 percent. As measured by the CPI, the five years of greatest inflation in the 1948–75 period were (in order of inflation rates) 1974, 1975, 1951, 1948, and 1973. Over these five years, inflation averaged 8.4 percent, while compensation per manhour grew at an average rate of 8.6 percent. The margin is clearly well below trend productivity growth. Conversely, the five years of lowest inflation were (in inverse order of inflation rates) 1949, 1955, 1954, 1953, and 1959, during which time inflation averaged a scant 0.1 percent per year. Over the same five years, compensation per manhour averaged 3.9 percent growth per year; the difference is well above trend productivity.

These gross statistics may or may not be compelling. A more serious job of answering the question requires some measure of the 'return on human capital' for the overall economy. It is not hard to see that compensation per manhour will not do. Its drawbacks are many. No allowance is made for the cyclical variation of hours of work per week, nor for weeks of work per year. Neither is allowance made for changes in tax burdens on labor income (payroll taxes and income taxes).

But what is a satisfactory empirical proxy? Problems abound in applying the rate-of-return notion to human capital. How does one value the stock at the beginning and end of the period? Even if this is answered, should capital gains be included? On the one hand, such gains cannot be cashed in. But, on the other hand, any revaluation of the human capital stock presumably means higher earnings at some future date; thus, by omitting the capital gains, we attribute these returns to subsequent years. Worse yet, human investment – not capital gains – accounts for some of the year-to-year increase in the market value of the human capital stock. Because I could neither isolate the capital gains, nor know what to do with them had I succeeded in measuring them, I concentrated instead on getting a more refined series on wage changes. As a representation of human capital returns, the series is probably too smooth.

Existing BLS data do most of the work for me. Their series on *Average Spendable Weekly Earnings in the Total Private Nonagricultural Sector* adjusts average gross hourly earnings for both variations in the work week and changes in payroll and income taxes (based on a worker with three dependants). Furthermore, it does not make any correction for inter-industrial movements of labor, which are, after all, elements of the return on human capital. I made only one adjustment to this series. Because it represents the return on human capital only to *employed* workers, I multiplied each yearly figure by one minus the unemployment rate.[26] The *rate of change* of the average earnings series so derived, henceforth denoted by h, is my rough empirical proxy for the returns to human capital.[27]

A simple regression of h on the rate of inflation[28] yields:

$h_t = 2.84 - 0.61\pi_t$

   (0.64) (0.15)

where π is the inflation rate and standard errors are in parentheses. The simple correlation between h and π is -0.62, which connotes a substantial negative covariance. The suggestion is clearly that real human-capital returns decline in inflation – and by quite a considerable amount.

It might be objected that the correlation between real returns on human capital and *unanticipated* inflation would be a more revealing statistic. Though possibly more revealing, it is difficult to obtain because the desired correlation is between two variables which are very hard to measure. I made an attempt to compute this correlation from data on expected inflation recently constructed by de Menil (1974). An annual series on *unanticipated* inflation, from 1955 to 1972, was constructed by the identity:

$u_t = \pi_t - \bar{\pi}_t$

where $\bar{\pi}_t$ is de Menil's series for expected inflation.[29] A simple regression of h_t on u_t yields:

$h_t = 1.51 - 1.10u_t$

   (0.58) (0.64)

The correlation in this case is -0.40. Given the wide margins of error in measuring each variable, the point estimate accords remarkably well with the notion that the expected rate of inflation is incorporated exactly into nominal human capital returns, so that real human capital returns decline point-for-point with unanticipated inflation.

Poole (1976), however, recently suggested an alternative hypothesis, 'that US experience has been for inflation surprises to be associated with lower real yields on human and physical capital independently of whether the inflation is higher or lower than anticipated' (p. 201). This can be tested, in a very rough way, by replacing u_t in the preceding regression by its absolute value. The result is:

$h_t = 3.75 - 2.90|u_t|$

   (1.17) (1.28)

and the simple correlation between h_t and $|u_t|$ is -0.49. While the standard error on the slope coefficient is regrettably large, the correlation slightly exceeds that between h_t and u_t, thus lending some credence to Poole's conjecture. However, the issue clearly cannot be decided on the basis of a difference of 0.09 between two correlation coefficients.

11.5.2 Inflation and the returns on financial instruments

To what extent are the financial instruments held by the typical household hedges against inflation? For some assets the answer is painfully obvious. Because of interest rate ceilings, deposits in thrift institutions, for example, often do not even compensate the holder fully for *anticipated* inflation. Short-term money market instruments such as Treasury bills and commercial paper probably offer adequate compensation for expected inflation, but none for unanticipated inflation; these instruments would have to be sold short in great volume to hedge against inflation. The practical difficulties of carrying this out need no elaboration, for there is a more fundamental point. Households with positive financial net worth *must* take a long position in *some* asset; they cannot sell everything short. Thus, inflation hedging requires the existence of some asset which actually gains from unanticipated inflation. Is there any?

Jaffe and Mandelker (1976) report strong negative correlations between monthly inflation rates and holding period returns on short-duration Treasury bills in the 1953–71 period, but very little correlation between inflation and holding period yields on long-term obligations. The more important question, however, concerns the correlation between real bond returns and unanticipated inflation, u_t. Both Bodie (1975) and Jaffe and Mandelker (1976) find almost no correlation between u_t and the *nominal* returns on bonds of various maturities, which must imply a negative correlation between real returns and u_t.[30]

Common stocks are the financial asset traditionally touted as a hedge against inflation. Yet Cagan's (1974) comparison of 24 countries over the 1939–69 period turned up a negative association between real stock market values and inflation rates.[31] Three recent studies, varying somewhat in statistical techniques and in period of coverage, all conclude that even *nominal* returns on common stocks in the United States are negatively correlated with unanticipated changes in the CPI. *Real* stock returns, therefore, must be affected extremely adversely by unanticipated inflation. Studying the United States from 1953 until the early 1970s, Bodie (1975), Jaffe and Mandelker (1976), and Nelson (1976) all found either a zero or negative correlation between *nominal* stock market returns and *unanticipated* inflation. The latter two studies even reported that *anticipated* inflation hurt common stock returns.[32]

The case for assuming that returns on households' financial portfolios decline with unanticipated inflation, then, seems quite strong. However, I have ignored owner-occupied homes, an important asset in the portfolio of many consumers.[33] Since prices of houses generally rise with the rate of inflation, while nominal payments on nonindexed mortgages do not, unanticipated inflation provides a windfall gain to homeowners. Essentially, homeowners enjoy a capital gain as the market value of their mortgage indebtedness falls.

11.5.3 Inflation and corporate profits

The last two sections suggest that the typical household – one which has positive net worth and receives most of its income from wages and salaries – stands to lose from unanticipated inflation. This, in turn, suggests that there would be substantial demand for NIMF deposits, and also ample supply of labor to firms which promised perfectly indexed wages (accomplished through NIMF, as explained earlier).

But will firms wish to participate? If they are risk neutral, they undoubtedly will, because workers and bondholders will be willing to pay for inflation protection by accepting lower expected real wages and expected real interest rates. However, the theoretical analysis reveals that risk-averse firms may or may not wish to participate, depending on their degree of risk aversion and on how their 'other income' fares in inflation.

The latter can be assessed empirically, at least in principle. Ideally, one would like several time series of complete income statements, aggregated to the industry level, in order to see how a concept like 'net income before wage and interest payments' behaves in inflation. Unfortunately, such ideal data are not available.

An indirect test can be designed as follows. The theory points out that firms whose positions improve when their industry's prices rise will be eager to hedge their positions by borrowing from NIMF, while firms who suffer when industry prices rise will want to avoid NIMF. The correlation between profits and prices, then, is an important datum in guessing whether or not NIMF would be well received by firms.

Matched profit and price data by industry are not readily available, but a close approximation can be created by linking the Federal Trade Commission's (FTC) quarterly data on profits of manufacturing corporations with the Bureau of Labor Statistics' (BLS) detailed breakdown of the Wholesale Price Index (WPI). These data are particularly suitable for this problem because the industrial classification is roughly at the level of disaggregation that I imagine NIMF would want to use (approximately two-digit industries in the Standard Industrial Classification). However, there are shortcomings. First, multi-industry firms are assigned to a single industry; this is not how I imagine NIMF would handle them. Second, precise matching of FTC and BLS classifications was not always possible. Judgment was exercised in deciding where a tolerably close match-up could be created; Appendix 11.1 explains the details. Third, profits as defined for corporate income tax purposes may be far from the ideal definition. Finally, the manufacturing sector may not be representative of the entire private business sector.

While theoretical interest attaches to the sign of $Y'(\pi)$, the usefulness of simple correlations between industry-specific *inflation rates* and *levels of profit* is vitiated by common time trends. To circumvent this problem, several alternatives were tried. The first two columns of Table 11.1 report correla-

Table 11.1 Correlations between profits and price increases for US manufacturing corporations, 1947–75

Industry groups[b]	Period	Correlations between inflation rate and: profits/sales ratio	Correlations between inflation rate and: profits/equity ratio	Correlation between deviations from logarithmic time trends
1. Food and kindred products (0.145)	Quarterly: 1947:I–1975:I[a]	+0.30	+0.42	+0.42
	Annual: 1948–74	+0.12	+0.52	+0.63
(a) Dairy products (0.017)	Quarterly: 1963:I–1973:IV	+0.05	+0.29	−0.19
	Annual: 1963–73	+0.05	+0.59	−0.26
(b) Bakery products (0.010)	Quarterly: 1962:I–1973:IV	−0.48	−0.34	−0.33
	Annual: 1962–73	−0.81	−0.63	−0.63
(c) Alcoholic beverages (0.012)	Quarterly: 1956:II–1973:IV	+0.16	+0.21	+0.01
	Annual: 1957–73	+0.31	+0.38	+0.04
2. Tobacco manufactures (0.012)	Quarterly: 1951:II–1975:I	+0.37	+0.23	+0.28
	Annual: 1948–74	+0.10	+0.21	−0.09
3. Apparel and other finished textile products (0.030)	Quarterly: 1947:I–1973:IV[a]	+0.62	+0.58	−0.03
	Annual: 1948–73	+0.26	+0.35	+0.30
4. Paper and allied products (0.025)	Quarterly: 1947:I–1975:I[a]	+0.55	+0.73	+0.46
	Annual: 1948–74	+0.35	+0.64	+0.49
5. Chemicals and allied products (0.080)	Quarterly: 1947:I–1975:I[a]	+0.32	+0.56	+0.31
	Annual: 1947–74	+0.27	+0.53	+0.38
(a) Industrial chemicals and synthetics (0.038)	Quarterly: 1956:II–1975:I	+0.12	+0.55	+0.22
	Annual: 1957–74	+0.10	+0.63	+0.48
(b) Drugs (0.015)	Quarterly: 1956:II–1975:I	+0.36	+0.05	−0.32
	Annual: 1957–74	+0.57	+0.26	−0.37
6. Petroleum and coal products (0.107)	Quarterly: 1957:I–1975:I	+0.26	+0.65	+0.51
	Annual: 1948–50, 1957–74	+0.30	+0.80	+0.71
(a) Petroleum refining (0.105)	Quarterly: 1954:II–1973:IV	−0.15	+0.24	+0.10
	Annual: 1951–73	−0.22	+0.28	+0.05

Industry (weight)	Frequency			
7. Rubber and miscellaneous plastic products (0.026)	Quarterly: 1951:II–1975:I			
	Annual: 1947–74	+0.66	+0.73	+0.32
8. Leather and leather products (0.006)	Quarterly: 1947:I–1973:IV[a]	+0.48	+0.48	−0.06
	Annual: 1947–73	+0.53	+0.48	+0.18
9. Stone, clay, and glass products (0.025)	Quarterly: 1951:II–1975:I	−0.28	−0.11	−0.21
	Annual: 1947–74	−0.06	+0.20	+0.48
10. Primary metal industries (0.064)	NA	NA	NA	NA
(a) Iron and steel (0.039)	Quarterly: 1947:I–1975:I[a]	+0.22	+0.41	+0.18
	Annual: 1947–74	+0.36	+0.68	+0.46
(b) Nonferrous metals (0.025)	Quarterly: 1947:I–1975:I[a]	+0.46	+0.56	+0.51
	Annual: 1947–74	+0.47	+0.62	+0.60
11. Electrical and electronic equipment (0.092)	Quarterly: 1951:II–1975:I	−0.20	−0.01	−0.41
	Annual: 1947–74	+0.40	+0.47	−0.41
12. Machinery, except electrical (0.086)	NA	NA	NA	NA
(a) Metalworking machinery and equipment (0.007)	Quarterly: 1956:II–1973:IV	+0.33	+0.37	−0.43
	Annual: 1957–73	+0.32	+0.44	−0.60
13. Transportation equipment (0.119)	Quarterly: 1969:II–1975:I	−0.34	−0.32	−0.41
	Annual: 1969–74	−0.61	−0.57	−0.43
(a) Motor vehicles and equipment (0.083)	Quarterly: 1947:I–1975:I[a]	−0.16	−0.09	−0.38
	Annual: 1947–74	−0.15	−0.04	−0.25
14. Furniture and fixtures (0.011)	Quarterly: 1947:I–1973:IV[a]	+0.58	+0.55	−0.06
	Annual: 1947–73	+0.71	+0.60	−0.39
15. Lumber and wood products except furniture (0.026)	Quarterly: 1947:I–1973:IV[a]	+0.53	+0.55	+0.53
	Annual: 1947–73	+0.79	+0.86	+0.66

Notes:
[a] Omitting 1951:II.
[b] Numbers below each title are the 1973:IV sales weights.   NA = not available.

tions between industry-specific *inflation rates* and the two measures of *profit rates* available in the FTC data. The rate of return on equity is generally regarded as superior to profits per dollar of sales for most purposes. However, for getting an indication of the sign of $Y'(\pi)$, the profits/sales ratio may be more appropriate, especially since the FTC's 'stockholders' equity' is based on book value rather than true market value.

An alternative approach is to compute the *deviations* of each industry's price and profit *levels* from their respective logarithmic time trends, and to calculate the correlation between these two deviations. This method of detrending is reported in the third column of Table 11.1.

For each of the three alternative measures of the price–profit correlation, the table reports results based on both quarterly and annual data.[34] Thus, for each industry, there are six measures in all.

In view of the many conflicting signs, what useful generalizations can be made from these correlations? Using the correlations between profits/sales ratios and inflation as the measure, price change and profitability are positively correlated in 17 of 23 cases in the quarterly data, and in 18 of 23 cases in the annual data. This looks highly favorable to NIMF. It is an unfair way to keep score, however, first, because it double-counts, and second, because the very large motor vehicle industry is among the industries showing the 'wrong' sign. A more relevant way to summarize the results is to compare the fractions of total sales accounted for by industries showing positive versus negative correlations.[35] Based on 1973:IV sales weights,[36] the set of industries with positive correlations is about 2.8 times as large as the set of industries with negative correlations.[37]

Using the correlation between profits/equity ratios and inflation rates instead, price change and profitability are positively correlated in 18 of 23 cases in the quarterly data, and in 20 of 23 cases in the annual data. The 18 industries with unambiguously positive correlation now account for 3.3 times as much sales volume as the three industries with unambiguously negative correlation.[38]

While these two measures agree quite well, a somewhat weaker picture emerges when we look at correlations between deviations of prices and profits from their logarithmic trends. In this case, a positive correlation emerges in only 12 of 23 cases with quarterly observations, and in 14 of 23 cases with annual data. The 11 industries with unambiguously positive correlation account for about 1.6 times as much sales volume as do the eight industries with unambiguously negative correlation.

In brief, then, a substantial majority of manufacturing industries, but certainly not all, seem to be characterized by the positive correlation between prices and profits which is necessary if NIMF is to work. While the theoretical discussion of Sections 2 and 3 suggests that we might learn more by looking separately at periods of 'supply side' versus 'demand side' inflation, a preliminary investigation of this was inconclusive.

One final shred of evidence pointing to a willingness of firms to borrow from NIMF is the apparent popularity of some recent financial innovations which can be viewed as halfway houses between conventional and index-linked borrowing. The best known of these are probably the floating prime rate loans now being made by Citibank in New York.[39] If instruments like these are attractive to businessmen, then perhaps NIMF loans would be too.

11.5.4 Conclusion: would NIMF work?

In Section 11.4, I argued that NIMF can be made to work if there is sufficient demand for NIMF deposits and a sufficient supply of bonds to NIMF. It seems to me that the evidence cited above on the effects of unanticipated inflation on the returns to human and financial assets and on corporate profits provides at least mild support for the notion that consumers and firms would welcome NIMF. However, the case remains weak enough so that the skeptic will rightfully remain unconvinced. The proof of this particular theoretical pudding will most assuredly come in the empirical tasting.

11.6 NOTES

1. The argument clearly assumes that firms are risk averse. If they are risk neutral, the relative absence of indexed contracts is truly mysterious.
2. The assumption of a two-period life probably is not restrictive if the forms of the wage contracts in different periods are not limited by some institutional constraint, e.g., a three-year contract which must involve the same escalator clause for all three years. In the latter case, since r and π may be serially correlated, the two-period problem misses some intertemporal linkages which might upset the conclusions.
3. This is just an application of the 'envelope theorem'. If γ is any parameter of the wage contract:

$$dJ/d\gamma = \partial J/\partial \gamma \mid_{k_1 = \text{constant}} + dk_1/d\gamma. \; \partial J/\partial k_1 \mid_{\gamma = \text{constant}}$$

$$= \partial J/\partial \gamma \text{ because } \partial J/\partial K_1 \mid_{\gamma = \text{constant}} = 0$$

4. A riskless indexed bond is a special case where the density function of real returns collapses to a spike. But one can conceive of other indexed securities which retain some risks unassociated with price-level fluctuations.
5. This is the technical representation of the notion that inflation lowers the real rate of return. Some empirical evidence supporting the proposition is presented later in the paper.
6. The relations between net worth and wage escalators are statements about *correlations*, not about *causation*, because both k_1 and $w(.)$ are selected in the same maximization process.
7. In general, ρ_F and ρ_W are not constants, but depend upon the income levels of firm and worker, respectively, and thus upon π. I note in passing that (11.6) can be modified to account for differences in subjective probability distributions. A similar problem is considered by Azariadis (1976).

8. $Y'(\pi) < 0$ does not mean, however, that no escalation will be offered, nor even that $w'(\pi) < 0$. See equation (11.6).

9. Siegel (1974) presents a similar argument in less mathematical form, using the capital assets pricing model.

10. The mean return, $\bar{H}$, may well depend on the expected rate of inflation, $\bar{\pi}$, but that is not of direct concern here.

11. This validates writing $h = H - \pi$.

12. This is not meant to imply that R is a constant unaffected by $\bar{\pi}$. That question is irrelevant for present purposes.

13. See Kuhmerker (1976) and David (1974) for documentation of these points.

14. A variety of other explanations is considered by Fischer (1976).

15. This proposition is stated rather too baldly; most of what follows is concerned with qualifications.

16. The following analysis abstracts from any risk that the firm will default. Thus, firms are distinguished only by the industry to which they belong. In practise, firms would have to be cross-classified by both industry and risk class (e.g., by their Moody's rating), and interest rates assigned accordingly. It is perhaps most useful to think of the r_i analyzed in the text as the prime rate charged to each industry.

17. The reader may have noticed that the question of self-insurance has no inherent connection with the aggregate inflation rate. Relative prices change with or without inflation, so the viability of NIMF is subject to the same questions in either regime. The difference is that the existence of money – or any other asset with a sure nominal return – makes NIMF superfluous if there is no inflation. NIMF deposits will be a 'riskless' asset for consumers in an inflationary environment only in the same limited sense that money is riskless in a world of zero inflation. Neither asset will move precisely in accord with the particular bundle of commodities any individual consumer might purchase, that is, neither asset offers insurance against relative price fluctuations.

18. This assumes that the recent past gives some ability to predict the near-term future, i.e., that relative prices are not a random walk. It should be noted, however, that while a mis-classification of a new driver is an inconsequential error to an insurance company, many industries will be of non-negligible importance to NIMF.

19. Literally, these are not arbitrage operations, for there is some risk.

20. The 'insulation' would only hold for the short run; nothing can insulate them in the long run.

21. I owe this point to Philip Friedman.

22. I owe this point to Edmund Phelps.

23. See Poole (1976).

24. The size of these 'insurance premia' depends on the willingness of firms to participate.

25. Data cited here and elsewhere in this section are from various tables in *Economic Report of the President, 1976*.

26. The labor force data and the wage data are not strictly comparable. See the footnote to Table B–7 in *Economic Report of the President, 1976*.

27. The rationale for using the rate of change is that the 'stock' of human capital should be roughly proportional to w_{t-1}, while w_t represents the 'yield' on the investment if capital gains are ignored. Thus, the rate of return should be proportional to w_t/w_{t-1}. Note that this can only be an approximation, since the factor of proportionality depends on the real rate of interest, and thus on the inflation rate.

28. The CPI is used both to deflate the nominal return on human capital and to measure inflation. The period of the regression is 1949–75.

29. de Menil's series is quarterly, 1953:IV–1972:III. An annual series was constructed as follows. Each quarterly expectation reported by de Menil pertains to the *average* inflation rate for the *following* four quarters. Since I seek expectations of the *year-over-year* inflation rate, it seems most appropriate to take an *average* of the expectations in the four quarters of year *t* as indicating the expected inflation rate from year *t* to year *t* + 1. I wish to thank George de Menil for furnishing me with his data.

30. One caveat must be entered here, although I do not know how important it is. Both Jaffe and Mandelker (1976) and Bodie (1975) make substantial use of Fama's (1975) analysis which suggests that the Treasury bill rate is the sum of a constant real interest rate plus the unbiased estimator of future inflation. However, there are well-known theoretical reasons–first spelled out by Mundell (1963)–for expecting *anticipated* inflation to lower real interest rates; this suggests that changes in the nominal bill rate should understate changes in inflationary expectations.

31. Using Cagan's (1974) data, I computed a rank correlation of −0.64 between real stock market appreciation and inflation.

32. Nelson (1976) proxied anticipated inflation by various leads and lags on actual inflation. Jaffe and Mandelker (1976) used the Treasury bill rate (see note 30 above). Bodie (1975) used both the bill rate and a variant of adaptive expectations.

33. I am grateful to Robert Barro for pointing out this oversight.

34. WPI data are reported monthly. Quarterly and annual inflation rates are computed from appropriately averaged quarterly and annual price *levels*. Similarly, FTC quarterly profit rates were aggregated to years by separately averaging numerators and denominators.

35. These two classes do not exhaust the manufacturing sector because some of the FTC industries could not be matched up with WPI price components, and because the electrical equipment and petroleum industries fall in neither category. The petroleum and coal products industry, 99 percent of which is petroleum refining, is not put in either category because of its puzzling behavior. Over some time periods, the correlation is positive; over others, it is negative.

36. This is the last quarter before several of the subdivisions listed in Table 11.1 were dropped from the FTC reports. It also avoids the distortions caused by the 1974–5 recession.

37. This ratio rises to 3.5 if petroleum is assigned a positive correlation, and falls to 1.6 if petroleum is assigned a negative correlation.

38. In this case, electrical equipment and stone, clay, and glass products fall in neither group, but petroleum and coal products clearly get a positive correlation. If electrical equipment is grouped in the positive category, the 3.3 ratio cited in the text rises to 4.

39. Thomas Huertas of Citibank pointed out to me the similarity between floating-rate loans and index-linked loans. However, I stress that it is only a loose kinship; floating-rate loans certainly are *not* indexed.

11.7 REFERENCES

Azariadis, C. (1976) 'Escalator clauses and the allocation of cyclical risks,' unpublished, Brown University.

Bodie, Z. (1975) 'Hedging against inflation,' unpublished PhD dissertation, MIT.

Cagan, P. (1974) 'Common stock values and inflation – The historical record of many countries,' Supplement to National Bureau of Economic Research Report.

Council of Economic Advisers (1976) *Annual Report*, in the *Economic Report of the President, 1976*, Washington DC: US Government Printing Office.

David, L. M. (1974) 'Cost of living escalation in collective bargaining, price and wage control: an evaluation of current policies,' Hearings before the Joint Economic Committee, 92nd Congress.

Fama, E. (1975) 'Short-term interest rates as predictors of inflation,' *American Economic Review* (June), vol. 65, no. 3, pp. 269–82.

Fischer, S. (1975) 'The demand for index bonds,' *Journal of Political Economy*, (June), vol. 83, no. 3, pp. 509–34.

Fischer, S. (1976) 'Corporate supply of index bonds,' unpublished paper, MIT.

Jaffe, J. F. and Mandelker, G. (1976) 'The "Fisher effect" for risky assets: an empirical investigation,' *Journal of Finance* (May), vol. 31, no. 2, pp. 447–58.

Kuhmerker, P. (1976) 'Scheduled wage increases and escalator provisions in 1976,' *Monthly Labor Review* (January), vol. 99, pp. 42–8.

de Menil, G. (1974) 'The rationality of popular price expectations,' unpublished paper, Princeton University.

Mundell, R. A. (1963) 'Inflation and real interest,' *Journal of Political Economy* (February), vol. 71, no. 1, pp. 280–3.

Nelson, C. R. (1976) 'Inflation and rates of return on common stocks,' *Journal of Finance*, vol. 31, no. 2, pp. 471–82.

Organization for Economic Cooperation and Development (1973) *Indexation of Fixed-Interest Securities*, Paris: OECD.

Poole, W. (1976) 'Indexing and the capital markets,' *American Economic Review* (May), vol. 66, no. 2, pp. 200–4.

Shavell, S. (1976) 'Sharing risks of deferred payment,' *Journal of Political Economy* (February), vol. 84, no. 1, pp. 161–8.

Siegel, J. J. (1974) 'Indexed versus nominal contracting: a theoretical examination,' unpublished paper, University of Chicago.

US Bureau of Labor Statistics (1974) *Handbook of Labor Statistics*, Washington DC: US Government Printing Office.

US Bureau of Labor Statistics, Wholesale prices and price indices, various monthly issues. Washington DC : US Government Printing Office.

US Federal Trade Commission, *Quarterly Financial Report for Manufacturing, Mining and Trade Corporations* (formerly *Quarterly Financial Report for Manufacturing Corporations*), various quarterly issues, Washington DC : US Government Printing Office.

APPENDIX 11· 1

This section explains the procedures used to match FTC data on profits by industry to components of the WPI. For convenience, the information is given in tabular form. The first column lists all industrial categories used by the FTC since 1947 to which a price series could be matched. Some of them do not go back to 1947; others were eliminated before 1975. The second column gives the component of the WPI which was used as a proxy for each industry's price. The final column (*Comments*) explains imperfections in the matching, gaps in the data, and so on.

Table A11.1.1 Matching of profits and price data

FTC industrial classification	Component of WPI	Comments
1. Food and kindred products	Processed foods and feeds	FTC carried this classification only from 1963 to 1973
(a) Dairy products	Dairy products	
(b) Bakery products	Cereal and bakery products	FTC carried this classification only from 1962 to 1973
(c) Alcoholic beverages	Alcoholic beverages	FTC carried this classification only from 1956: II to 1973: IV
2. Tobacco manufactures	Tobacco products	Prior to 1951, insufficient data were available to construct quarterly price series
3. Apparel and other finished textile products	Apparel	This FTC industry includes nonapparel textile products made *outside* of textile mills. Products manufactured in textile mills constitute a separate industry in FTC's classification, to which no price series could be matched
4. Paper and allied products	Pulp, paper, and allied products	
5. Chemicals and allied products	Chemicals and allied products	
(a) Industrial chemicals and synthetics	Industrial chemicals	
(b) Drugs	Drugs and pharmaceuticals	
6. Petroleum and coal products	'Petroleum products, refined' and 'coal'	A price series was created by averaging (with BLS weights) the WPI components, 'petroleum products, refined' and 'coal.' Monthly data on the former began only in 1954. 1951–6 are omitted because FTC did not use this industrial classification for those years

(a) Petroleum refining	Petroleum products, refined	Monthly price data began only in 1954
7. Rubber and miscellaneous plastic products	Rubber and plastic products	Monthly price data began only in 1951
8. Leather and leather products	Hides, skins, leather, and related products	
9. Stone, clay, and glass products	Nonmetallic mineral products	Monthly price data began only in 1951
10. Primary metal industries	NA	No suitable price index
(a) Iron and steel	Iron and steel	
(b) Nonferrous metals	Nonferrous metals	
11. Electrical and electronic equipment	Electrical machinery and equipment	Monthly price data began only in 1951
12. Machinery, except electrical	NA	No suitable price index
(a) Metalworking machinery and equipment	Metalworking machinery and equipment	
13. Transportation equipment	Transportation equipment	
(a) Motor vehicles and equipment	Motor vehicles and equipment	Monthly price data began only in 1951
14. Furniture and fixtures	Furniture and household durables	
15. Lumber and wood products, except furniture	Lumber and wood products	

ACKNOWLEDGEMENTS

We are grateful to the following for permission to reproduce copyright material:

Chapter 1: *Journal of Public Economics*. Article reproduced from November 1973 issue, pp. 319–37.

Chapter 2: *American Economic Review*. Article reproduced from May 1983 issue, pp. 297–302.

Chapter 3: *Economic Journal*. Article reproduced from June 1987 issue, pp. 327–52.

Chapter 6: *American Economic Association Papers and Proceedings*. Article reproduced from May 1988 issue, pp. 435–9.

Chapter 7: *Eastern Economic Journal*. Article reproduced from July–September 1986 issue, pp. 209–16.

Chapter 8: *American Economic Review*. Article reproduced from May 1987 issue, pp. 130–6.

Chapter 9: Philip Allan. Article reproduced from Peston, M. H. and R. E. Quandt (eds) (1986) *Prices, Competition and Equilibrium: Essays in Honor of William J. Baumol*, London: Philip Allan.

Chapter 10: *American Economic Review*. Article reproduced from May 1988 issue.

Chapter 11: *Journal of Monetary Economics*. Article reproduced from Brunner, K. and A. H. Meltzer (eds) (1977) *Stabilization of the Domestic and International Economy*, Carnegie-Rochester Conference Series (a supplement to the *Journal of Monetary Economics*), vol. 5, pp. 69–105.

INDEX